CHINA AND THE WORLD ECONOMY

Anti-Crisis and Rebalance

CHINA AND THE WORLD ECONOMY

Anti-Crisis and Rebalance

Edited by

LEI Da

Renmin University, China

World Scientific

NEW JERSEY • LONDON • SINGAPORE • BEIJING • SHANGHAI • HONG KONG • TAIPEI • CHENNAI • TOKYO

Published by

World Scientific Publishing Co. Pte. Ltd.
5 Toh Tuck Link, Singapore 596224
USA office: 27 Warren Street, Suite 401-402, Hackensack, NJ 07601
UK office: 57 Shelton Street, Covent Garden, London WC2H 9HE

Library of Congress Cataloging-in-Publication Data
Names: Lei, Da (College teacher), editor.
Title: China and the world economy : anti-crisis and rebalance / Lei Da, Renmin University, China.
Description: New Jersey : World Scientific, [2022] | Includes bibliographical references and index.
Identifiers: LCCN 2022007619 | ISBN 9789811247613 (hardcover) |
ISBN 9789811247620 (ebook) | ISBN 9789811247637 (ebook other)
Subjects: LCSH: China--Economic policy--2000– | China--Economic conditions--2000– |
Global Financial Crisis, 2008–2009.
Classification: LCC HC427.95 .L478 2022 | DDC 330.951--dc23/eng/20220218
LC record available at https://lccn.loc.gov/2022007619

British Library Cataloguing-in-Publication Data
A catalogue record for this book is available from the British Library.

B&R Book Program
《中国与世界经济: 反危机与再平衡》
Originally published in Chinese by China Renmin University Press

For any available supplementary material, please visit
https://www.worldscientific.com/worldscibooks/10.1142/12567#t=suppl

Desk Editors: Aanand Jayaraman/Lixi Dong

Typeset by Stallion Press
Email: enquiries@stallionpress.com

About the Author

Lei Da, a professor at the School of Economics, Renmin University of China, served as director of the Department of International Economics, vice dean of the School of Economics, vice president of the China World Economic Society and the executive director of the China Society for International Cooperation. Professor Lei Da has been engaged in the studies of world economy and international political economy, especially the US economy and finance for more than 20 years. He has published more than 100 high quality paper in many top journals, such as *Xinhua Digest*, *The Journal of World Economy*, *World Economics and Politics*, *International Economic Review*, *Journal of Renmin University of China.*

Contents

Chapter 1

Introduction*

The overall situation of the world economy in 2015 had basically continued the momentum of a slow recovery since 2010, but the growth had been lower than expected. At the same time, the emergence of many over-expected events in the world economy and the increasingly severe geopolitical situation made people doubt and concern about the development trend of world economy in the future. Such doubts and concerns are highlighted in the over-reaction, over-concern and over-interpretation of the market, the government and the media to some unexpected and over-unexpected events. In fact, from the perspective of the world economic development after the Second World War, the core law is the imbalance in the economic development of the participating countries in the world economy, as well as the continuous strategic and tactical adjustments made by the core countries of the world economy in response to the imbalance of the world economic development. However, the manifestation of this phenomenon has never been explained by established theories and cognition. For example, the global economic crisis triggered by the U.S. financial crisis in 2008 was not accurately predicted by economists, and the booming economic globalization driven by the IT revolution in the 1990s also emerged amid the noisy discussion of the "hollowing-out" of American industry. Therefore, before making a judgment on the overall situation of the world economy, we must establish a logical analysis framework for the long-term trend of world economic development, and

---

*This chapter was written by Lei Da, Zhao Yong and Yu Chunhai.

then explicate the characteristics of the world economic operation in 2015 on the basis of this framework.

1. Overall Analysis Framework

The basic framework of our analysis is to add the characteristics of economic operation for different countries to the national income identity under the condition of open economy, and based on that, to explain the different risks which are brought to core and peripheral countries by the global economic imbalance caused by the rapid development of globalization.

1.1. *The emergence of global economic imbalances and the demand for rebalancing adjustments*

The current account imbalance in the United States emerged at the beginning of the "New Economy", and the scale of the imbalance has been relatively large since the end of the "New Economy" (see Figure 1). The question is, whether the supporting factors behind the current account deficit of the United States have changed, in addition to its scale expansion, before and after the "New Economy"? We found that the import growth of the United States remained a steady upward trend before and after the "New Economy", but the factors supporting this imbalance model at the domestic level have undergone fundamental changes. As the prosperity of the Nasdaq market faded and the "capital effect" of the stock market disappeared, the "wealth effect" formed by the capital market in the real estate subprime mortgage boom has become a new force supporting the high consumption of the United States, which has further boosted the export growth of the peripheral countries. However, unlike the "New Economy" period, the sustained U.S. trade deficit is increasingly dependent on the inflow of foreign capital, which is equivalent to relying on external debt to sustain high consumption and rapid growth of the United States.

What are the reasons that trading partners keep lending money to the United States for consumption? There are three reasons: the first one is the purchasing power of international goods and services brought by U.S. dollar hegemony; the second one is the demand for high technology and high-level services of the United States; the third one is the inherent

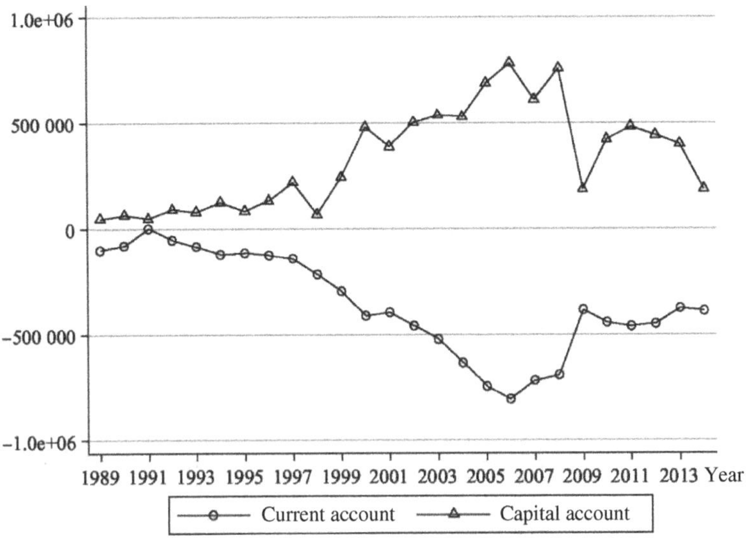

Figure 1. The Scale of the U.S. Current Account Deficit (in Million Dollars)

dependence on the U.S. consumption structure for the production structure of the periphery. Then why does the United States worry about the economic growth model under the consumption on debt? Firstly, the United States is concerned that the decline of the dollar exchange rate index will threaten world dominance of the U.S. dollar. Secondly, if the United States has been dependent on consumption on debt and lacks competitive tradable goods, its central position in the world economy will not be sustainable. Thirdly, since the 21st century, the counterpart countries of the U.S. trade deficit have turned to the emerging economies represented by China. However, there is a lack of mechanism for the macroeconomic policy coordination between the U.S. and emerging economies in the existing world economy system, while exploring a new type of coordinating mechanism among big countries, the United States and China are also testing the sincerity of their adversaries. Of course, the emerging economies represented by China also have the endogenous desire for re-balance, mainly because:

(1) For export-oriented economic countries that rely on export development, the trade deficit of the United States has reached about

700 billion dollars, which has already been at a very high level, while China's share of exports to the United States has also been close to its limit. It is difficult to make any breakthrough in either trade creation effect or trade transfer effect, and the sustainability of economic growth must depend on new ways for growth. The concentration of manufacturing centers in a country or a certain region will inevitably lead to pressure on world manufacturing centers in terms of population, resources, environment, etc. Such a bottleneck to growth was already apparent around 2006.

(2) A large proportion of China's manufacturing industry lies in the assembly. This trade mode does not have high added value in the international value chain, and the trade benefits for participating countries are relatively limited. Although this can be compensated by the growth of scale in the era of rapid growth for external demand, once the rapid growth disappears, the disadvantages of the limited effect of international trade on improving national welfare will be fully exposed. With bread-and-butter issues becoming the main content of China's national policy, the effect of international trade on welfare improvement is bound to become the focus of China's economic policy.

1.2. *The ideas of rebalancing adjustment for core and peripheral countries*

From the perspective of country-specific economy, we can see that countries with current account imbalances, whether surplus countries or deficit countries, have inherent requirements for rebalancing (see Table 1). As for the adjustment method of imbalance, it is also very simple if we look at it from the perspective of national income identity. The surplus

Table 1. Comparison of Motivations for Rebalancing between Core and Peripheral Countries

U.S.A.	China
1. Considering the international status of the U.S. dollar	1. Considering the scale of external demand
2. Considering the core status in the world economy	2. Considering environmental and resource constraints
3. For geopolitical considerations	3. For the consideration of domestic livelihood issues

side expands its domestic demand and imports, while the deficit side increases its exports and reduces its demand. Under the Gold standard, this adjustment is realized through the automatic balancing mechanism for balance of payments. However, while adjusting the scale of imbalances, the automatic balancing mechanism under the Gold standard also limits the scale of international trade. Before that, the rapid growth of the world economy was achieved by the approaches of expanding constantly the scale of international trade, so the ideal adjustment approach should also achieve the rebalance of the world economy under the circumstances of maintaining the scale of international trade. Therefore, in terms of the choice in the balance approaches, there are two completely different choices: globalization and liberalism, anti-globalization and protectionism. The principle for this choice is based on the benefits that different countries have gained in globalization.

From the perspective of national interests of the United States, it would not choose the anti-globalization strategy, because the annual benefit of the United States from the globalization in the 1990s was about 100 billion dollars, while the annual cost of globalization was only about 5% of the annual benefit of globalization (Bernstein, 2004). As a result, the goal of the rebalancing strategy adjustment of the United States and the growth direction of the trade scale should be consistent in theory. However, the United States is unwilling to simply rely on the wealth effect of capital markets and maintain the trade scale through imbalances in the current account; thus there are only two approaches. One is to balance imports through technological innovation, and the other is to balance imports through exports of competitive industries. In the global division of labor, the competitive industries in the United States are increasingly concentrated in the service sector, which belongs to non-trade sector in the traditional sense. Thus, it can be seen that the approach to realize the rebalancing strategy of the United States should be innovative reindustrialization and enhancing the tradability of services. Among them, the final result of reindustrialization will also be reflected in the competitive edge of service trade. In this sense, we can understand that the core goal of TPP agreement is to promote the export of American service trade.

However, for the emerging economies, the approach to achieve rebalance is somewhat passive, because both their economic structure and industrial structure are highly dependent on the demand scale and structure of the United States in the process of globalization. If demand in the United States falls, inevitably, there will be over-capacity of manufacturing industry in emerging economies. From the perspective of sustainable development, the manufacturing industry must be transferred to the service industry. In recent years, the development of service industry in China has accelerated significantly (see Table 2), which actually corresponds to the rebalancing adjustment process in the United States. However, it must be noted that the service trade of emerging economies is mainly concentrated in consumer service trade, which is quite different from the service trade represented by financial services and high-tech

Table 2. GDP Composition of Major Countries and Regions in the World (%)

Countries and Regions	Primary Industry			Secondary Industry			Tertiary Industry		
	1995	2008	2014	1995	2008	2014	1995	2008	2014
U.S.A.	1.6	1.2	1.4[a]	26.8	19.5	16.6[a]	71.7	79.3	82.0[a]
U.K.	1.6	1.0	0.7	28.2	23.3	14.7	70.2	77.7	84.6
Germany	1.2	0.9	0.7	30.1	29.0	25.7	68.7	70.1	73.6
Japan	1.9	1.3	1.2[a]	38.2	29.4	20.4[a]	59.9	69.3	78.4[a]
France	3.0	2.0	1.7	24.4	20.5	13.8	72.6	77.5	84.5
Italy	3.0	2.0	2.2	28.3	27.1	18.5	68.7	70.9	79.3
Spain	4.3	2.8	2.5	28.5	29.1	17.0	67.2	68.1	80.5
Netherlands	3.3	1.7	1.8	25.9	25.4	16.7	70.8	72.9	81.5
Czechs	5.0	2.3	2.7	44.2	37.6	32.4	50.8	60.1	64.9
Russia	7.9	5.0	4.0[a]	39.2	37.2	29.0[a]	52.9	57.8	67.9[a]
Australia	3.4	2.6	2.5[a]	25.2	29.1	18.6[a]	71.5	68.4	78.9[a]
Mexico	5.5	3.8	3.3[a]	27.9	37.1	27.1[a]	60.6	59.1	69.6[a]
Brazil	9.0	6.7	5.1[b]	36.7	28.0	20.9[b]	54.0	65.3	74.0[b]
South Africa	3.9	2.8	2.4[a]	34.8	31.3	23.8[a]	61.3	65.9	78.3[a]
Thailand	11.2	11.7	12.0[a]	39.1	44.1	42.5[a]	49.7	44.2	45.5[a]
India	28.4	17.6	18.0[a]	27.9	29.0	30.7[a]	38.9	53.5	51.3[a]
South Korea	6.2	2.6	2.3	43.2	37.1	33.3	47.0	60.3	63.4
Singapore	0.2	0.1	0.0[a]	34.0	27.8	25.1[a]	65.9	72.2	74.9[a]
Hong Kong, China	0.1	0.1	0.1[a]	16.1	9.8	7.2[a]	68.0	90.1	92.7[a]
China	19.9	11.3	9.2	47.2	48.5	42.6	28.7	40.1	48.2
The World	5.4	3.0	—	34.5	28.0	—	59.4	69.0	—

Note: [a]Represents the data of 2013; [b]Represents the data of 2011.

Source: OECD statistics (http://stats.oecd.org/), International Statistical Yearbook (2001, 2010, 2011, 2014) and China Statistical Yearbook (2015).

producer services in the United States. This point can be seen from the comparison that the share of service export in China and other countries is growing rapidly while the service sector output of GDP in the United States is still rising. In other words, in the field of service trade, there is no such relationship of industrial transfer and undertaking as in the field of goods trade. The import and export of service trade also reflect this point. Although the service sector output of GDP in emerging economies is rising, the status of service trade deficit countries has not changed substantially. Therefore, without changing structural factors, passively transferring resources to the service trade sector is not an effective way for rebalance in emerging economies.

In recent years, the emerging economies have witnessed the rapid development of service sector and the decline of overall economic growth. If the economic structure cannot develop toward the service sector, can the emerging economies try to find a way out in the direction to upgrade industrial structure? We can see that under the condition of modern economy, some conditions are required for upgrading industrial structure in terms of technology stock and institutional arrangement of equity financing market, etc. Since 2006, it has entered a steady development period for world technological innovation. The emerging economies do not have the advantage in the accumulation of science and technology stock. In the absence of technology stock, they attempt to stimulate enterprise innovation by expanding the scale of equity financing. This kind of exploration did not achieve the expected results in the practice at least in 2015. In addition to the aforementioned two attempts, there is a third possible approach for emerging economies, which is to increase their domestic production section in the international value chain and increase value increment of their domestic goods in international trade. Although such an attempt is meaningful to a country's economy, the implementation of this rebalancing policy will also lead to a decline in the scale of intra-industry trade among emerging economies. This also constitutes an important reason for the decline of the overall growth rate of international trade, especially those of goods trade in recent years. Besides the aforementioned three self-fulfilling approaches for rebalancing, the emerging economies also have a passive one, that is, to adjust their internal economic structure and industrial structure according to the rebalancing of the United States. However, it is not clear which direction a new round of manufacturing innovation is in the United States, resulting in the wait-and-see stage still in those countries which follow the U.S. strategic adjustment. This can actually explain why some peripheral countries can accept the high standard TPP clauses led by the United States, which aims to be able to participate in a new round of international industrial division system led by the United States (see Table 3).

In the specific analysis, the year 2006 is chosen as the historical starting point for our analysis. When Bernanke became the Federal Reserve Chairman in 2006, the U.S. trade deficit also reached a historical peak. More importantly, in 2006 before the crisis, some major countries had already adopted strategic and policy adjustments to avoid the "hard landing" of economic growth caused by the adjustment to global economic imbalance. However, the crisis over the adjustment to global economic imbalance was not averted after all. With the bursting of the U.S. real estate bubble, the U.S. demand, which relied on the support of the U.S. financial wealth effect, began to shrink. The demand-level shocks then became the first issue that governments had to face in their anti-crisis policies. At the same time, the trade-off between the anti-crisis and rebalancing goals also made the road to recovery complicated after the 2008 crisis, due to the conflict between anti-crisis policy and rebalancing policy in terms of growth effect, which was still reflected in the world economy in 2015. Based on this understanding, the major challenges faced in the world economy are summarized as the dilemma of the anti-crisis and the rebalancing policies.

2. Main Characteristics of World Economy in 2015

In 2015, the world economy was still in the process of slow recovery, but the momentum of economic growth slowed down and showed obvious differentiation characteristics. According to data released by the IMF, the growth rate of world economy was 3.1% in 2015, that of developed countries was 2.0%, and that of developing countries and emerging economies was 4.0%, of which the economic growth rate of CIS countries was –2.7%, that of Latin America and the Caribbean was –0.3%, and that of the Middle East and North Africa was 2.5%. Except for Japan, the economic growth rate was 6.5% in East Asian economies, which was still the region with the highest economic growth rate in the world, while China's economic growth rate was 6.8%, slightly higher than the overall growth rate of East Asia. India's growth rate exceeded that of China, and became the fastest growing country in the world. However, on the whole, the

Table 3. Comparison of Rebalancing Approaches between the United States and the Emerging Economies

The United States		The Emerging Economies	
Approaches	**Corresponding Risks**	**Approaches**	**Corresponding Risks**
1. To choose a closed economic growth model	1. To lose the benefits of Globalization	1. To adjust economic structure and transform from manufacturing industry to service industry	1. The non-tradability of the consumer service industry determines that the service industry cannot replace the manufacturing industry in driving the national economy
2. To continue to maintain the scale of current account through financial advantages	2. To threaten the international currency status of U.S. dollar, affect the international competitiveness of the United States, and have geopolitical risks	2. To upgrade industrial structure	2. Under the premise of lack of technology stock, asset bubbles are caused by equity financing reform
3. To revitalize the manufacturing sector and enhance the tradability of services	3. To challenge the existing world economy pattern	3. To extend industrial chain	3. The scale of intra-industry trade declines among emerging economies
		4. To adapt to the rebalancing approach of the United States	4. There is no clear direction at present, and the expected long-term benefits cannot solve the short-term economic problems

Table 4. Economic Growth in Different Regions of the World (%)

Countries and Regions	2013	2014	2015
World	3.3	3.4	3.1
Developed countries	1.1	1.8	2.0
U.S.A.	1.5	2.4	2.6
Eurozone	−0.3	0.9	1.5
Japan	1.6	−0.6	0.9
Developing countries and emerging economies	5.0	4.6	4.0
Developing and emerging economies in Europe	2.9	2.8	3.0
CIS countries	2.2	1.0	−2.7
Latin America and the Caribbean	2.9	1.3	−0.3
The Middle East and North Africa	2.3	2.7	2.5
East Asian economies (except Japan)	7.0	6.8	6.5
China	7.7	7.3	6.8
India	6.9	7.3	7.3
Quantum of world trade (including goods and services)	3.3	3.2	3.1
Import			
Developed economies	2.0	3.4	4.0
Emerging economies	5.2	3.6	1.3
Export			
Developed economies	2.9	3.4	3.1
Emerging economies	4.4	2.9	3.9

Source: IMF, World Economic Outlook, 2015.

economic growth rate of all regions declined significantly, compared with that of 2010–2011 (see Table 4).

According to the data, the overall world economy in 2015 has the following characteristics.

(1) The world economy was still in the process of recovery after the global economic crisis in 2008, but the overall growth rate tended to decline.

(2) Economic growth was differentiated among countries, with the growth performance of developed economies better than that of emerging economies. Among the developed economies, the growth of the United States was better than that of Europe, which was better

than that of Japan. The growth of emerging economies had been declining for six consecutive years, but the situation of manufacturing exporters was better than that of resource exporters.

(3) The growth of world trade was slower than that of world output, which indicated that the world economy has not been rebalanced in the crisis adjustment, and the recovery of the world economy still depends on the effect of anti-crisis policies of individual countries.
(4) The increase in the total imports of the developed countries did not have an obvious pull effect on the exports of the emerging economies. The severe decline in imports of emerging economies is a noteworthy issue. From the perspective of the reasons, it can be seen that the policy spillover of internal structural adjustment in emerging economies led to the decline in the volume of goods trade of emerging economies. The decline of import trade has a direct impact and influence on lower global commodity prices. The endogenous growth rate of emerging economies was declining, and a negative feedback shock was formed among emerging economies.
(5) China's economic growth rate dropped below 7%, which has become the focus of global concern.

In our view, the main reasons for the aforementioned characteristics of the world economy are as follows.

2.1. *The cycle of science and technology development has led to the decline of the world economic growth rate*

The rapid growth of the world economy mainly depends on technological progress and institutional innovation. However, since the 21st century, the world economy has entered a steady period of science and technology development. Around the world, whether from the scale of input and output of science and technology research and development, or from the characteristics of industries and countries, it can be found that new technology flashpoints have not appeared, and the promotion of existing science and technology stock on global total factor productivity is also weakening, which is the most fundamental reason for the slowdown in real economic growth.

With the Malmquist index approach of DEA non-parametric estimation, we made a quantitative analysis of the overall characteristics and trends of the technological progress in the world. The basic conclusion is that world scientific and technological innovation still lacks a clear direction for breakthrough, which is mainly in the following five aspects.

Firstly, the R&D investment in the OECD countries shows an inverted U-shaped downward trend. In particular, from 2000 to 2014, the R&D expenditure saw an inverse U-shaped change that first rose then declined. From 2000 to 2008, the proportion of R&D expenditure in GDP was fluctuating upward, but the proportion has declined significantly since 2009. From the perspective of different industries, from 2006 to 2014, the R&D expenditure in those areas like manufacturing, services, construction, mining and agriculture industries also showed a characteristic of the inverted U-shaped change, which also first rose, then declined. Among them, the industry of machinery and equipment for metal products and the petrochemical industry are two sub-sectors with the largest R&D expenditure in manufacturing, their trends all took the peak in 2008 as the boundary, and also showed the inverted U-shaped trend that first rose then declined.

Secondly, the overall R&D output of the OECD countries is decreasing. From the perspective of the total output of technological innovation, the number of EPO patent applications in OECD countries has fluctuated around 130,000 since 2001, and the R&D output has not shown a significant upward trend, even with a certain degree of decline. From the perspective of the field of technological innovation, the number of patent applications in the OECD countries is mainly concentrated in five major fields such as network telecommunications (ICT) and power transmission. Among them, network telecommunications accounts for the highest proportion of patent applications, which shows that currently network telecommunications are still the core fields of technology research and development. At the same time, the proportion of patent applications is relatively low and the technology R&D is still immature, in the fields of those technologies corresponding to the new technology frontier, such as biotechnology, nanotechnology and technologies for pollution and waste management as well as for addressing climate change. On the whole, with the declining trend of R&D output in the OECD countries, the effect of technological revolution brought by information technology is gradually weakening. Those emerging technology fields such as biotechnology and nanotechnology do not show a strong promotion of technical change. And network telecommunication technology still occupies a dominant position in the field of patented technologies, though its technological innovation growth decreases rapidly.

Thirdly, the industry R&D innovation has a significant trend of differentiation. As for R&D expenditures in different industries, from 2000 to 2014, the manufacturing industry had the largest R&D expenditure, followed by that in service industry, construction industry, mining industry and agriculture. Among them, the growth rate of R&D expenditure in service industry was significantly higher than that in manufacturing industry, and the decline trend of the R&D expenditure in agriculture was most significant, falling from the peak of 840 million dollars in 2007 to 80 million dollars in 2013. Furthermore, in terms of R&D output of different industries, those five technology fields with higher average annual growth rates were nanotechnology, medical technology, electricity, mechanical engineering and human necessities. From 2009 to 2011, the R&D output in most industries declined in fluctuation, while the innovation activities in the technology fields that maintained rapid growth, such as nanotechnology, medical technology, electricity and so on, accounted for a relatively small proportion in the overall scale of patent innovation. It can be found that the main reason for the slowdown of technological progress in the OECD countries lies in the decrease of R&D expenditure growth in manufacturing industry, at the same time, it is also related to the fact that the increase of R&D expenditure in service industry failed to bring about significant improvement in overall technology.

Fourthly, the country-specific characteristics of technological innovation have a significant differentiation trend. From the perspective of the R&D expenditure of different economies, the proportions of R&D expenditures (in GDP) are all above 2% in some technological powers, such as the United States, Japan, Germany, France and Britain. However, the R&D expenditures of those countries are mainly in the manufacturing industry, while the R&D expenditure of the service industry is much lower than that of the manufacturing industry. Moreover, the R&D expenditures of both those industries show a trend of slower growth. However, in some economies such as Australia, France, Israel, Austria, Mexico, Czech Republic, Switzerland and Denmark, the R&D expenditure of service industry is significantly higher than that of manufacturing industry, showing a rapid upward trend. From the perspective of technological innovation, those traditional industrial powers such as the United States, Germany,

Japan and France, still occupy a dominant position in the number of patent applications. However, in the fields of emerging technology, for example, in those five major fields, including nanotechnology, medical technology, electricity, mechanical engineering and human necessities, the patent applications of the above-mentioned countries are all at a relatively low level, resulting in the lack of innovation leading force in the field of emerging technology.

Fifthly, from the perspective of the improvement of scientific research input and output changes on the production frontier since 1991, it is very obvious that the improvement of total factor productivity caused by the change in scientific and technological input and output had promoted the production frontier from 1991 to 1999. However, since 2000, this promoting effect has weakened, and during the period from 2006 to 2014, it has basically been relatively stable.

2.2. *Trade overshoot in the emerging economies has led to insufficient growth momentum of the world economy*

From the perspective of the history after the Second World War, the cycle of world economic growth is not completely consistent with that of technological progress. Therefore, it is hard to fully explain the mediocrity of economic growth, just with the current steady development of science and technology input and output. At the same time, it can be seen from the data that the sustained downturn of international trade growth is synchronized with the sluggish economic growth. Therefore, to explore the reasons for the decline in world trade growth will be helpful to explain the stagnation of world economic growth.

In the traditional mode of global economic imbalance, the import of developed countries is the main demand source to pull economic growth of emerging economies. However, after the crisis, under the impact of the financial transmission channels of the crisis, Europe reverted to the old way of improving and repairing regional economic integration, and its influence on the world economy has declined significantly. Meanwhile, during the European economic recovery in 2013 and 2014, EU trade basically maintained a negative growth trend, indicating that its foreign trade was no longer the main driving force of the EU economic recovery. On the contrary, the foreign trade played a negative role. From the perspective of domestic and foreign trades of EU 28 countries, after 2013, the growth rate of internal trade began to exceed that of external trade, indicating that

EU countries increasingly choose internal trade. In Japan, Abe's economic policies not only failed to achieve the expected goals in terms of growth but also did not change Japan's position and role in the world economy. In both the history after World War II and the current rebalancing process, Japan, like other East Asian countries, plays the role of a supplier in the world economy. Therefore, Japan cannot play a role in stimulating the demand of developed countries in the process of world economic growth. On the whole, the growth of world trade in the anti-crisis process mainly depends on the change in U.S. import demand.

From the perspective of the external balance of the United States, after the financial crisis in 2008, its current account deficit had been adjusted from 806.726 billion dollars in 2006 to 389.526 billion dollars in 2014, which greatly reduced the potential risk of economic imbalance. However, it should be noted that from the specific content of current account adjustment in the United States, the narrowing of the imbalance scale was not entirely due to the reduction of trade scale, and the rapid increase of capital gains after the crisis also played a very crucial role. Since 2007, the capital gains in the U.S. current account have increased from −13.268 billion dollars to 118.798 billion dollars (see Table 5). The corresponding question is why did the limited decline in the U.S. trade deficit scale lead to a sharp decline in world trade growth? It is nothing more than two reasons. Firstly, the scale of trade imbalance had reached

Table 5. U.S. Current Account and Capital Account Net Amount (In 100 Million Dollars)

Year	Current Account	Goods Trade	Capital Gain	Capital Account
2005	−7,454.34	−7,142.45	−311.89	11 311.1
2006	−8,067.26	−7,617.16	−450.1	26,914.54
2007	−7,186.43	−7,053.75	−132.68	30,506.72
2008	−6,907.89	−7,087.26	179.37	−5,641.43
2009	−3,840.23	−3,837.74	−2.49	667.8
2010	−4,419.61	−4,946.58	526.97	18,551.36
2011	−4,603.54	−5,486.25	882.71	9,247.68
2012	−4,496.7	−5,367.73	871.03	2,463.36
2013	−3,767.6	−4,783.94	1,016.34	12,074.8
2014	−3,895.26	−5,083.24	1,187.98	12,612.42

Source: Database of BEA—U.S. International Transaction, the United States.

its extreme value around 2006, and it was with relatively low possibility to stimulate the world economic growth by increasing the scale of trade deficit. Secondly, when the crisis occurred, the emerging economies had already made adjustment for the possible decline in U.S. trade scale, resources flowed to non-trade services, and the change of trade structure eventually led to the overshoot of world trade growth.

2.3. *The pulling effect of external demand of core countries cannot be replaced by the growth of domestic demand in peripheral countries*

Whenever the imbalance adjustment is started up in the world economy, core countries and international economic organizations all hope that peripheral countries can replace their growth of external demand by boosting their domestic demand. In the 1980s, the G7 countries all put pressure on Japan and required it to open its domestic market. However, the efforts to increase the domestic demand in Japan did not change the basic pattern of consumption in the core countries while production in peripheral countries in the world economy. The conclusion at that time was that Japan's economic scale could not be compared with that of the United States. Therefore, Japan's economic rise could not be counted on for replacing the position and role of the United States in the world economy. In this round of adjustment of the world economic imbalance, the United States and the international economic organizations also repeatedly called on the East Asian economies to increase their domestic demand. In fact, the East Asian economies did increase their domestic consumption levels in response to the crisis, as manifested by the fact that the growth rate of final consumption in East Asia was much higher than that in North America and the European Union after the crisis. In 2010 and 2011, the growth rate of final consumption in East Asia reached about 15%, higher than the growth rate of GDP in East Asia in the same period. In 2013, the total final consumption of 10 East Asian economies reached 11.1 trillion dollars, exceeding the level of 11 trillion dollars of the 15 European Union countries. The gap was also narrowing, compared with the level of 13.9 trillion dollars in North America. This phenomenon of East Asian economies has also been verified in China's macro-economic data. In the process of declining aggregate demand in China, the

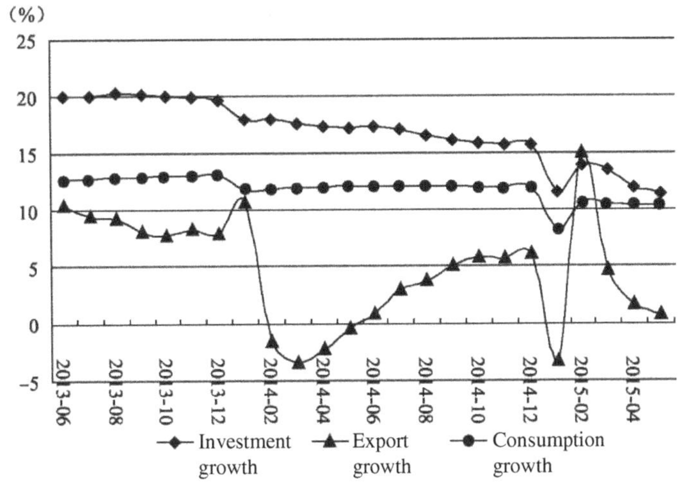

Figure 2. Changes in Growth Rates of Three Major Demands in China

Source: China's Macroeconomic Analysis and Forecast (Mid-2015) Report — China's Macro-Economy with a coexistence of Depression and Prosperity, Depression and Bubble, by Research Group of Macroeconomic Analysis and Forecast, Renmin University of China, published in *Economic Theory and Economic Management*, 2015(8): 5–35.

consumption demand has maintained a steady development trend, without obvious fluctuations (see Figure 2).

The growth of internal consumption demand in emerging economies did not promote the growth of international trade. On the contrary, while the internal demand of emerging economies increased, the import scale was shrinking, which reflects that in the traditional imbalance adjustment, the supply structure of peripheral countries served the demand structure of core countries, and the growth of internal consumption demand could not absorb the excess capacity brought by the decline of external demand. Formally speaking, the growth of domestic demand in emerging economies is mainly manifested by the transfer of demand from manufacturing to service industries, while the international competitiveness of service industries in emerging countries is at a distinct disadvantage. Especially after the 2008 crisis, except for the significantly improvement of India's service industry advantage index, the service industry advantage index of other emerging economies is declining, including that of China and South

Korea, while the service industry advantage index of the United States is rising obviously. This phenomenon can reveal at least three points as follows: (1) the internal consumption demand of the peripheral countries cannot replace the external demand of the core countries. The reason lies not only in the relatively small economic scale of the peripheral countries, but more important in the constraints of economic structure, especially of global supply and demand structure. (2) As the emerging economies have a relatively low position in the division of labor in the field of service trade, when impacted by external demand, the output growth of the service industry cannot replace the export demand of emerging economies. (3) Considering the weak trade competitiveness of the service industry in the emerging economies, it is impossible for the emerging economies to obtain more trade gains in the future service trade, either. Therefore, it is not an advisable choice for these countries to transfer resources from manufacturing industry to service industry through economic restructuring, at least in terms of welfare and growth outcomes.

2.4. *Booming stock markets in the emerging economies cannot change the downward trend of the world economic growth*

The phenomenon of concern in the world economy in 2015 was the deviation between "stock market prosperity" and "economic fundamentals". The stock market was no longer the "barometer" of the real economy. In both the developed countries and the emerging market countries, their stock markets had a negative correlation with their economies and for those countries with sluggish economic growth, their stock markets rose faster instead.

In the first half of 2015, among the mature stock markets, the European market and the Japanese market performed well. Since the beginning of 2015, the CAC40 index of France, the DAX index of Germany and the Nikkei 225 index of Japan had increased by 18.95%, 15.33% and 17.96%, respectively. However, for those three countries, their real GDP growth rate year-to-year was only 0.36%, 1.61% and –0.42%, respectively, in 2014. Australia, the United Kingdom and the United States, with their real GDP growth rates of 2.71%, 2.55% and 2.39%, respectively, had relatively mediocre stock market performance in the first half of 2015. The stock market trend of emerging economies was similar to that of developed countries. China's economy entered a new normal, and there were no bright spots in economic growth for Russia and other countries, but their stock markets performed better instead. The economies of India and Indonesia performed better, but their stock markets were also relatively mediocre.

In addition, corresponding to this deviation is the situation of small and medium-sized enterprises. The performance of innovative companies in the stock market is better than that of traditional enterprises and large blue-chip companies. On the one hand, it shows that the market and the government have high expectations for technology innovation. On the other hand, we must also point out that the risk aggregation process is very rapid for both developed countries and emerging economies which want to support corporate innovation or reduce enterprise debt leverage ratio through the stock market, on the premise of lacking technology stock. According to the experience of the United States in the 1990s, the promotion of economic growth by the capital market, including the stock market, must be with two premises of "wealth effect" and "capital effect" together at the same time (see Figure 3). If the factor of technological progress no longer exists, then the earnings expectations of an enterprise will decline, and then the decline of expectations will lead to the decrease of the investment. At this time, the "capital effect" of the capital market no longer exists, and all that left for the rising of stock market price is the pursuit of "wealth effect", which must result in the gradual accumulation of bubbles and risks. The relationship between investment and consumption in the capital market has already been shown in the U.S. Subprime Crisis. In

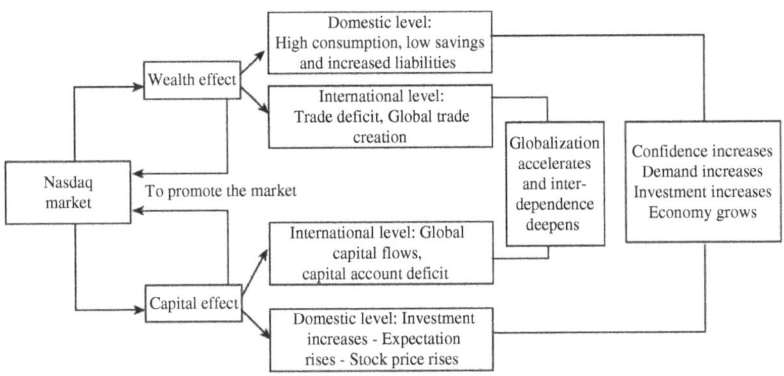

Figure 3. Transmission Mechanism of Economic Growth Effect in Stock Markets

2016, risks accumulated rapidly once again while the stock markets in the emerging economies were deviating from the real economy.

2.5. *The attempt to establish a new international economic order makes the economy rebalancing more complicated*

If the decline in global economic growth in 2015 is related to the rebalancing adjustment of the global economy, then whether the policy coordination among countries is successful or not is the key issue related to the future trend of world economy. From the perspective of the changes of world economy imbalance pattern in 2006, the rise of China's economy and its position in the world trade greatly reduce the importance of the G7 coordination mechanism, which played a decisive role in the 1980s. The developed countries led by the United States need to find a global coordination mechanism with the participation of emerging economies, and the G20 is undoubtedly a good alternative mechanism. However, no effective agreements have been reached yet on major issues related to the future development of the world economy since the establishment of the G20, due to the large differences among emerging economies themselves covered by the G20. At the same time, the World Trade Organization only applies the means of free trade to border policy, and from the perspective of the adjustment of American rebalancing, whether for the intellectual property rights related to high-tech and service trade, or for the fair trade rules restricting subsidies and dumping, it is necessary to extend the implementation means of fair trade to the interior of a country. Therefore, even the world economic system dominated by the United States after the Second World War cannot meet the demand of rebalancing adjustment of global economy in the 21st century.

In this context, the major countries involved in rebalancing in 2015 all made bold attempts in the aspect of establishing a new international economic order. China has taken substantial steps in the "The Belt and Road" and "Asian Infrastructure Investment Bank", and adopted a positive attitude in the aspect of RCEP, while the United States has started with TPP and TIPP to build a high standard trade system to replace the WTO.

The contents of different agreements have conflicts of interest, for example, the rules of origin in TPP will have discrimination on the trade goods of non-members, then trigger the interruption of the value chain among the emerging economies, and such impact will destroy the existing world division of labor, however, if different regional trade agreements can have an impact on free competition, then the separated exploration on the new international order will also have a positive impact on the establishment of the new international economic order in the future. What is more, from the published text of TPP, there is a certain conflict between its content and the rules of free trade.

Therefore, in our view, the existing provisions may be rejected or made major changes by members (including the United States) in the future implementation, due to such logical contradictions in the existing TPP texts. That is to say, the actual effect when TPP landings may be quite different from the effect currently envisaged by the United States. Of course, our view may not be true eventually, which is mainly because the TPP is not just a trade agreement, it is a pillar in itself for the Asia-Pacific rebalancing strategy of the United States. Therefore, considering the geopolitical factors, whether the existing members and potential TPP members accept the TPP agreement is not entirely out of their economic interests. And they may accept such an institutional arrangement of the United States from the perspective of political security. This will make the conflict of interests between regional coordination organizations become the mainstream, and the world economy in the future will become more complex in this conflict.

3. The Impact of Policy Conflicts among Great Powers on World Economy

Before the U.S. economic crisis in 2008, the U.S. concerns about the global economic imbalance adjustment risks were mainly focused on the expansion of current account imbalances, the decline of the dollar exchange rate index, the rise of commodity prices represented by petroleum, and interest conflicts among countries, especially those interest conflicts arising from the rise of China's economic aggregate and the eastward expansion of the Eurozone. After experiencing an economic crisis and seven years of slow recovery, for those risks that the United States was concerned about, the only risk left is caused by uncoordinated policies among countries. Based on this, the judgment of country-specific policy risks is an important content for us to predict the future world economic trends.

3.1. *The Eurozone has separated from the rebalancing framework of the United States when improved the regional integration mechanism*

After experiencing the sovereign debt crisis, the Eurozone began to embark on the track of growth recovery in 2015 by implementing the intra-regional rescue package. At the same time, the overall economy in the Eurozone has become less connected with the outside region. Therefore, for a period of time in the future, the main challenge the Eurozone faces will come from the impact of the intra-regional integration system, rather than the adjustment process of world economy rebalancing.

From the perspective of reasons of the Eurozone economic recovery in 2015, in addition to the improvement of production costs and the pull of consumption demand which were caused by the decline of oil prices, the effective implementation of regional relief programs has played a crucial role.

Among them, the introduction of supranational European stability mechanism in the financial field, the choice of various loose monetary policies, the implementation of monetary policies independent of external influences, and the promulgation of the Euro Convention and The European 2020 Strategy, have all played a leading and promoting role in the structural reform and competitiveness improvement for EU Member States.

In order to promote investment in EU countries, Mr. Juncker, the new President of the European Commission proposed the European Investment Plan (also known as the Juncker Plan) with a seed funding of 21 billion euros (expected to drive 315 billion euros) in the next three years, and the plan was officially announced on November 26, 2014. According to the Juncker Plan, the European Commission will cooperate with the European investment bank to establish the European Fund for Strategic Investments (EFSI), with the European investment bank taking full responsibility for the investment and financing of the European investment plan. The financing form of the EFSI is mainly through the "seed funding" of 21 billion euros, of which the European Union invests 16 billion euros budget funds and the European Investment Bank contributes 5 billion euros, to encourage the EU member states to contribute directly or indirectly (through their national promotion banks) to the expansion of refinancing the seed funding, as well as attracting private and foreign investors. Of the total 21 billion euros EFSI, 16 billion euros will be used to drive long-term investment in transportation and energy infrastructure (transportation, energy, broadband), education, research, innovation, renewable energy and other fields, planning to leverage 240 billion euros funds into those above-mentioned long-term investment fields; and 5 billion euros will be used to promote investment in small and medium-sized enterprises, planning to leverage 75 billion euros investment in small and medium-sized enterprises. In January 2015, the European Commission put forward the proposal on the Regulation of the EFSI, which was approved by the EU Finance Ministers' Meeting on March 10. The European Parliament voted on the Regulation on April 20, and the proposal is under legislative discussion in European legislatures.

Although the European investment plan has not yet been formally implemented, it has already been supported by major European countries. Germany, Spain, France, Italy and Luxembourg had successively announced that they would provide supporting funds for the projects supported by the Juncker Plan through their national promotion banks. In February 2005, Germany and Spain respectively announced an injection of 8 billion euros and 1.5 billion euros into the EFSI, in order to support projects supported by the Juncker Plan in their own countries. In March, France and Italy each pledged to inject 8 billion euros into the European investment plan to support their own approved projects. On April 9, Luxembourg announced that it would inject 80 million euros into the projects supported by the Juncker Plan through its national promotion bank. On April 21, the Polish government announced that it would inject 8 billion euros into the projects in its country supported by the EFSI. According to the estimation of the European Commission, during the three years from 2015 to 2017, the European investment plan would add additional 330 billion to 410 billion euros to GDP, and increase employment by 1 million to 1.3 million.

Those highlights in the economic policy of the Eurozone have not completely overcome the institutional defects that led to the sovereign debt crisis, the asynchrony of fiscal policy and the difficulties of structural reform. In addition, the geopolitical factors may interrupt the recovery process of the economic growth of the Eurozone at any time. But even if Europe's growth is interrupted again, its impact on the world economy will be limited. The main reason is that after the sovereign debt crisis, the spillover impact of the Eurozone economy on the global economy has declined significantly.

First of all, with the EU monthly import and export growth rate, import growth rate and export growth rate from January 2008 to July 2015, the EU's foreign trade grew rapidly in 2010 and then declined rapidly. In 2013 and 2014 when the economy was recovering, the growth rate of these three indicators in the EU basically maintained a negative growth trend (see Figure 4). This shows that foreign trade is no longer the main driving force of the EU's economic recovery; on the contrary, it has become a negative constraint.

Secondly, from the perspective of the structure of intra-regional and extra-regional trade in the 28 EU countries, the intra-regional trade volume is far greater than the extra-regional trade volume (see Figure 5). Although the extra-regional trade in the EU region grew rapidly after 2010, and its growth rate was higher than that of the intra-regional trade, but the growth rate of intra-regional trade begun to exceed that of extra-regional trade after 2013, which indicates that EU countries are increasingly choosing intra-regional trade rather than the extra-regional trade (see Figure 6).

Finally, from the perspective of the contribution of final consumption expenditure, total capital formation and foreign trade to GDP, the EU household final consumption expenditure is replacing the foreign trade as the main driving force to promote the EU economic growth from the third quarter of 2013. In the first quarter of 2015, the contribution of the EU

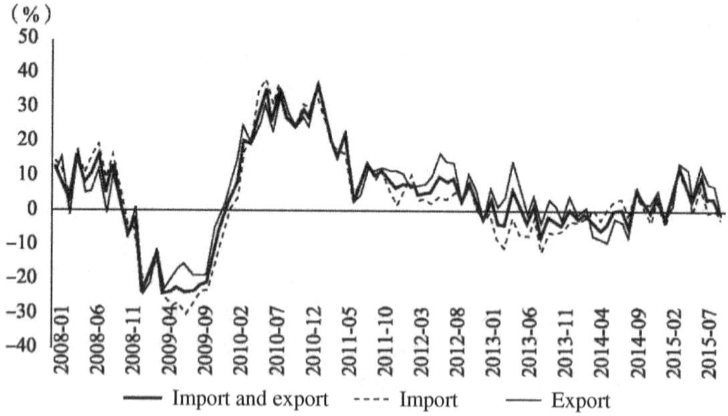

Figure 4. Changes in the Foreign Trade of the EU

Source: Wind Information.

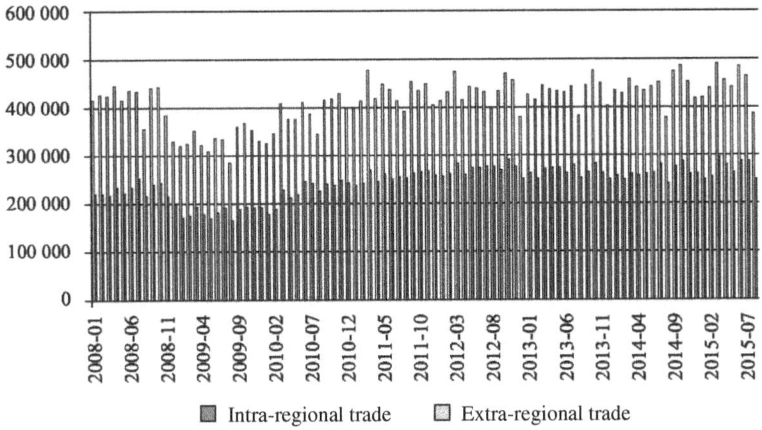

Figure 5. The Intra-Regional Trade Volume and the Extra-Regional Trade Volume in the EU (In Million Euros)

Source: Wind Information.

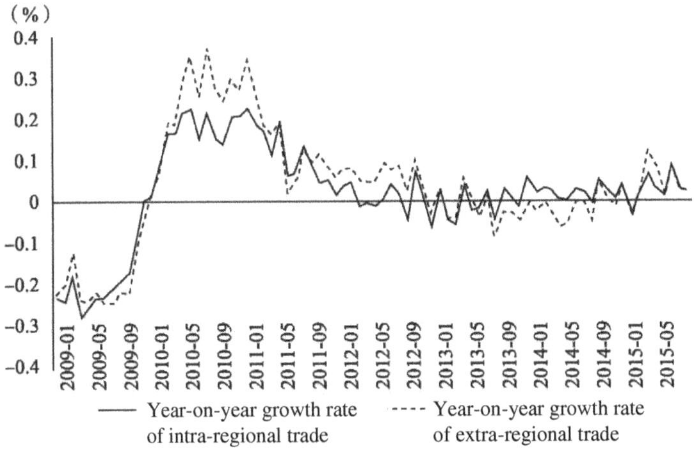

Figure 6. Growth Rates of Intra-Regional Trade and Extra-Regional Trade in the EU

Source: Wind Information.

household final consumption expenditure to regional GDP was 1.54%, while the contribution of foreign trade to economic growth was −0.14% (see Figure 7).

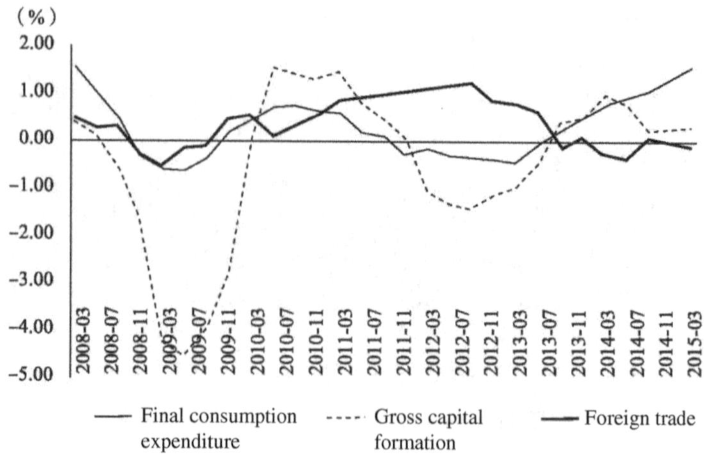

Figure 7. Principal Components of the EU's GDP

Source: Wind Information.

From the aforementioned three points, it can be seen that the economic growth of the EU is becoming less dependent on its foreign trade, and in its foreign trade, the growth rate of the intra-regional trade of the EU is far greater than that of extra-regional trade. It indicates that recent economic recovery of the EU is in the relatively closed conditions.

3.2. *The economic policies led by the right-wing politics in Japan can hardly change the economic downturn*

Abenomics is actually an anti-crisis policy. Fundamentally speaking, with this kind of anti-crisis policy, it is difficult to solve the structural problems in Japan's economy. From the perspective of the growth of Japan from 2014 to 2015, Japan has already lagged behind Europe. However, in Japan, Abenomics still had certain support. This is mainly because the logic of Abenomics in terms of international strategic adjustment accords with the mentality of Japan's social and economic development.

Japan is the first country to succeed in developing an export-oriented economy after the Second World War. However, under the impact of economic globalization, Japan also experienced the painful "lost 20 years". If we compare Japan's prosperous 20 years with its lost 20 years, we can find that, during the "prosperous 20 years", Japan's economic growth rate exceeded that of other major developed countries in most years, with the exception of a few years. In the 1960s, the average annual growth rate of Japan's industry exceeded 14%, corresponding to three times that of the United States and five times that of the United Kingdom, which made the economic gap between Japan and Western countries narrowed rapidly and achieved continuous transcendence. Japan's GDP surpassed that of Britain and France in 1967 and that of federal Germany in 1968, making Japan become the second largest economy after the United States. However, after the 1990s, with the exception of 1996, Japan's economic growth rate was at the lowest level among developed countries for most of the time (see Table 6). The result of this comparison inevitably led to the conclusion that the external conditions of the prosperous period are conducive to the revitalization of Japan's economy. The beginning of Japan's economic prosperity was in the Cold War strategic period of the United States. The United States not only provided Japan with a Marshall assistance program, but more importantly, it also tolerated the controlled economy thought of Japan's right-wing political party headed by Kishi Nobusuke. Therefore, that the Cold War mentality of containing competitors was conducive to reshaping the external environment of Japan's economic development became the idea for Japan to push its economy back to prosperity. From this perspective, regardless of the effect of the Abe administration's economic policies, its political right-wing turn has been successful in Japanese politics. For this reason, Mr. Abe has never shied away from comparisons between his grandfather and him by other people, because Kishi Nobusuke had also achieved the high-speed economic growth while striving to achieve the political right-wing goals. However, the 20-year comparison based on Japan's economy will ignore the basic trend of world economic development. If we compare Japan's economic history of the 70 years before and after the Second World War, the conclusion is quite different (see Figure 8).

It can be seen from Table 6 and Figure 8 that the speed of Japan's economic development was very fast after the Second World War. Such economic performance of Japan is mainly due to the existence of global market, which strengthens the role of technological progress in promoting growth. Therefore, a peaceful international economic environment is conducive to the long-term development of Japan's economy. In recent years, under the interference of the right-wing politics of the Abe

Table 6. The World's GDP Growth Rate and GDP Growth Rates of Japan, U.S.A., U.K. and China (%)

Country	1820–1870	1870–1913	1913–1950	1950–1973	1973–2001
U.S.A.	4.2	3.94	2.84	3.93	2.94
U.K.	2.05	1.9	1.19	2.93	2.08
Japan	0.41	2.44	2.21	9.29	2.71
China	−0.37	0.56	−0.02	5.02	6.72
World	0.93	2.11	1.82	4.9	3.05

Source: [U.K.] Angus Maddison. *Millennium Statistics on the World Economy*. Beijing, Peking University Press, 2009.

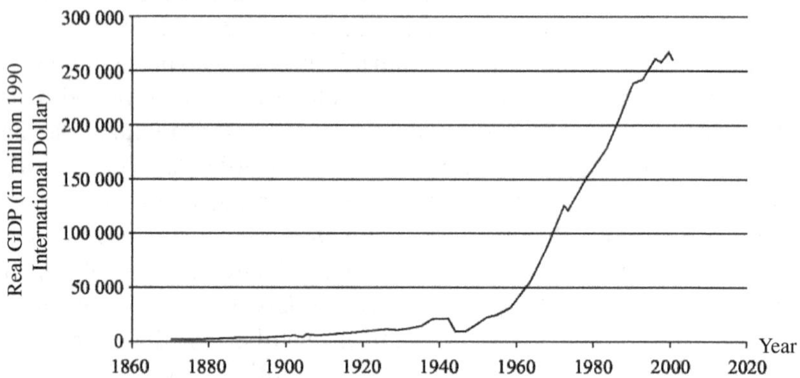

Figure 8. Changes in Japan's GDP before and after the Second World War (1870–2001)

Source: [U.K.] Angus Maddison. *Millennium Statistics on the World Economy*. Beijing, Peking University Press, 2009.

administration, Japan's foreign economic relations have quietly changed in the course of the escalating island disputes with its neighbors, including China. For example, Japan's direct investment in China is undergoing a reverse change in recent years. After 2009, Japan's foreign direct investment decreased due to the impact of the financial crisis, but its direct investment in China increased continuously. In 2009, Japan's direct investment in China was 4.117 billion dollars, which rose to 7.352 billion dollars in 2012. However, in 2013, Japan's direct investment in China began to decline, only 7.058 billion dollars, about 4% lower than the previous year. In 2014, it dropped sharply by 38.8% compared with the previous year. In fact, in 2014, China's FDI inflows grew moderately as a whole, and it surpassed the United States to become the world's largest direct investment inflow country for the first time. However, under such circumstances, Japan's direct investment in China declined significantly, indicating that the change in Japan's investment was completely opposite to the pattern of international capital flows. The pattern of capital flow changed, at the same time, the trade dependence between China and Japan also had certain changes. Japan's trade dependence on China increased from 4.12% in 2005 to 6.68% in 2014, while China's trade dependence on Japan decreased from 8.31% in 2005 to 2.97% in 2014 (see Table 7). This shows that Abe's right-wing strategic adjustment has neither solved the problem of Japan's domestic economic growth nor changed Japan's role in the world economic structure, worldwide and within the region.

Table 7. China's Trade Dependence on Japan and Japan's Trade Dependence on China from 2005 to 2014

Index	2005	2010	2011	2012	2013	2014
China's GDP (in 100 million dollars)	22,686	60,397	74,924	84,616	94,906	103,601
China's exports to Japan (in 100 million dollars)	1085.2	1533.7	1840.6	1883.9	1807.6	1,810
China's export dependence on Japan (%)	4.78	2.54	2.46	2.23	1.91	1.75
China imports from Japan (in 100 million dollars)	799.7	1496.9	1620.4	1442	1291.2	1264.8
China's import dependence on Japan (%)	3.53	2.48	2.16	1.7	1.36	1.22
Bilateral Trade between China and Japan (in 100 million dollars)	1884.9	3030.6	3461.1	3325.8	3098.9	3074.8
China's trade dependence on Japan (%)	8.31	5.02	4.62	3.93	3.27	2.97
Japan's GDP (in 100 million dollars)	45,719	54,954	59,056	59,545	49,196	46,015
Japan's export dependence on China (%)	1.75	2.72	2.74	2.42	2.63	2.75
Japan's import dependence on China (%)	2.37	2.79	3.12	3.16	3.67	3.93
Japan's trade dependence on China (%)	4.12	5.51	5.86	5.58	6.3	6.68
Japan's trade deficit (in 100 million dollars)	285.5	36.8	220.2	441.9	516.4	545.1

Source: World Bank statistics and Japan Customs statistics database.

3.3. *The U.S. economy is still in the balance between anti-crisis and rebalancing*

From the perspective of the policy orientation of the U.S. government after the financial crisis, under the dilemma of balanced growth, the anti-crisis policy and the rebalancing policy have been in a dynamic trade-off adjustment. One of the most prominent performances is the repeated delay of the Federal Reserve on the time of withdrawing from quantitative easing monetary policy. And this hesitation in policy choices began to appear in 2010 and has continued up to now.

3.3.1. *The rebalancing policy in the anti-crisis process of the United States*

In the early stage of the crisis, the external economic imbalance of the United States was quickly adjusted to the equilibrium. The proportion of the current account deficit in GDP was rapidly adjusted from the historical high point of 6.2% in the third quarter of 2006 to 2.7% in early 2009 (see Figures 1–9). However, the adjustment of the economic imbalance of the United States in this period was mainly due to the disappearance of the real-estate wealth effect under the background of the real-estate bubble

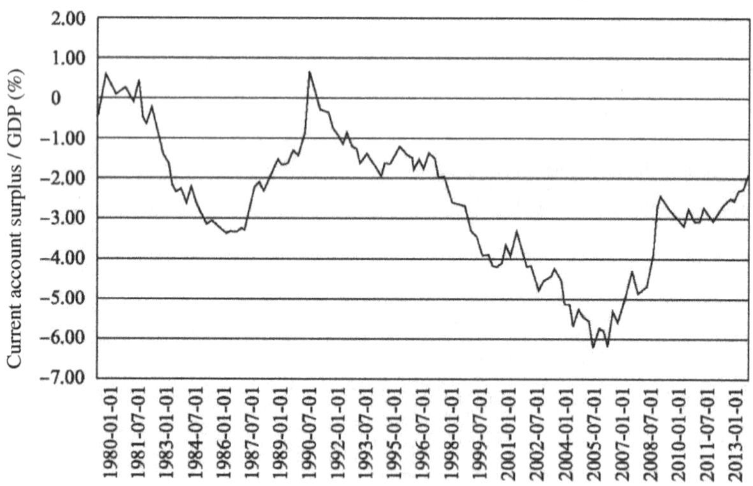

Figure 9. Dynamic Adjustment of the U.S. Economic Imbalance

Source: Federal Reserve Bank of St. Louis.

burst, which has typical characteristics of market adjustment and has little connection with the macroeconomic policies of the U.S. government. In fact, during this period, the policies of the U.S. government had relatively more anti-crisis characteristics, and its policy direction was opposite to that of rebalancing. In the early stage of the crisis, coping with the sharp economic decline was the primary goal of the policy, and differences in economic growth pattern were not critical. However, from the perspective of specific policy orientation, the stability of the financial sector and the maintenance of consumer demand was the core objectives of the government's anti-crisis policy, still corresponding to the maintenance of the competitive advantage of the U.S. financial services sector and the leading role of consumption in the development of deficit economy, which essentially emphasized the return of the economic growth mode to the unbalanced growth mode before the crisis. This also explains why the economic growth of emerging economies did not show a significant decline in the early stages of the crisis.

After 2010, with the gradual recovery of the U.S. economy and the further understanding of the risk attributes of economic imbalance, "avoiding the unreal and taking the practical" and "avoiding the trivial and taking the important" have become the main industrial adjustment ideas. Economic rebalancing has begun to be taken as the primary policy objective by the system and policy design represented by the Manufacturing Promotion Act, the National Manufacturing Strategy Act and the Five-Year Export Doubling Plan. As a result, since 2010, the proportion of the U.S. current account deficit to GDP has been stabilized at a moderate level of about 3% for a long period of time. However, after the characteristics of the U.S. economic recovery were basically determined from 2012, such value even gradually dropped to about 1.9%, showing a certain overshoot characteristic.

3.3.2. *Changes in the U.S. economy under its rebalancing adjustment*

The dynamic change of the U.S. anti-crisis policy and rebalancing policy is essentially a trade-off between growth gains and growth risks, and the result must be in accordance with the overall interests of the U.S. economy in a specific period. But the problem is that, as the core country of the world economy, the adjustment of U.S. economic policy will inevitably produce very obvious spillover effects. When the U.S. anti-crisis policy being as policy leading, and under the background of lack of major technology and institutional innovation, the growth model of the world economy will certainly follow the old pattern of unbalanced growth before the crisis, and the gains derived from the financial services and manufacturing industries remains as the main source of growth for core and peripheral countries. At this time, the economic interests of the core and peripheral countries are relatively consistent, and the world economy will also benefit from the positive externality of the U.S. macro policies. However, when the U.S. rebalancing policy represented by re-industrialization is taken as the leading one, along with the transfer of the U.S. economic barycenter from the financial services industry to the manufacturing sector, at least in the short term, it is difficult for the peripheral countries to form a new source of comparative advantage, and the individual interests of the core countries will conflict with the overall interests of the world economy. The country differentiation of world economic growth will also have the most basic necessary condition. From the perspective of several major characteristics of the current U.S. economy, such a conflict in the mechanism of realizing interests is also reflected in consumption and investment.

First of all, at the consumption level, there has been a substitution of domestic product consumption for imported product consumption in the United States.

With the external transfer of the U.S. manufacturing sector, the gap between U.S. domestic product consumption and output, especially that between durable goods consumption and output, has been increasing constantly. The consumption demand for imported products has gradually increased, and the proportion of imported products in residents' commodity consumption and total consumption has also been increasing. Although such a trend eased in the early stage of the financial crisis, from 2010, the proportion of imported products consumption still continued rising, as before the Crisis. It was only in 2012 that the proportion of consumption derived from domestic products in U.S. residents' consumption began to rise. And the proportion of imported product consumption, whether in commodity consumption or in the total consumption, has begun to decline, showing a certain replacement of domestic product consumption for imported product consumption (see Figure 10).

Secondly, at the investment level, the U.S. foreign investment began to transfer to domestic investment.

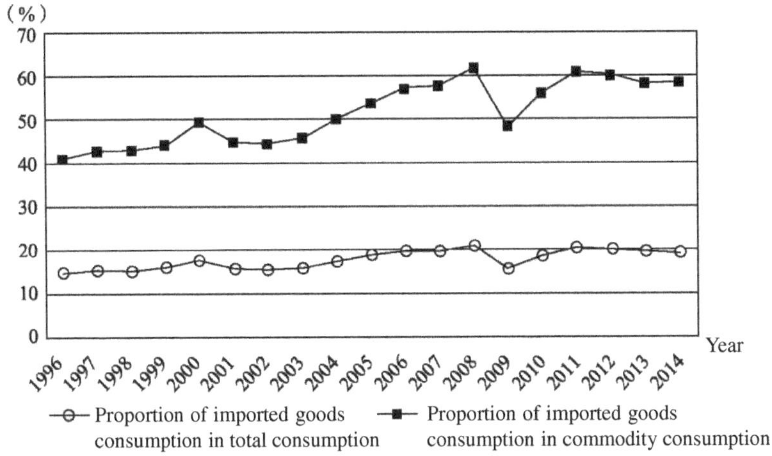

Figure 10. Changes in U.S. Residents' Consumption of Imported Goods

Source: U.S. TIC trade database and Bureau of Economic Analysis, the U.S. Department of Commerce.

Similar to the field of consumption, the same change trend also happens in the investment field. In the context of global economic imbalance, the two-way circulation flow of international capitals characterized by capitals with "large outflows and inflows" has become a realistic carrier for the realization of economic gains in the United States and the world. As can be seen from Figures 1 to 11, since 2010, although the overall pattern of two-way international capital flows has been maintained, the speed of capital inflows into the United States begun to greatly exceed that of capital outflows from the United States, and the net capital flowing into the United States has gradually increased. In 2014, this value has risen to 7 trillion dollars, which was 4.5 times higher than that in 2007. Such a change in the capital flow pattern reflects the difference in growth between the United States and the peripheral countries, while it further strengthens the differentiation characteristics of world economic growth. More importantly, in terms of the reasons for the slow growth of U.S. foreign investment, the transfer from foreign investment to domestic investment may be a very critical factor. As can be seen from Figure 12, before 2010, the growth rate of the U.S. foreign direct investment was much higher than that of domestic investment. The U.S. economy showed a very distinctive export-oriented characteristic, and the outflow of

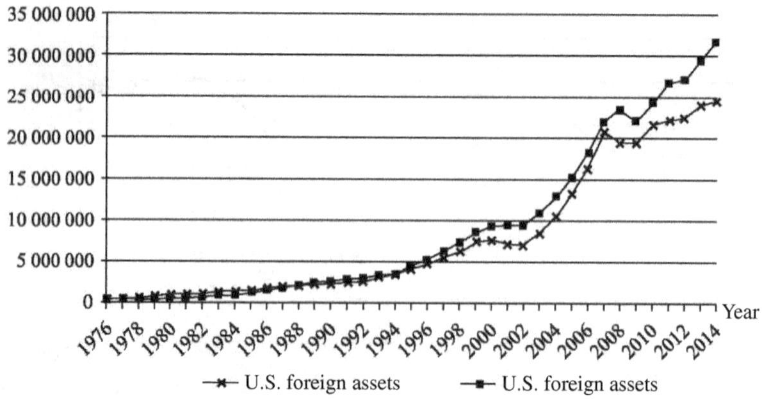

Figure 11. Capital Flow of the United States (in Million Dollars)

Source: Bureau of Economic Analysis, the U.S. Department of Commerce.

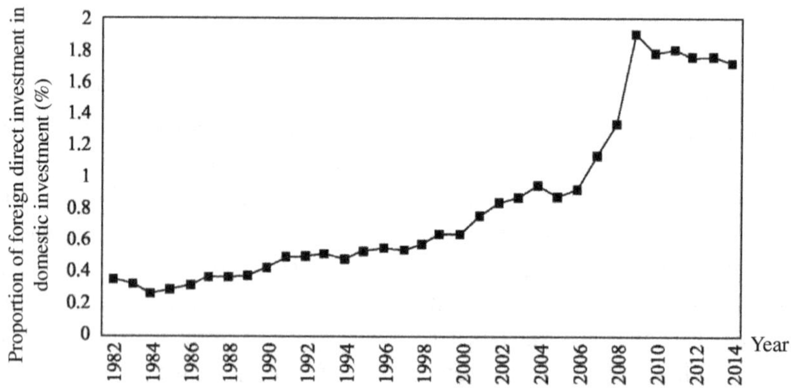

Figure 12. Changes between the U.S. Domestic Investment and Foreign Direct Investment

Source: Bureau of Economic Analysis, the U.S. Department of Commerce.

foreign direct investment has become a practical carrier for the outward transfer of U.S. manufacturing industry, while it has also become a favorable means to promote the economic growth of the peripheral countries. However, from 2010, the growth rate of foreign direct investment and domestic investment began to reverse. The growth rate of foreign direct investment slowed down, while the scale of domestic investment began to increase rapidly. It was also very obvious that there were the substitution characteristics of domestic investment for foreign investment in capital field.

3.3.3. *The underlying reasons for the economic growth differentiation in various countries due to the U.S. economic policy adjustment*

As mentioned earlier, when the macro policies of the core countries are more focused on the adjustment of economic imbalances, in the short term, conflicts of interest between core countries and peripheral countries will be inevitable. However, the problem is that the U.S. unilateral policy adjustment has only brought about the conflict between the core countries and peripheral countries in the mechanism of realizing interests, and does not necessarily show that the core countries are unilaterally improving their economic growth. The fundamental reason for the outstanding performance of the United States in the current world economic recovery still lies in its dual advantages in the service and manufacturing sectors and the inherent drawbacks of dependent development of peripheral countries.

On the one hand, although in terms of expression form, the wordings such as re-industrialization and the revitalization of manufacturing industry all emphasize the return of manufacturing competitiveness of the United States in the context of de-industrialization. But in fact, although the share of manufacturing industry in the domestic output of the United States is declining, globally speaking, it has not really lost its absolute manufacturing competitiveness. On the contrary, for a very long period of time, the United States can be said as the most competitive manufacturing country in the world. From the perspective of industrial added value, before 2010, the United States had been the country with the largest added value of manufacturing industry in the world. It was only after 2010 that the status of the United States as the largest country in world manufacturing industry was replaced by China, and became the country with the manufacturing output only next to China. But even so, in the global manufacturing output share, the current proportion of U.S. manufacturing value added in global manufacturing value added still accounts for nearly 20%. That is to say, in terms of pure competitiveness, both the service sector and the manufacturing sector represented by financial services in the

United States have absolute competitiveness, but just from a relative perspective, the U.S. financial services industry has more obvious comparative advantages. This also means that, the United States can still form the absolute competitiveness on a global scale in the field of manufacturing industry, under the circumstances that the United States takes the revitalization of the manufacturing sector as the main policy of rebalancing adjustment and abandons the financial services industry in the short term. In fact, it is also precisely the dual advantages of the United States in its service and manufacturing sectors that enable the United States to maintain a relatively high economic growth rate in the process of short-term rebalance adjustment.

On the other hand, for peripheral countries, it is just the opposite. From the perspective of the process of domestic adjustment in the U.S. economic structure, in the context of the increasingly consolidated status of the U.S. financial center, the United States has gradually concentrated its domestic resources on the service sector through the external transfer of the manufacturing sector. However, the peripheral countries have gradually taken the earnings of manufacturing sector production. In the process of promoting domestic economic growth, they also provided cheap goods and capital supply for residents' consumption and enterprise production in the core countries. In such a process, the economic growth of the peripheral countries actually benefited from the elimination of backward production capacity in the process of high-end oriented adjustment for industrial structure in the core countries. Although there is an interest realization mechanism from the perspective of absolute returns, as far as the interest distribution mechanism is concerned, the peripheral countries must be the party with less relative interests. More importantly, although the peripheral countries have the internal impetus to upgrade their industrial structure and catch up with the developed countries in the long term, due to the limitations of technology and innovation capabilities, the peripheral countries cannot accurately judge and lead the direction of technological innovation and industrial upgrading, and can only attach themselves to the industrial structure adjustment of the core countries in the short term. When the industrial adjustment of the core countries tends to be high-end oriented, the industrial upgrading space of the peripheral countries will expand accordingly. However, when the upgrading of industrial structure in the core countries is weak and even there is a return demand for traditional sectors, in the absence of additional competitive advantage sectors, the natural defects of dependent pattern growth in peripheral countries will be further exposed, and the output contraction will also become even more severe.

3.3.4. *Double external shocks faced by China's economy*

Different from the economies of the Eurozone and Japan, China's macro economy in 2015 is more closely related to the world economic rebalancing, and has a stronger correlation with the rebalancing adjustment of the U.S. economic policy. With the withdrawal of the U.S. quantitative easing monetary policy, China will have more severe challenges.

Similar to the rebalancing adjustment of the United States, China also has an inherent need for rebalancing. Therefore, in 2005, China's macroeconomic policy began to enter a rebalancing adjustment period, which was specifically manifested in the correction of factor price distortions marked by the promulgation of the new "Labor Law" and the adjustment of export growth by export tax rebates. However, such initiative adjustment measures of the Chinese government did not achieve the expected results in the face of strong external demand. This actually reflected that as a large peripheral manufacturing country, China's domestic macro policy has limited impact on micro economic behavior. In the early stage of the U.S. financial crisis, as the Chinese economy was directly faced with the impact of the decline in external demand for the first time after the Reform and Opening up, plus we need a cognitive process of the transmission of the U.S. economic crisis and the U.S. anti-crisis policy, so when we dealt with the impact of external demand, the macro demand policy was excessively adjusted, which led to the further deterioration of the overcapacity in China's traditional manufacturing industry. The voice for adjusting structure and promoting upgrade within China was rising gradually. However, in our process of adjusting structure and promoting upgrade, the U.S. trade imbalance has actually risen again quietly under the stimulus of U.S. anti-crisis policy. From the perspective of the policy analysis of China and the United States at the corresponding time, as the two ends of the global economic imbalance, China and the United States lack an effective coordinating mechanism in their anti-crisis policy coordination.

From the practical perspective of an economy, China's economic structure has indeed undergone great changes after the Crisis. With the policies to stimulate domestic demand, the proportion of China's tertiary industry has been continuously increasing, from 40.46% in 2005 to 44.59% in 2012 and further increased to 48.1% in 2014. However, while the proportion of China's service industry output value has increased, China's economic growth rate has declined significantly. The reasons are as follows. Beside that China's service industry has weak competitiveness and no substitute relationship with goods trade export, the decline is also related to the development bottleneck of the service industry itself in the peripheral countries. In the context that China's economic policies are generally conducive to the development of the service industry, the growth rate of China's service industry in 2013 reached 8.3%. However, without any change in policy orientation, the growth rate of China's service trade declined in 2014, with a growth rate of only 7.8%. Moreover, in fact, China's service industry also faces another risk. Once the high-tech industry of the core countries enters the stage of external transfer of international industry, the tradability of the high-tech service industry will increase, and the development of international service trade will have an impact on China's traditional service industry.

During the industrial transformation and upgrading, China has witnessed the differentiation of industry growth, and the growth of traditional manufacturing industry has declined, while emerging industries and strategic industries have still maintained a certain growth momentum. However, the development of emerging industries cannot make up for the decline in the overall performance of traditional manufacturing sectors in terms of profits, which makes China's economy face huge adjustment costs in the process of promoting industrial upgrading.

The adjustment directly related to the imbalance of the world economy is the change in the mode of Chinese goods trade. According to Table 8, it can be seen that, in the era of global trade imbalance, the mode of China's trade participation is mainly processing trade. This mode of trade has not changed much until 2012, and its output value has also been in the rising stage. However, in the global value chain, the counterpart to this mode of trade is the low value-added product assembly at the end of the industrial chain. Therefore, the increase in the general trade and the decline in the processing trade after 2008 indicate that the industrial upgrading of China's export industry has made achievements. At the same time, it is noted that China's import had a very significant decline in 2015. The cumulative growth rate of imports for the whole year was −15.0%, which was 15.4 percentage points lower than that in the same period of the previous year. However, this phenomenon is not entirely a

Table 8. China's Export Trade Volume (by Trade Modes) (In 1,000 Dollars)

Year	General Trade Exports	Processing Trade Exports	Feeding Processing Trade Exports	Total Exports
1995	71,405,752	20,669,962	53,048,744	148,820,336
1996	62,938,184	24,246,122	60,096,404	151,173,952
1997	78,060,912	29,460,176	70,203,088	182,840,576
1998	74,150,872	30,737,386	73,624,272	183,746,496
1999	79,172,184	35,797,672	75,146,992	195,192,256
2000	105,187,944	41,121,076	96,525,352	249,239,664
2001	112,178,280	42,237,408	105,289,232	266,661,120
2002	136,236,128	47,463,136	132,510,512	325,642,080
2003	182,129,360	54,233,216	187,614,160	438,472,544
2004	243,677,376	68,610,584	259,643,440	593,647,168
2005	315,195,680	83,988,528	332,697,280	762,326,784
2006	416,383,968	94,487,800	416,069,024	969,324,800
2007	538,840,768	115,735,608	501,798,048	1,218,155,520
2008	662,770,880	110,381,440	564,922,496	1,428,869,248
2009	530,083,776	93,395,472	493,663,840	1,201,947,520
2010	721,010,112	112,344,432	628,194,240	1,578,446,592
2011	917,577,152	107,626,744	727,955,776	1,899,280,640
2012	988,530,880	98,885,928	764,448,512	2,050,109,184
2013	1,087,947,520	92,498,448	768,534,784	2,210,662,144
2014	982,428,096	73,245,624	640,744,768	1,904,046,976

Note: As the export trade modes also include consignment trade and small-scale border trade, the sum of the general trade exports and the processing trade exports is less than the total exports.
Source: CEInet Statistics Database.

manifestation of declining demand in China, but also the result of changes in the trade mode at the same time, this beneficial adjustment to the economy may be reflected in the reduction of China's imports from emerging economies on a global scale, which will reverse the already existing intra-industry trade relations among the members of the East Asian production network system, and may have a negative spillover effect on China's economic diplomacy with its neighboring countries.

Since 2008, China's economy has been facing many difficulties in the process of adjusting structure and promoting transformation. Under such circumstances, the cumulative growth rate of China's export fell to −1.3% in 2015, 7.4% lower than that of the same period in the previous year, showing a continuous decline in growth rate. Taking into account the factor of falling export prices, the decline in year-on-year growth rate of export volume is actually a slightly smaller. However, in the face of the dual impact of anti-crisis and rebalancing, the trend and status of China's export-oriented economic development have not changed. Its specific performance is that, China has obtained initial achievements in exploring the new international economic order, the establishment of "The Belt and Road", the Asian Infrastructure Investment Bank (AIIB) and the Silk Road Fund has promoted the implementation of the "Go globally" strategy of China's economy, and progress has also been made in the strategy for internationalizing Chinese RMB, which will play a positive role in China's initiative to realize the rebalancing strategy. The most important thing is that China's status as a major country absorbing FDI in manufacturing industry did not lose in the adjustment of this round of crisis. Although the proportion of U.S. overseas investment has declined in the process of rebalancing, the scale of U.S. investment in Asia has also leveled off, the scale of its investment in China's manufacturing industry still shows a certain upward trend, to a certain extent, which indicates that China is still the core producer of manufacturing industry in Asia, and the world status of "Made in China" has not changed significantly.

4. External Risks That Need to be Paid Attention to for China's Economy

Despite the trend of severe differentiation in growth performance in 2015, the world economy was still at the stage of slow recovery after the 2008 crisis. With the withdrawal of the U.S. quantitative easing monetary policy, rebalancing has become the primary goal of U.S. economic policy, while other developed countries will still remain in the process of anti-crisis. At the same time, from the perspective of the crisis transmission cycle in 2008, the transmission process at the real economy level will continue, while the process of rebalancing in the United States has started again, and China's economy will face the dual impact of anti-crisis and rebalancing adjustment in the future. From the analysis of the policy effect of great powers, the anti-crisis policies of Europe and Japan have limited impact on China's economy in the future, and the trend of the U.S. economy is the focus we must pay attention to. In this context, we believe that there are some external risks which need to be paid special attention to for China's economy in the future, including the risk of misjudgment of the U.S. rebalancing adjustment, the risk of "double dip" in emerging economies and the impact of the TPP agreement dominated by the U.S. with geopolitics on China.

4.1. *Correct judgement on the rebalancing approaches of the United States*

The first potential risk that China should pay close attention to in the future is the misjudgment of the adjustment approaches in the U.S. rebalancing process. From the perspective of the possible approaches of rebalancing adjustment in the United States, one is the return of the manufacturing sector under the existing pattern of division of labor, and the other is to form the trade surplus of the newly introduced sectors by introducing new trade elements on the basis of the existing imbalance. The former is essentially a denial of the globalization model on the basis of converse comparison advantage, and is more characterized by short-term imbalance adjustments, while the latter corresponds to the emergence of new driving force for economic growth, and is the most likely a rebalancing approach in the long run. We make this judgment based on the following three reasons.

4.1.1. *To adjust the imbalanced economic base which lacks long-term sustainability by returning to the traditional manufacturing sector*

From the simple logic of economics, the rebalancing adjustment of the return to the traditional manufacturing sector is faced with the constraints of diminishing capital returns and the differentiation of world economic growth.

(i) The output expansion of the manufacturing industry is faced with the natural limitation of diminishing marginal return of capital.

The expansion of manufacturing production capacity means the shrinkage of other production sectors, especially the service sector. From the perspective of U.S. endowment conditions, technological level, production mode and so on, the expansion of manufacturing output mainly depends on the deepening of capital, the improvement of total factor productivity and the improvement of labor quality, rather than the increase of labor input. However, in the context of the excessive development of the U.S. financial sector, along with the improvement of the external financing environment, the risk premium of external financing is constantly declining, and the return on physical capital of the U.S. manufacturing sector will enter a diminishing interval. Under the condition of opening up, this means that the return on overseas investment in the U.S. manufacturing sector is far greater than the return on domestic investment. Therefore, from this perspective, in the context of the highly developed financial service industry, such a rebalancing adjustment strategy is contradictory to the principle of optimal allocation of resources and lacks micro-conditions for welfare improvement. Although it can be used as a short-term measure to avoid risks and balance industrial development, in the long run, such a rebalancing adjustment strategy of returning to the traditional manufacturing sector lacks a long-term sustainable economic foundation.

(ii) The growth differentiation of the world economy is the reverse resistance of the traditional rebalancing adjustment.

The U.S. rebalancing adjustment of returning to the traditional manufacturing sector corresponds to the transformation of the driving force of U.S. economic growth. With the dependent pattern growth of peripheral countries, the prosperity of the U.S. economy corresponds to the sluggish economic growth of the peripheral countries. Although such a situation can be maintained in the short term, in the long term, the stagnation of economic growth in peripheral countries will lead to the deterioration of overseas business environment of U.S. multinational companies, and then lead to the reduction of overseas profits of the parent companies of the U.S. multinational companies. On the contrary, this is not conducive to the sustained improvement of the U.S. economy. In fact, since 2012, such a situation has begun to emerge. As can be seen from Table 9, for most of the time after 2010, the value-added and net income of the parent companies of the U.S. multinational companies showed a steady growth trend, which reflects the improvement of the domestic economic situation in the United States. However, at the same time, since 2012, with the continuous deterioration of economic growth in peripheral countries, the value added and net income of overseas subsidiaries of the U.S. multinational companies had been deteriorating for two consecutive years, which is in sharp contrast to the improvement of economic indicators of the parent companies.

Table 9. Key Economic Indicators in American Multinational Corporations

Year	Value Added			Net Income		
	Total	Parent Company	Subsidiary	Total	Parent Company	Subsidiary
2010	4,191 (12.03%)	2,949 (13.59%)	1,242 (8.50%)	1,936 (38.17%)	910 (46.16%)	1,026 (31.79%)
2011	4,577 (9.21%)	3,161 (7.20%)	1,416 (13.98%)	2,160 (11.58%)	1,062 (16.72%)	1,099 (7.03%)
2012	4,664 (1.90%)	3,249 (2.79%)	1,415 (−0.09%)	2,061 (−4.59%)	995 (−6.32%)	1,066 (−2.93%)
2013	4,853 (4.05%)	3,469 (6.76%)	1,384 (−2.18%)	2,221 (7.75%)	1,159 (16.54%)	1,062 (−0.45%)

Note: In the table, the unit is 1 billion dollars for numeric values of the relevant economic indicators corresponded by the figures outside the brackets, and the figures in the brackets are the growth rate of the relevant economic indicators.
Source: Bureau of Economic Analysis, the U.S. Department of Commerce.

With the deteriorating overseas operation of the multinational companies, a possible choice is to transfer overseas investment to domestic investment through "Manufacturing Reshoring". However, from the micro level, the re-accumulation of production capacity will face tremendous difficulties after losing market share, fixed capital, input supply network, output marketing network, production skills, know-how and related systems. Coupled with the changes in the international market structure and the establishment of the dominant position of low-cost producers in labor-intensive industries, it is undoubtedly with enormous difficulty for the United States to re-enter relevant industries after de-industrialization. Furthermore, even if the U.S. manufacturing industry successfully returned from abroad, it would only reflect the regression of economic globalization. In other words, although the U.S. has a huge market space, compared to the global market, it still cannot avoid the small market attribute under the closed condition.

Therefore, from this perspective, although the rebalance adjustment of returning to the traditional manufacturing sector will lead to the differentiation of world economic growth in the initial stage, the differentiation characteristics of world economic growth in turn limit the further development of such a rebalancing adjustment mode.

4.1.2. *The tradability of the service sector is the optimal choice for the U.S. rebalancing adjustment*

In the absence of breakthrough in technological progress or institutional innovation, it is unlikely to make major adjustments either in the global labor division system or in the domestic supply structure of the United States. In the context that there are difficulties in rebalancing adjustment under the traditional mode, the expansion of export can only be realized through the marginal adjustments brought by the introduction of new trade elements. The employment increase and trade rebalancing can be driven by relying on the U.S. industries with competitive advantages, through their production capacity expansion and export growth.

As for the choice of industries with competitive advantages, the U.S. service industry is undoubtedly the most advantageous industry sector, but under the restriction of high trade costs, many service industries have become *de facto* non-trade sectors. If the bilateral and multilateral trade and investment system can be improved, the trade cost of the U.S. service industry for entering the international market can be can be reduced, and the tradability of related industries can be improved, then the U.S. export will grow rapidly and the trade deficit will be reduced substantially. This adjustment is mainly achieved by improving the tradability of the original non-tradable industries, especially that of services and high-tech products. The change happening here is not the cross-industry flow of resources, but the change in the tradability of the output of related industries, especially the reduction of policy barriers to trade. Therefore, this change will not lead to the decline of employment creating ability, the losses of productive efficiency or of positive externality, and the total output will not be reduced either. Moreover, with the improvement of the tradability of the service industry, the output of the service industry can get rid of the constraint of domestic demand and grow at a faster speed, thereby creating more employment opportunities and providing a greater driving force for the overall economic growth. This is a way to promote the improvement of U.S. trade balance with minimal cost and negative impact.

With the restriction of high trade costs, from the perspective of the composition of the present U.S. external current account balancing adjustment, the role of service trade export in the U.S. rebalancing adjustment is gradually emerging, although the U.S. service industry does not have the conditions for comprehensive export. As can be seen from Figure 13, from the perspective of export growth rate, the growth rate of

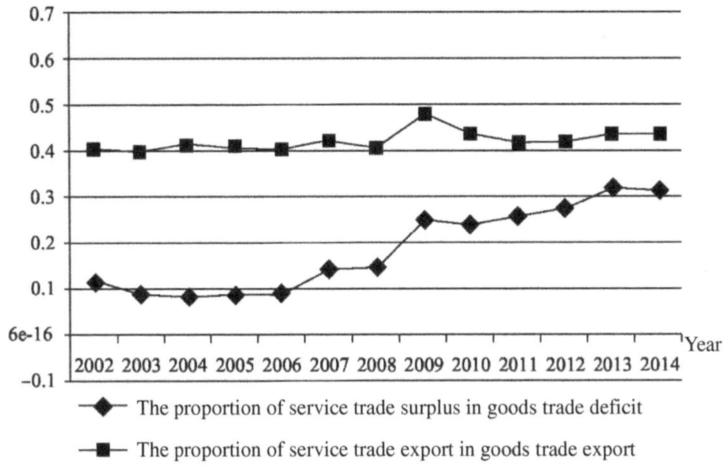

Figure 13. The Development of U.S. Services Trade and Goods Trade

service export is generally faster than that of goods trade. In the case of relatively small export base of service trade, the proportion of service trade export in goods trade export still slowly increased from 0.4 in 2002 to 0.44 in 2014. More importantly, the service trade surplus has become an important means of U.S. trade rebalancing. In 2002, the proportion of service trade surplus was only 12% in goods trade deficit, while the proportion had rapidly risen to 31% by 2014. Therefore, from the trend, with the establishment and development of the U.S. international consultation mechanism at all levels within bilateral and multilateral scopes in the future, especially with the conclusion of high-quality free trade agreements such as TPP and TTIP, the trade costs of the U.S. service industry will be further reduced, and the export expansion of the service sector will also become the most likely approach for the U.S. rebalancing adjustment.

4.1.3. *The reindustrialization strategy is essentially the consolidation and reinforcement to the advantages of the U.S. service industry*

How to understand a series of U.S. re-industrialization strategies for the rebalancing adjustment at present, since the optimal approach for the U.S.

rebalancing adjustment lies in the improvement of the tradability of the service sector?

Obama once proposed that the United States should be made as the center of the next revolution in manufacturing by creating a network of a series of manufacturing hubs, in his State of the Union address, 2013. From the perspective of the advantages of the U.S. manufacturing industry, the advantages in technology and human capital are the basis of the actual realistic comparative advantage, and it would only be new technology innovation in the long term. Then, how to obtain economic benefits from the comparative advantages brought by technology innovation more effectively? For this question, we must realize that whether they are new technologies in manufacturing or those in energy and environment. The greatest value for the United States is not to use those new technologies to rebuild the production process of manufactured goods and compete with emerging economies, but to transform new technologies into corresponding equipment and services, so as to provide key equipment and service inputs for the proliferation and wide application of new technologies. In other words, the effective carrier is not the products produced by using new technologies, but the equipment and services for the application and proliferation of new technologies, in order to realize the potential benefits of technological advantages.

In addition, for the peripheral countries, with constantly rising labor costs in the major industrial producers, the existing manufacturing value chain will face more and more challenges, resulting in the demand for the application and proliferation of new technologies, which in turn provides huge potential demand for the U.S. technical equipment and services. It just accords with the ways as defined above in which the United States realizes the potential benefits of new technologies.

From this perspective, the purpose of the U.S. reindustrialization strategy is to pursue breakthroughs and innovation in manufacturing production technology. However, the purpose of technology innovation is not limited to the demands of internal product production in the manufacturing sector, but to obtain maximum benefits by reshaping the global division of labor network and controlling key technologies and equipment. Furthermore, although the realistic carrier of the re-industrialization strategy originated from the manufacturing sector, the realization of the ultimate benefits cannot be separated from the development and export of the producer service sectors. This is not only the historical logic of the domestic industrial structure adjustment in the United States but also the relative unification of the short-term adjustment strategy and the long-term adjustment strategy in the process of U.S. economic rebalancing adjustment.

4.2. *The risk of "double dip" appears in the emerging economies*

According to our analysis of the characteristics of world economy operation in 2015, the risk that asset bubbles are being accumulated by stock market development deviating from economic fundamentals, together with the difficulties in structural adjustment and industrial upgrading of emerging economies, will probably lead to the "double dip" phenomenon in economic growth of emerging economies including China, in the process of their crisis recovery. This endogenous "double dip" in emerging economies may be due to the following possible reasons.

Firstly, the decline in domestic investment caused by continuous external demand shocks will affect innovation at the supply level, resulting in the decline of total factor productivity, the overall shrinkage of the domestic production system and the collapse of the real economy growth.

Secondly, in the absence of technology stock and real economy performance support, irrational investment in the innovation field through equity financing is prone to a large amount of capital sinking, leading to the collapse of the stock market, and thus triggering a crisis.

Thirdly, the potential risks brought by the transfer of the economic structure of emerging economies to the service industry. Since the service industry of the emerging economies does not have comparative advantages in general, the enhanced tradability of the service industry in developed countries will inevitably have an impact on the traditional service industry of the emerging economies, and then affect the clearance of the employment market in emerging economies, resulting in an increase in unemployment and a decrease in income, thus triggering a typical form of crisis.

Fourthly, the interruption of international value chain caused by the transformation of trade mode of each country may affect the rebalancing process of the core countries, thus triggering a global economic crisis.

Fifthly, the continuous decline of international commodity prices may lead to the aggravations of social upheaval and geopolitical instability in resource exporting countries, and interrupt the economic recovery process of their neighboring countries.

4.3. *The impact of the TPP agreement dominated by the U.S. with geopolitics on China*

The TPP itself is not terrible, because the implementation of any international agreement must take into account the interests of its members. Therefore, eventually there is always a big difference between the effect of the TPP implementation and the assumption of the dominant country of the agreement. Even the Bretton Woods system agreed upon by the U.K. and the U.S. after the Second World War has also exposed mistakes in the system design in the process of its implementation, and the TPP will have the same problems as well. At present, from the perspective of the TPP text that has been disclosed, it is at least logically in conflict with the international economic order advocated by the United States, and there is a phenomenon that the U.S.-dominated TPP challenges the U.S.-dominated international economic structure after the Second World War.

Firstly, if the "fair trade" principle emphasized in the TPP Agreement has surpassed the corresponding clauses of WTO in terms of labor, society, environment and so on, then the factors to promote the growth of international trade will completely depend on the differences in technology (including enterprise management techniques and production scale) among countries, and the basis of international trade will become the "absolute advantage" rather than the "comparative advantage" among countries, which is actually a denial of the basis of international trade development since the Second World War. If the international trade is based on the absolute advantage, the existing TPP member countries, with the exception of Japan, have almost no goods that can be exchanged with the United States in industrial manufacturing. If there is no trade, there would not be any creative effect of trade, or any increase in employment opportunities in the United States either.

Secondly, the U.S. government emphasizes that the goal of TPP is to establish a high-standard international trade system, which means that the United States will abandon the existing WTO. In the 20th century, the United States was also constantly trying to sign bilateral trade agreements with other countries. However, the purpose of such attempts was to make up for the defects in coordination ability of multilateral agreements through bilateral agreements, so as to promote the negotiation process of multilateral trading system. From the perspective of the attitude of the United States toward TPP, the United States tried to replace the bilateral trade agreements with a regional trade agreement, which was another self-challenging trial and error of the United States. After the Second World War, with the collapse of the Western colonial system, the United States changed the regional group distribution pattern of imperial preferential system adopted by the United Kingdom when it dominated the world economy through the multilateral world trade system. Therefore, the regional groups will inevitably have opportunistic behaviors. Only a global multilateral agreement can avoid opportunistic behavior. For a sovereign country, to choose the multilateral means the choices of opening up and the world; and to abandon the multilateral means the choices of the closure and rejecting the world.

Therefore, the United States abandoned the multilateral and chose the form of regional group, which attempt has a series of uncertain consequences. (1) The United States must take sufficient economic measures to ensure the interests of the member states, in order to avoid the opportunistic behavior of the member states. With the principle of fair trade, merely opening markets cannot guarantee the benefits of all member states, unless the United States implements a new round of Marshall Plan among the TPP member states, out of consideration of the Cold War mentality. (2) On the basis of the Seattle Agreement, the scope of TPP Member States is expanded rapidly, so that it can be developed from a regional group to a global trade organization. To achieve this goal, the existing framework of the TPP must produce a demonstration effect to promote trade growth. From what we have analyzed previously, it is difficult to achieve the rapid trade growth, because there are not many countries with the absolute trade advantages among the TPP member countries. (3) On the basis of the successful operation of TPP, through the integration with other cross-regional groups, the transformation of the regional groups to the global multilateral system will be realized, but this also depends on the operation effect of TPP itself.

Thirdly, the Rules of Origin in TPP has exclusiveness, which is a symbol of a typical regional group pursuing trade diversion effect. As the arrangement of the Trans Pacific strategic partnership agreement, it will have an impact on the East Asian network production system. In the East Asian network production system, there are some TPP member states, while the TPP Agreement excludes some important countries. The Rules of Origin will hinder the trade exchanges between the member countries in the East Asian network production system and interrupt the industrial chain. As the main country in the East Asian network production system, China is bound to be greatly impacted consequently. However, the crux of the problem is that while impacting the existing global network production system, TPP is unlikely to recreate a new network production system in a short time. In fact, after the formation of the East Asian network production system, the economic development of East Asian countries has been beyond the traditional growth model relying solely on labor-intensive industries. Some East Asian countries (except Japan) in TPP cannot simply rely on the advantage of demographic dividend to replace the existing East Asian network production system. If the East Asian network production system no longer exists, then the pattern of interdependence between the United States and the global economy will also change. The United States must make major adjustments to its domestic economic structure, and there will be enormous costs for such adjustments.

However, if geopolitical factors were taken into consideration, then, for existing TPP members and potential ones, why they choose to join the TPP would not be entirely out of considerations of economic interests, and also of political security. This result will affect China's foreign economic policies at least from three aspects. First of all, the U.S.-led TPP will directly affect the actual operation effect of the regional economic cooperation framework that China participates in. It is the soft power of U.S. diplomacy that the United States utilizes to implement TPP while China is utilizing its hard power such as real money, whether for the "The Belt and Road" or for the "Asian Infrastructure Investment Bank". The result of such a struggle for the discourse power in economic order is likely to be changed by non-economic factors. Secondly, the TPP may affect the promotion of China's position in the Global Value Chain Division System. The certification of the origin for final goods depends on the value of the member countries contained in components and parts, due to the Rules of Origin in TPP. If the overseas added value of Chinese manufactured products is low, then China cannot enjoy the treatment of member States when exporting to the United States. To enjoy the treatment of member states, China has to accept the current pattern of value chain specialization. Finally, if China is excluded from the TPP framework for a long time, it is likely to be excluded from the new international division of labor in the process of global economic rebalancing in the future, which will further narrow the policy space for China's export-oriented economic development.

Chapter 2

The Arduous Recovery of World Economy*

Today, eight years after the Subprime Crisis, the world economy is still in the process of arduous recovery. New words such as New Mediocre and Secular Stagnation have become buzzwords to describe the current state of the world economy. The Quantitative Easing Monetary Policy, which emphasizes demand management, has not yet brought the spectacular recovery of the world economy. Compared with the Great Moderation growth period for more than two decades in developed economies before the Subprime Crisis, the current dynamic mechanism of world economic growth has been weakened, lacking not only new and explosive drivers of growth but also pull factors to significantly improve short-term demand. At the same time, in the stage of the Great Moderation before the Crisis, as a long cycle of world economic growth, it had the nature of debt leverage accumulation. In addition, lending was further stimulated by the extremely low interest rates brought by the global quantitative easing monetary policy after the Subprime Crisis, and the whole economy entered a stage of high leverage, leading to the emergence of the so-called super debt cycle. The lack of new growth engines and excessive debt leverage together determine that the road to recover the world economy will be an arduous one. The arduousness of recovery has determined that global macro policies are characterized by that "each one will go a

---

*This chapter was written by Wang Jinbin and Ma Man.

separate way when disaster strikes" and further determines that the road to recover the world economy is the one of interest redistribution, with less win–win cooperation than "imaginative collaboration". We can see that some effects will be revealed in this round of arduous recovery for world economy, that are, the wealth redistribution effect brought by the expectation of stronger U.S. dollar and commodities on the low price, the global dividend distribution effect caused by market competition which was then triggered by the sharp decrease of international market capacity led by "Trade Overshoot", the wealth distribution effect of asset price which was caused by capital flow resulting from the U.S. dollar system born with over-elasticity, as well as the policy of spillover effect caused by the non-synchronization of monetary policy accompanied by unbalanced recovery. Moreover, all kinds of frictions and impacts produced will increase the difficulty and uncertainty for the road of world economic recovery.

In the context of the declining potential growth rate of world's major economies, the risks brought by the aforementioned interest redistribution mechanism and channels determine that the process of recovery for world economy may not be a win–win one. This chapter is divided into two parts, in order to demonstrate the judgment that world economy is arduous to recover but may not be in a win–win situation. The first part will explain why world economy is still in the process of arduous recovery, the second part will illustrate why the road to arduous recovery may not be a win–win one, and the third part is a brief conclusion.

1. Why is World Economy Still in the Process of Arduous Recovery?

1.1. *The decline in the potential GDP growth rate of world economy, especially of the developed economies, determines that it will be moderate for the road to recovery*

It is a basic trend that the potential GDP growth slows down in the global economy, while the potential GDPs of the developed countries and regions have decreased significantly, which was particularly obvious after the Subprime Crisis. Figure 1 shows that after 2010, the decline in economic growth in developed economies was accompanied by the slow narrowing of the output gap, which clearly indicates that the potential

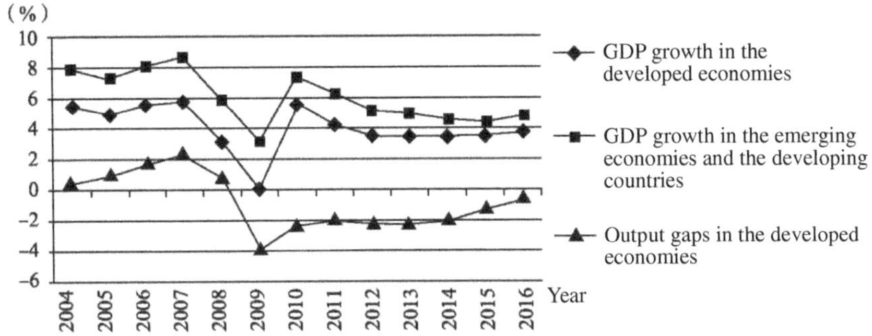

Figure 1. GDP Growth in Different Economies and Output Gaps in the Developed Economies

Source: The author drew the above figure based on the data provided by IMF and World Economic Outlook Database. The developed economies include 37 countries; and the emerging economies and developing countries include 152 countries.

output of the developed economies has declined; and the slow narrowing of the potential output gap also indicates that the process of economic recovery will be moderate. The decline in potential GDP growth is the immediate cause of the slowdown in world economic growth. IMF (2015b) estimates show that 60% of the decline in economic growth in developed economies is caused by the decline of potential output level, while 70% of the decline in output in emerging economies is caused by the decline in potential output.

There are mainly four reasons for the decline in global potential GDP as follows. First of all, in most countries and regions, the number of the traditional working-age population (aged 15–64) has declined steadily, despite the population growth in South Africa and India. However, with the current population policy unchanged, OECD (2014a) research shows that the population of OECD countries will increase by 17%, while the working-age population (aged 15–74) will decrease by 7% from 2010 to 2060. Recent OECD (2015) research shows that the traditional working-age population in high-income countries will decline by 5% on average in the next 30 years. The rise in wages and the decrease in the working-age population, as well as the accompanying problem of aging population will make the demographic dividend decline in the process of globalization. Secondly, the growth of capital deepening for production in developed countries is slow, and the growth of capital investment scale after the Crisis has declined, which makes the growth of capital stock decline. The data of capital deepening in developed countries before and after the crisis given in Table 1 show that the capital deepening had increases and decreases before and after the crisis, but the growth was not fast on average. Thirdly, the labor productivity has declined rapidly. With the exception of South Korea, Iceland and Spain, the labor productivity has declined in almost all OECD countries. Finally, from the perspective of multi-factor productivity that reflects technological progress, the multi-factor productivity of all countries has declined, and the decrease is relatively large. After the crisis, there was a negative growth in multi-factor productivity in more than 60%

Table 1. Source of Economic Growth in the Developed Countries: Comparison before and after the Crisis (%)

	2001–2007			2007–2011		
	Capital Deepening	The Growth of Multi-factor Productivity	The Growth of Labor Productivity	Capital Deepening	The Growth of Multi-factor Productivity	The Growth of Labor Productivity
South Korea	1.23	3.38	4.61	1.44	3.29	4.70
Sweden	0.62	2.20	2.82	0.61	−0.33	0.26
Finland	0.29	2.22	2.51	0.50	−1.04	−0.56
Iceland	0.72	1.68	2.38	2.27	1.14	3.36
U.S.A.	0.58	1.41	2.00	0.67	0.83	1.46
Australia	0.52	1.46	1.98	0.60	0.07	0.66
Netherlands	0.83	0.91	1.75	0.69	−0.70	−0.02
Japan	0.49	1.12	1.61	0.47	0.33	0.78
Germany	0.45	1.14	1.59	0.14	0.05	0.25
France	0.56	0.91	1.48	0.54	−0.34	0.19
Belgium	0.65	0.80	1.45	0.36	−0.93	−0.57
Denmark	1.08	0.35	1.44	0.93	−0.69	0.22
Portugal	1.34	0.06	1.39	1.47	−0.32	1.25
New Zealand	0.60	0.55	1.16	0.52	−0.83	−0.33
Switzerland	0.35	0.79	1.15	−0.04	−0.28	−0.32
Canada	0.65	0.19	0.85	0.73	−0.27	0.43
Spain	0.75	−0.01	0.73	1.72	−0.05	1.64
Italy	0.48	−0.32	0.16	0.62	−0.72	−0.12

Source: OECD, Science, Technology and Industry Outlook (2014).

of OECD countries (see Table 1). A recent study also shows that the global total factor productivity (TFP) declined by 0.5 percentage points from 2007 to 2012 (Eichengreen *et al.*, 2015). This is why the so-called economic recovery since the Subprime Crisis can be called a recovery without technological progress, which essentially refers to the significant slowdown of global technological progress.

After the Subprime Crisis, despite the sharp decline in the aggregate demand of the global economy, the proportion of R&D expenditure in GDP (R&D/GDP) did not decline, but increased. According to OECD country studies data, the R&D/GDP of EU28 increased from 1.76% in 2007 to 2.07% in 2012, the proportion of the United States increased from 2.63% in 2007 to 2.79% in 2012, and the proportion of China increased from 1.40% in 2007 to 1.98% in 2012. The proportion of South Korea increased from 3.21% in 2007 to 4.36% in 2012, making it the country with the highest R&D intensity in the world. Among the developed economies, only a few countries, such as Japan, showed a slight decline in R&D intensity. However, the top 10 countries spent 80% of global R&D expenditures, and the country-specific concentration of R&D was still high. Comparing the rise of R&D expenditures with the decline of multi-factor productivity reflecting technological progress, it is certain that the global technological innovation speed has entered a significant diminishing region, and technological progress has entered a bottleneck period. Therefore, in addition to the decline in economic aggregate demand growth itself, to a large extent, it can be said that this round of global economic growth decline has the nature of real business cycle, which is manifested in the slowdown of technological progress, and the process of recovery will definitely be moderate.

1.2. *The nature of the debt super-cycle determines that the road to recovery will be very long and moderate*

The "Great Moderation" period of more than 20 years before the Crisis led to the accumulation of debt, and the anti-crisis stimulus plan led to the rapid growth of debt. The underlying reason is that Keynesian economic thought has dominated the macro policies of important global economies for a long time, and demand management has become a magic weapon to deal with the crisis and economic downturn, and supply management has been ignored. Today, the global economy is generally faced with the dilemma of low growth and high debt (Ali *et al.*, 2013), and the economy as a whole is in a moderate recovery of debt super-cycle rather than stagnation.

For the developed economies, government debt grew rapidly after the anti-crisis (see Figure 2). The government debt/GDP of the developed economies and the G7 countries reached the highest level in 2012, at about 106% and 121%, respectively; moreover, the rate of decline will be slow in the future, and it will be in a long-period stage of high debt, and much higher than 60% of the warning line internationally recognized. In terms of different countries, the United States is roughly equivalent to the average level of developed economies, with its government debt/GDP maintained at about 104% from 2013 to 2015; however, Japan, with the highest government debt/GDP, was as high as about 245% during the same period. Excessive government debt has forced the developed countries to adopt extremely loose monetary policy, maintain extremely low interest rates so as to reduce debt pressure and stimulate investment and consumption; at the same time, excessive government deficit make it difficult for the developed economies to adjust their economic structure through fiscal policies or to stimulate economic growth by improving the aggregate demand structure, making fiscal policies almost lose the basic function of promoting economic recovery. Therefore, the biggest feature of the recovery of developed countries is to maintain extremely low

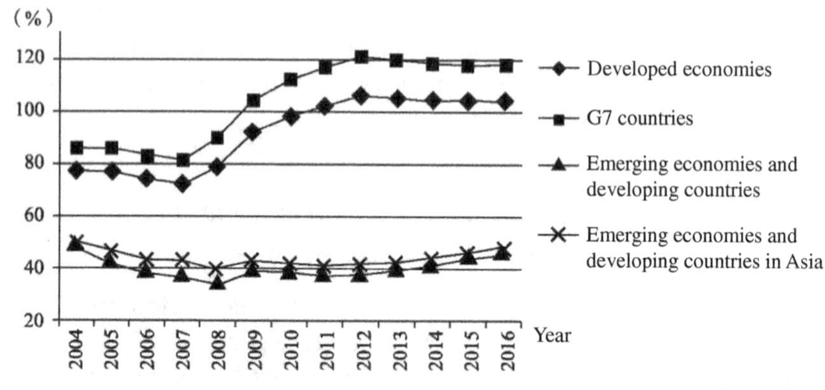

Figure 2. Changes in Government Debt/GDP in Different Economies

Source: The author drew the above figure based on the data provided by IMF and World Economic Outlook Database. G7 countries refer to the United States, Britain, Germany, Japan, France, Canada and Italy. Emerging economies and developing countries in Asia include 29 countries, including China and India.

interest rates with loose monetary policies, reduce debt pressure and make the markets self-repaired slowly. All these determine that it will be very long and moderate for the road to recovery.

Figure 2 also shows that the government debt levels of emerging economies and developing countries (including developing countries in Asia) are generally in a healthy state. The current government debt/GDP is only about 45%, although it has risen since 2011. In terms of different countries, in 2014, except for the government debt/GDP of several small economies such as Egypt, which were close to or reached 100%, the government debt/GDP of China, India, Russia, Brazil and Indonesia were about 41%, 66%, 18%, 65% and 25%, respectively. There is still large space for the governments of these countries to regulate the economic operation through fiscal policies.

The debt risks in emerging economies are mainly concentrated on corporate debt risks. The anti-crisis stimulus policies have encouraged corporate lending. However, corporate profits have declined and corporate debt has been rising, due to the shrinking aggregate demand. At the same time, low interest rates in developed countries and regions, such as the United States, Europe and Japan, have stimulated cross-border corporate lending and lending for cross border capital flows, leading to a significant increase in corporate financial leverage. IMF survey data in 2015 showed that corporate debt/GDP in emerging economies increased by 26 percentage points from 2002 to 2014 (see Figure 3), and the loose financial conditions worldwide significantly increased the vulnerability of corporate financial leverage.

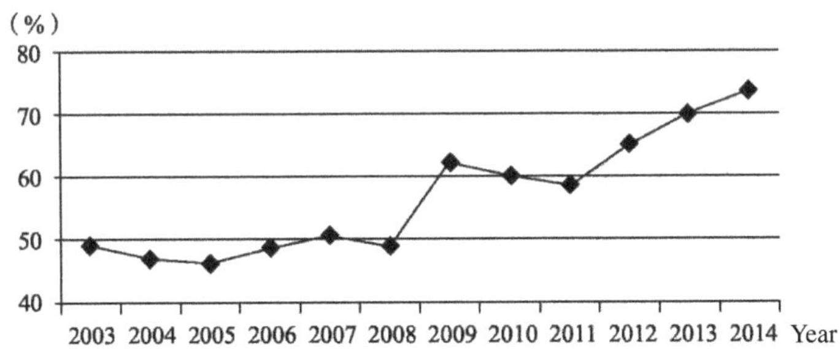

Figure 3. Changes in Corporate Debt/GDP in the Emerging Economies: From 2003 to 2014

Source: IMF Survey, September 29, 2015.

This super debt cycle is characterized by high risk of government debt in the developed countries and high leverage of corporate debt in the emerging economies. The high risk of government debt makes the fiscal policy almost ineffective, while the high leverage of corporate debt makes the financial profit erode the corporate profits and reduces the viability of corporate surplus. Under the conditions of leverage reduction and no major changes in the financing environment, the reduction in market capacity caused by the demand dilemma and the weakening of the viability brought by the decline in profit doubly squeeze the survival and development space of the corporate, thus leading to a significant decline in corporate investment, which also determines that it will be very long and moderate for the economic recovery.

2. Why the Road to Recovery May Not Be a Win–Win One?

The road to recover world economy is the one of interest redistribution, with less win–win cooperation than "imaginative collaboration". We will find that it is unbalanced for the road to world economic recovery, the international monetary system is asymmetric, the export structure of countries is differentiated, and there are frictions between trade and exchange rate policies. All of these factors determined that the recovery process of world economy will inevitably accompany with the wealth redistribution effect, and lead to a recovery that is not necessarily a win–win result.

2.1. *The "resource curse" phenomenon has appeared in commodity exporting countries in the low-price operation cycle*

After the Subprime Crisis, both commodity price index and crude oil spot price have experienced a sharp decline. With the implementation of large-scale economic stimulus plan, especially the implementation of China's stimulus plan of up to 4 trillion yuan, the prices of commodities and crude oil also rose rapidly and reached the peak in 2011–2012. However, with the withdrawal of the economic stimulus plan and the recurrence of economic weakness, the expectation of U.S. interest rate hike led to the strengthening of the U.S. dollar, and OPEC's abandonment of the pricing strategy of restricting production and maintaining prices pushed oil prices down. More importantly, shale oil supply has grown rapidly, and the marginal effect of increased crude oil supply has pushed oil prices into rapid decline (IMF, 2015a). Important oil-producing countries did not cut down their production, in order to compete for the international crude oil market share, which made the pricing rule of the international crude oil market evolved from the original cartel pricing to the competitive pricing with the characteristic of Bertrand (Wang and Ma, 2015). Other types of commodities were constrained by economic demand dilemma, and their prices have also fallen sharply. The prices of commodities and crude oil have almost been halved relative to their peak prices in 2011–2012 (see Figure 4). Meanwhile, some large developing countries, such as China, are gradually reducing heavy industrial production, and their economies are developing more toward consumption-driven and cleaner production models, due to the high sensitivity of shale oil prices to the supply, as well as the gradual change in world production models. The vigorous development of clean energy has gradually reduced the crude oil intensity in

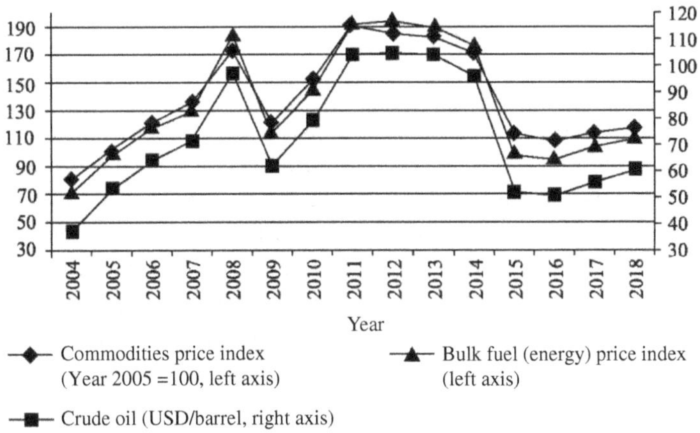

Figure 4. The Price Index of Commodities, Bulk Fuel (Energy) and Crude Oil Price Trend

Source: The author drew the above figure based on the data provided by IMF and World Economic Outlook Database. The commodities price index includes the price indexes of fuel and non-fuel; the bulk fuel (energy) price index includes the price indexes of crude oil, natural gas and coal; the crude oil price is the simple average of the three major spot market prices of Dated Brent, West Texas Intermediate and Dubai Fateh.

global economic growth. These mean that crude oil will be on the track of low and medium prices in the next few years (IEA, 2015).

From the perspective of countries exporting commodities and energy, commodity exporting countries are faced with a "resource curse" on prices due to the dimmed prospects for commodities (including crude oil) prices, and the increase in marginal exports has a greater downward pressure on prices, leading to a sharp reduction in export profits. Meanwhile, compared with 2012–2014, the annual growth rate of more than 40 commodity exporting countries in the world may drop by 1 percentage point in 2015–2017. Moreover, in energy exporting countries, the adverse impact is expected to be even greater, reaching an average of about 2.25 percentage points (IMF, 2015b), although the drop in oil prices will boost world economic growth by 0.5 percentage points in 2015–2016 (Husain *et al.*, 2015). This also means that the potential outputs of commodity exporting countries are falling. Correspondingly, commodity importing countries obtain the benefits of price distribution and the economic growth brought by low-cost input of commodities.

2.2. *The "mediocre period" of trade caused by "trade overshoot" will lead to a battle for dividends in international markets*

Affected by the Subprime Crisis, the economic aggregate demand dropped sharply. However, the changing scope in world trade growth is significantly greater than that of GDP. The short-term response of trade to the impact worldwide showed a situation that exceeded its long-term stable equilibrium value, resulting in the phenomenon of "trade overshoot" (Escaith *et al.*, 2010). Figure 5 shows the comparison between the growth rate of world GDP and that of trade, from which we can see the "overshoot" of world trade volume to the impact of the Subprime Crisis. Moreover, after 2012, this impact made the growth rate of world trade gradually converge to the global GDP growth rate, which is in sharp contrast to the fact that the growth rate of world trade was significantly greater than the economic growth rate 20 years before the crisis, and started the "Mediocre Period" of world trade.

Accompanied by the "Mediocre Period" of trade, trade frictions occur frequently, and thus counter cyclical trade policies prevail. Many countries especially the developed countries have introduced some temporary international trade and investment protectionist measures within the scope

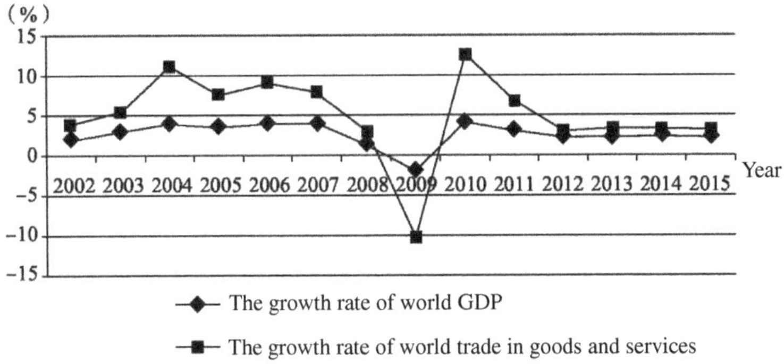

Figure 5. Changes in the Growth Rate of World GDP and the Growth Rate of World Trade in Goods and Services

Source: The author drew the above figure based on the data provided by IMF and World Economic Outlook Database.

permitted by the WTO, in order to maintain their international market share and promote their domestic employment. There have been cases in which the developing countries have implemented trade facilitating measures while the developed countries have reversed trade liberalization. According to the data provided by the WTO, from October 2008 to May 2015, WTO members implemented a total of 2,416 trade measures, of which there are 1,828 trade restriction measures, accounting for 75.7%, and 588 trade restriction measures eliminated, accounting for 24.3%. In the last five years, there has been a sharp increase in the number of trade restriction measures, from 464 to 1,828, with an average increase of 273 measures per year. Since the Subprime Crisis, the trade restriction measures implemented by the G20 countries have continued to increase, with 1,360 trade restriction measures implemented, only less than a quarter of the trade restriction measures eliminated. Up to now, there are still 1,031 trade restriction measures left. The trade restriction measures implemented by the G20 countries account for 74% of the global total, and the monthly trade restriction measures implemented are higher than the global average, which has a significant negative impact on the growth of global trade volume.

From the perspective of specific countries and regions, since the global financial crisis, major developed countries and regions such as the United States, the European Union, Japan, Canada and Australia have implemented 163, 171, 4, 50 and 74 trade remedy measures respectively, while very few trade facilitating measures have been implemented in the same period, namely 3, 5, 5, 17 and 3, respectively. The number of trade remedy measures implemented is 14 times that of trade facilitating measures. Major emerging market economies such as China, India, Mexico, Russia and Indonesia have implemented 73, 181, 71, 29 and 46 trade remedy measures respectively; and those countries have implemented 32, 69, 24, 92 and 17 trade facilitating measures respectively. The number of trade remedy measures implemented is 1.7 times that of trade facilitating measures. Moreover, in the future, as the geographical center of Global trade will gradually shift to emerging economies, the share of OECD in Global trade will drop from 50% in 2012 to 25%, while the trade share within the Asian economy will rise from 6% to 16% (OECD, 2014b). Therefore, it is predictable that it will be normal for the developed countries to use various trade restrictive measures to cope with the rapid growth of trade in the developing countries. For example, the recent TPP mainly emphasizes high standards and non-tariff measures, and the developed countries like the United States and Japan hope to set global trade standards, which will undoubtedly affect the developing countries. This leads to a vicious circle of trade: the decline in exports will inevitably bring about the decline in the economic growth of emerging economies, because the export-oriented emerging economies are the most potential ones for growth, which in turn will affect imports from the developed countries and regions, and the developed countries are also exposed to the trade decline risk. For example, on average, the products exported by G20 countries to China accounted for 6.6% of their total exports in 2007, and this proportion rose to 10.3% by 2013. For some countries, such as Australia, South Korea and Japan, this proportion was as high as 36.1%, 26.1%, and 18.1%, respectively, in 2013. The decrease in China's imports will undoubtedly have a significant impact on the growth of these countries. Therefore, the TPP program that excludes China will only have a negative effect on the recovery of world trade.

On the whole, the so-called "Post-Washington Consensus" flaunted by the developed countries in the 20th century has become obsolete due to the "Mediocre Period" of trade, and the battle for the dividend of international market trade will continue and may be escalated.

2.3. *Capital flows caused by the excessive flexibility of the U.S. dollar system will lead to exchange rate exposure risks in the emerging economies*

The policy combination of fiscal tightening and monetary expansion becomes the main way for the developed economies to promote economic recovery, and the result will inevitably be the devaluation of their currencies, but the competitive devaluation of global currencies will be a zero-sum game. The "beggar-thy-neighbors" competitive devaluation of global currencies from 1929 to 1933 is a typical historical case of zero-sum game. In the international monetary system dominated by the U.S. dollar, the competitive devaluation of major currencies caused by the excessive elasticity of the U.S. dollar system will have a significant negative impact on the emerging economies. Once the developed economies promote economic recovery due to the devaluation of their own currencies, the withdrawal of quantitative easing monetary policy will be put on the agenda, and the reflux of capital will bring the pressure of exchange rate fluctuations in the emerging economies. As early as June 2013, Bernanke, the former Chairman of the Federal Reserve, pointed out that once there was a clear signal of improvement in the labor market, the Federal Reserve would consider withdrawing from the quantitative easing policy, and the emerging market economies would respond immediately, so a large amount of capital flowed back to the United States. If there are large capital outflows from emerging market economies and the international balance of payment becomes seriously unbalanced, then the local currency is bound to depreciate and exchange rate risks will occur. The export-oriented emerging market countries are generally afraid of exchange rate fluctuations (Calvo and Reinhart, 2002). Violent fluctuations of exchange rates are detrimental to the import and export trade, and the transmission effect of exchange rate will also affect the stability of domestic prices. After the financial crisis in 2008, the exchange rates of most emerging market economies were relatively volatile, such as that of India, Russia, South Africa, Brazil and Mexico. Russia was the country with the largest currency depreciation, and the ruble depreciated by half after the crisis. The emerging market economies have weak bearing capability for currency mismatch. If the exchange rate is not managed, the large fluctuation of exchange rate will have a significant negative impact on a country's economy.

The implementation of unconventional monetary policies in major developed countries amplifies the risks of exchange rate fluctuations and capital turmoil in the emerging market economies. Unexpected changes or non-anticipated trends in the normalization of monetary policies in the developed countries will have a significant impact on the emerging market economies, which is closely related to the dollar system with excessive elasticity. The emerging market economies generally face the risk of capital reversal and the challenge of managing large-scale and continuously fluctuating liquidity.

A considerable part of the liquidity released by the quantitative easing policies of the developed economies has flowed to the emerging market economies, and the vast majority of capitals were private ones (the proportion of private capitals from 2011 to 2015 was 96%). The proportion of fast-flowing securities investment increased from about 4% in 2001 to about 12.7% in 2015, which rose more than twice, especially after the financial crisis. IIF (2015a) research shows that capital inflows to the emerging market economies have declined sharply in recent months. The non-resident capital inflows to the emerging market economies were lower in 2015 than that of in 2008 while the resident capital outflows were on the rise; in 2015, the net capital inflow to the emerging market economies were negative for the first time since 1988. The profit-seeking characteristic of private capitals determines its volatility, and the impact of the reversal of private capitals on the emerging market economies has become a reality.

Under the condition of financial opening, the government intervention capacity declines, and international investors will forcibly correct the distorted structure through arbitrage in a broad sense, and the consequences of such forcible correction are vulnerability and crisis (by Economic Growth Frontier Research Group, 2005). Especially when the traditional monetary policy of the developed economies causes the real interest rate to be close to or equal to zero, the exchange rate becomes the main international transmission channel of monetary policy. The fluctuation of exchange rate will affect the investment strategy of market investors, amplify the impact of monetary policy spillover and trigger the financial cycle. The degree of domestic liquidity tightness in the United States is closely related to the reversal of capital inflows to the developing countries. When the United States tightens monetary policy and enters an interest rate hike cycle, the emerging market economies may face a new round of large-scale capital reversal, thus greatly increasing the probability of financial crisis (Li *et al*., 2009). The IIF report pointed out that, since the Federal Reserve expressed its willingness to withdraw from the quantitative easing policy in May 2013, the emerging market economies have encountered three waves of market shocks. Every time international capitals reversed and outflowed, the emerging market economies experienced currency devaluation and financial market turmoil. Considering that the Federal Reserve may raise interest rates for the first time in 2015, the IIF estimates by using a model that there will be more than three financial crises in the emerging market economies in 2015 (IIF, 2015b).

Subject to many uncertainties in the process of economic recovery, the primary problem in regulating capital flow with interest rate instruments is whether it is allowed by the domestic economic status. An alternative approach is that the emerging market-oriented economies can implement capital controls in order to cope with capital reversals, namely, implement prudent capital account management. In the 1990s, the IMF spared no effort to promote the free flow of capital and prohibited its members from regulating capital accounts. After the financial crisis in 2008, witnessing that some emerging market economies were affected by the crisis due to insufficient control of their own capital markets, the IMF changed its attitude toward the capital controls. It believed that capital flows can be properly controlled under certain circumstances, and in 2011, it set out the proposed framework for capital controls in response to capital flows, in which it believed that in the face of large-scale capital flows, it may be appropriate for some countries to implement prudential measures or capital controls based on their exchange rate status. In general, the implementation of capital controls in the emerging market economies can basically play a certain role of "firewall" (Wang *et al*., 2013).

Therefore, under the guidance of expectation of the Fed's interest rate hike, the backflow of dollar capital has always kept the currency associated with the dollar under continuous depreciation pressure. The emerging economies, especially export-oriented ones, should place a high value on practical exchange rate arrangements, and any action in hurry to embrace financial globalization and fully open the capital account may have disastrous consequences.

2.4. *The non-synchronization of the monetary policy accompanied by the imbalance of recovery will bring about the risk of negative externality of the monetary policy*

After the global financial crisis, the quantitative easing monetary policies that began in developed economies produced a "pass the parcel" effect. However, the results are quite different due to the differences in financial market conditions, the intensity of quantitative easing monetary policies, and the transmission mechanism of monetary policy and so on. Therefore, the time for withdrawing from quantitative easing monetary policies will also be different. The asynchrony of monetary policy caused by the asynchronous recovery cycle has also become a reality.

The differentiation of unconventional monetary policy in the developed economies began with the expectation that the U.S. Federal Reserve started the withdrawal from the quantitative easing monetary policy, while the European economy entered the era of negative interest rates. These two landmark events reflect the asynchronous economic recovery of the United States and Europe. At present, the United States and the United Kingdom are expected to raise interest rates, while Europe and Japan continue to be easing. As the United States had better economic recovery, the momentum of its economic growth has been gradually restored and its employment situation has been improved, it officially withdrew from the quantitative easing policy in October 2014. This means that the United States has shifted from the unconventional easing monetary policy to the conventional monetary policy. The momentum of economic recovery in Britain is not abating, the expectation of interest rate hikes also appeared in 2014, and its monetary policy has been tightened. However, the economy in Eurozone is still struggling in the quagmire, with its unemployment rate at a record high, and the risk of deflation is also continuing to ferment. The easing policy announced by the European Central Bank will continue until September 2016. Under the background of weak economic recovery in Japan, its easing monetary policy will continue. There is a clear differentiation of monetary policies within the developed economies.

Monetary policies of the emerging economies have also begun to differentiate gradually. Some emerging economies, such as Russia, Brazil and South Africa, continue to tighten monetary policies to control inflation and prevent currency devaluation. Since March 2014, there has been vast capital flight in Russia, the ruble has continued to depreciate, and inflation has risen. In response to the deteriorating economic situation, the Central Bank of Russia raised interest rates five times in 2014, increasing the benchmark interest rate from 5.5% to 17%. Since 2015, the Central Bank of Russia has cut the benchmark interest rate five times, reducing the benchmark interest rate from 17% to 11%, in order to boost its economy. Brazil's economy has experienced stagflation, on the one hand, its economy is in recession, on the other hand, the inflation rate is as high as double digits, which is more than twice the target value. In early August 2015, the Brazilian real depreciated nearly 30% against the U.S. dollar in a free fall. The Central Bank of Brazil has raised interest rates six times to 16.25% consecutively, and currently interest rates in Brazil have been still at their highest level since July 2006. South Africa raised interest rates to 5.5% in January 2014 (which is also the first increase in South Africa's benchmark interest rate in five and a half years), and it raised interest rates to 6% in July 2015, in order to alleviate the trend of rapid depreciation in the rand, reduce inflationary pressures and inhibit capital flight. Some important emerging economies, such as China, India, Turkey and South Korea, are implementing easing monetary policies to cope with the continued decline in economic growth and the risk of deflation. China's GDP growth began to decline after the financial crisis. In 2014, the GDP growth rate was 7.4%, a 24-year low. The pressure of GDP growth rate falling below 7% in the third quarter of 2015, once again made the People's Bank of China implement the "double reduction" of reserve ratio and interest rate at the time of "First Frost" in 2015. As India's economic prospects became increasingly uncertain, coupled with the continued decline in commodity and agricultural prices, India reduced its benchmark interest rate from 7.25% to 6.75% in September 2015, which is the fourth rate cut by the Reserve Bank of India (RBI) in 2015. The RBI believes that the monetary policy orientation must remain easing and the debt investment regulations to overseas investors should be relaxed. In addition, the monetary policies of South Korea and Turkey are also on the way of interest rate cuts, due to the lack of impetus for their economic development or unsatisfactory recovery.

It can be seen that the current global monetary policy has appeared obvious differentiation: among the developed economies, the U.S. and the U.K. have expectation of interest rate hikes while the EU and Japan have easing monetary policies. Among the emerging economies, Russia and Pakistan have raised interest rates while China and India have cut interest rates. In world economy where financial correlation is gradually strengthened, the differentiation of monetary policies will inevitably bring about the negative externality. This negative externality is mainly embodied in two aspects. First of all, the monetary policies of the emerging economies are in a dilemma, and they can only be forced to integrate into the monetary policies of the developed economies, in order to maintain the relative stability of exchange rates. Inflows and outflows of capitals cause the loss of partial independence to monetary policies. Namely, there is an "impossible trinity". Secondly, even for the peripheral countries with floating exchange rate systems, as long as there is capital flow, the currencies of the core countries will affect the peripheral countries in the form of credit or leverage, and the peripheral countries cannot obstruct the impact of the financial cycle of the core countries through exchange rates (Rey, 2013). The research of Frankel *et al*. (2004) shows that the interest rates of countries that implement floating exchange rates can only be adjusted slowly in line with the international market interest rates. That is to say, they can obtain certain monetary policy independence. However, in the long run, even in countries that implement floating exchange rates, their interest rates will also be affected by interest rates in international markets. Only a few developed countries are exceptional, and they can choose their own interest rates in the long run. Therefore, the emerging economies cannot consider their own economic reality, and have to passively choose the monetary policies of the core countries. This negative spillover effect will be a practical problem faced by the emerging economies.

3. A Brief Conclusion

The global potential GDP decline caused by the impact of the Subprime Crisis together with the long debt cycle caused by the stimulus policies emphasizing demand management determine that world economy is in the process of arduous recovery. The imbalance of the recovery process, the asymmetry of the international monetary system, the differentiation of national export structures and the friction between trades and exchange rate policies determine that the recovery of world economy will inevitably accompany with the wealth redistribution effect, and lead to a recovery that is not necessarily a win–win result.

Constrained by the demand dilemma and the fact of slow technological progress, the global economic recovery is arduous and moderate. Initiating economic structural reform is undoubtedly an alternative choice to activate or reshape new sources of growth from the aspect of the supply. However, the structural reform is beset with difficulties. Many countries and regions have lost their capital and capacity for structural reform due to the impact of the Crisis. Those countries that are unable to carry out structural reforms and can hardly hedge the negative spillover of monetary policies in the core countries will lose the initiative of economic development in the process of recovery, can hardly share the dividends brought by the recovery of world economy, and will also lead to a recovery that is not necessarily a win–win result.

Chapter 3

Comparison of Unconventional Monetary Policies in the U.S., Europe and Japan

After the outbreak of the Subprime Crisis and the European Sovereign Debt Crisis, both the United States and Europe had the problem of zero lower bound in their monetary policies, and then successively adopted quantitative easing or unconventional monetary policies. Some economists believe that Japan is the earliest country to implement the unconventional monetary policy among large economies, because long ago, Japan's interest rate had been at zero for a long time. However, 8 years since the outbreak of the Crisis, although unconventional monetary policies have been increasingly implemented, so far, only the U.S. economy has shown signs of recovery, and entered the stage of discussing the withdrawal procedure of its unconventional monetary policy. But Europe and Japan, by contrast, still remain in the quagmire of economic recession.

What on earth are the reasons for such huge differences in the effects of unconventional monetary policies in various countries? About the differences in the effects of monetary policies in various countries, this chapter studies emphatically on the causes, operating procedures, characteristics and differences of unconventional monetary policies in the United States, Europe and Japan, and then analyzes why the unconventional monetary policies have different effects in different countries.

This chapter is divided into the following parts: the first part briefly generalizes the basic characteristics of unconventional monetary policies from the perspective of monetary policy theory; the second part summarizes the process of unconventional monetary policy implementation in the United States, Japan and Europe. The third part summarizes the differences and causes of unconventional monetary policies in different countries and regions by means of comparison. The last part is a conclusion.

1. The Unconventional Monetary Policy and Its Basic Characteristics

The unconventional monetary policy refers to the policy adopted by the central bank to stimulate the aggregate demand when the nominal interest rate drops to zero. From the perspective of monetary policy operation itself, the unconventional monetary policy can be simply understood as the monetary policy implemented through the balance sheet of the central bank.

1.1. *Implementation of unconventional monetary policies*

As a synonym for unconventional monetary policy, the quantitative easing policy was initially adopted by the Bank of Japan in 2001 to cope with the deflation that appeared in the early 20th century, and continued until 2006. Faced with the economic stagnation that began in the 1990s and the serious problem of distressed debt, the Bank of Japan began to implement the "zero interest rate" policy in early 1999. However, the effect of this policy was not obvious. In 2001, Japan's economy continued to deteriorate; deflation was severe; the losses of bank's own capital increased sharply; corporate investment decreased. As the traditional monetary policy had lost its operation space, Japan had to adopt other methods to implement further easing policy. In March 2001, the Bank of Japan introduced the quantitative easing policy and eventually withdrew in 2006.

For the quantitative easing policy of the Bank of Japan in 2001, there are three core aspects (Franta, 2011). Firstly, the monetary policy target of the Bank of Japan has changed from the call rate to the deposit reserve of financial institutions. Since the deposit reserve of financial institutions is the liability of the central bank, the last round of quantitative easing policy in Japan is considered to be the monetary policy actively implemented by the central bank through the "liabilities side" in its balance sheet. Secondly, The Bank of Japan promised to continue to adopt quantitative easing until core consumer price index (CPI) deflation disappeared, which is quite similar to the "Forward Guidance" in the unconventional monetary policy of the United States. Thirdly, the Bank of Japan promised to purchase long-term treasury bonds to increase liquidity for the market, which is also similar to the Operation Twist in the unconventional monetary policy of the United States. It can be seen that the first round of quantitative easing monetary policy in Japan is similar to the unconventional monetary policies in the United States, Britain and other countries after the Subprime Crisis, in many aspects such as operation modes.

In 2006, the Bank of Japan withdrew from the quantitative easing monetary policy, and readjusted its monetary policy target to the call rate, and continued to implement the zero-interest-rate policy. However, when the Bank of Japan withdrew from the quantitative easing policy in 2006, the year-on-year growth rate of the core CPI did not return to a positive number, and only the year-on-year growth rate of CPI was a positive number in the short term, but it was extremely unstable and fell back into deflation after the beginning of 2007. From the perspective of the scale of the quantitative easing policy, the scale of the quantitative easing policy from 2001 to 2006 was much smaller than that of the Bank of Japan after 2013. The total assets of the Bank of Japan increased from about 105.45 trillion yen at the beginning of 2001 to about 155.6 trillion yen at the end of 2005, with an average annual growth rate of only 6.7%. Moreover, after withdrawing from the quantitative easing policy in 2006, the balance sheet of the Bank of Japan experienced a rapid tightening process. By the end of June 2006, the total assets of the Bank of Japan rapidly dropped to 113.8 trillion yen, which was 27% lower than that at the end of 2005.

After restarting the quantitative easing policy in 2013, the Bank of Japan has greatly increased its asset purchases. At the beginning of 2013, its total assets were 157.94 trillion yen and have reached 373.55 trillion yen by the end of October 2015, increasing by nearly 1.4 times in the past 3 years, with an average annual growth rate of 33%, which was much higher than that of the quantitative easing policy from 2001 to 2006.

After 2008, the Federal Reserve took the lead in implementing the unconventional monetary policy among the major central banks, followed by the Bank of England. On the one hand, it was because that the United States and the United Kingdom were directly hit by the Subprime Crisis, on the other hand, it was also related to the monetary policy theory of Bernanke, then chairman of the U.S. Federal Reserve. When Japan initially implemented the quantitative easing policy, it mainly targeted the reserves of financial institutions, which was somewhat different from the "Credit Easing" implemented by the United States after the Subprime Crisis. In addition to the so-called Credit Easing, the Federal Reserve also proposed the concept of the so-called Forward Guidance. After April 2013, the Bank of Japan started a new round of unconventional monetary policy and defined it as "Quantitative and Qualitative Monetary Easing" with additional Forward Guidance, namely QQE. Within this monetary policy framework, the Bank of Japan will continue to adopt the unconventional monetary policy of quantitative easing until the annual growth rate of the consumer price index stabilizes at 2%.

Therefore, this chapter will use the term of "unconventional monetary policy" rather than call it "quantitative easing policy" in general. Table 1 shows the changes in the balance sheets of central banks after the implementation of quantitative easing monetary policies by central banks in various countries. In terms of the extent of expansion, the Federal Reserve, the Bank of Japan and the Bank of England have expanded to the same extent. From 2007 to July 2015, the ratio of assets to GDP of the abovementioned central banks roughly increased by 3.3 times. The ratio of total assets to GDP of its central banks only increased by about 1.1 times, due to the relatively late implementation of the unconventional monetary policy in the Eurozone.

Table 1. Unconventional Monetary Policies of Central Banks in Major Countries (Regions)

	Time	Total Assets (% GDP)	Monetary Base (% GDP)	Asset Purchase (% GDP)
ECB	2007	9.9	8.8	—
	July 2015	20.7	15.2	5.2
The Federal Reserve	2007	5.8	5.7	—
	July 2015	24.5	22.7	24.3
Bank of Japan	2007	16.3	17.1	—
	July 2015	70.1	66.0	63.6
Bank of England	2007	5.4	4.4	—
	July 2015	23.4	21.7	20.9

Note: The assets scale of the ECB (European Central Bank) reached 26.2% of GDP during the European Sovereign Debt Crisis in June 2012, and the monetary base reached 18% of GDP.

1.2. *The basic transmission mechanism of unconventional monetary policies*

Although there are some differences in the implementation of specific policies, basically the unconventional monetary policies pump money into the economy through purchasing government bonds or private assets by the central banks. Through purchasing financial assets, the unconventional monetary policies can have the following effects:

> Firstly, counterparties of the central banks can obtain the necessary liquidity by selling assets, so as to enhance their own security and benefit the stabilization of the financial market.
>
> Secondly, the central banks push up asset prices by purchasing specific financial assets. On the one hand, this will produce a wealth effect and stimulate consumption or investment. On the other hand, the decline in the rate of return caused by rising asset prices is also conducive to reducing financing costs.
>
> Thirdly, for private financial institutions, selling assets to the central banks will obtain reserves, and the increase of reserves may promote financial institutions to increase credit supply to households and businesses.
>
> Fourthly, in addition to the tangible channels mentioned earlier, the increase in the amount of money will also generate inflation expectations, driving down the real interest rates and contributing to the recovery of the real economy. The transmission channels of unconventional monetary policies are shown in Figure 1.

Since the risk appetite of financial institutions tends to be reversed during economic crises, the effectiveness of unconventional monetary policy depends on whether it can effectively affect both supply and demand in credit markets to a great extent. From the perspective of credit supply, the effectiveness of unconventional monetary policy depends on whether it can reduce loan costs and increase credit supply, that is, whether households and businesses can borrow more loans at cheaper prices. From the perspective of credit demand, the effectiveness of unconventional monetary policy depends on whether it can effectively repair the balance sheets of households and businesses, and achieve the deleveraging of businesses. Only when both the supply and demand of credit are improved can the unconventional monetary policy achieve the desired effect.

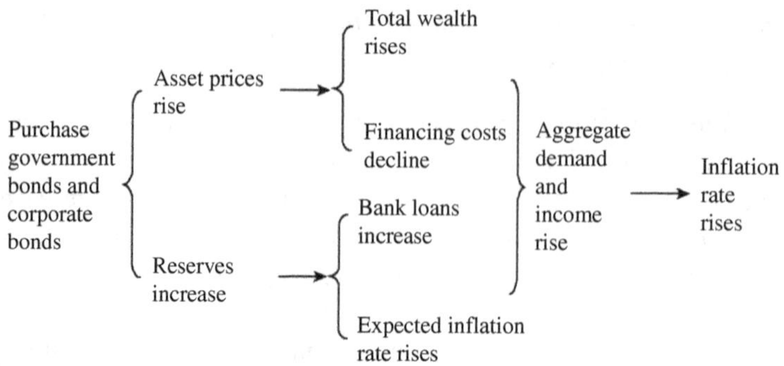

Figure 1. Main Transmission Channels of Unconventional Monetary Policy

1.3. *The theoretical basis of unconventional monetary policies*

The theoretical basis of unconventional monetary policies can be traced back to Friedman's research on monetary policy at zero interest rate, and later Krugman and Bernanke developed the theory of unconventional monetary policy.

Krugman has developed the generalized liquidity trap theory, and defines it as the state in which aggregate demand continues to decline when the nominal interest rate drops to zero. Krugman attributes the liquidity trap to information or expectation problems. When the economy falls into the liquidity trap, the economy is in a state of stagnation, which will also affect the expectation of people. Worried about future credit problems, consumers reduce investment and consumption, which eventually makes the economy to further deteriorate. Managing expectation is an important approach to get the economy out of the deflation trap. If the public believes that inflation will recur in the future, the real interest rates will fall, thus stimulating the aggregate demand and economic growth.

Bernanke systematically demonstrated the possible coping strategies of the central banks when monetary policies reached the zero-interest-rate boundary under the condition of deflation. Bernanke believes that after the short-term nominal interest rate reaches the zero-interest-rate boundary, the central banks can continue to stimulate the economy with unconventional monetary policy instruments. He proposed three major measures: managing public expectations of future interest rates, changing the structure of the central bank's balance sheet and expanding the scale of the central bank's balance sheet. The specific measures include: the central bank can control the market interest rate at a low level by purchasing or promising to buy long-term treasury bonds and agency bonds, expand the number and types of assets purchased, pump money into the economy, or put liquidity by providing low interest loans to banks and coordinating with the financial sector, etc. Bernanke formally referred to the policy relating to central bank's balance sheet regulation as the central bank's balance sheet policy, and the related policy of expanding the scale of the balance sheet as Quantitative Easing, and the related policy of changing the composition of the balance sheet as Credit Easing. These theories eventually became the blueprint of the Fed's unconventional monetary policy during the 2007–2008 financial crisis.

Anderson *et al.* (2010) summarized the basic principles of unconventional monetary policy implementation based on the practice of unconventional monetary policies in various countries: Firstly, if the scale of balance sheet of a country's central bank increases rapidly in the short term, it can provide the impetus for economic recovery. Secondly, the central banks should communicate with the public about the purpose of implementing unconventional monetary policies. Thirdly, compared with purchasing assets, the scale of balance sheet expansion is more important. Finally, when the crisis is over, the balance-sheet expansion should be lifted in time.

1.4. *The effects of unconventional monetary policies*

Then what are the effects for implementing an unconventional monetary policy? The research of Ncube (2014) found that the effects of an unconventional monetary policy were asymmetric in stabilizing prices and stimulating economic growth. Thereinto, the unconventional monetary policy is very effective for stabilizing prices. If unconventional monetary policies are not adopted, inflation rates in major economies will fall to more unfavorable levels. However, the research results also show that the impact of quantitative easing on economic growth is limited. There was no significant impact other than the 0.7 percentage point increase in the GDP growth rate of the U.K., and no direct impact of the quantitative easing was found on GDP growth in major economies.

In addition, Ncube's analysis also found that the quantitative easing policy contributed to the reduction of unemployment rates in the United

States and Japan, and also led to rising inflation expectations in the United States, the United Kingdom and the Eurozone. However, it is uncertain with the impact of quantitative easing on house prices, stock prices, consumer confidence and exchange rates.

Therefore, without structural reforms and other policy measures, it is difficult to succeed in overcoming the global economic crisis just with the monetary policy alone.

2. The Basic Process and Characteristics of Unconventional Monetary Policies in the United States, Europe and Japan

2.1. *The implementation of unconventional monetary policies in the United States*

In the implementation of unconventional monetary policies, Bernanke (2009) classified monetary policy instruments into three types.

The first type of financial instruments provides healthy financial institutions with the extended liquidity in the financial market. But the Fed's provision of liquidity to the interbank market is not a panacea for the economic crisis. Although there is sufficient liquidity in the interbank market, the willingness of financial institutions to extend credit is greatly reduced, due to changes in risk appetite. The Fed's expansion of liquidity supply for the financial institutions cannot completely eliminate the lack of credit in non-bank markets such as the commercial paper market and the asset-backed securities market.

The second type of financial instruments provides liquidity for borrowers and investors directly in the credit market, such as direct purchases of commercial paper and money market mutual funds. The purpose of this type of financial instrument is to attempt to transfer the liquidity in the interbank market to the lending market, avoid the volatility of the credit market when facing a large number of short-term asset redemptions, at the same time, reduce the rollover risk of those assets with relatively long terms, and encourage private investors to provide credit funds to the market.

The third type of financial instruments reduces long-term interest rates by purchasing long-term assets and supports the credit market to function normally.

What these three types of unconventional monetary policy instruments have in common is to achieve the expansion of monetary policies

Table 2. The Implementation of the U.S. Unconventional Monetary Policies

Time	Unemployment Rate (%)	Inflation Rate (%)	Unconventional Monetary Policies
November 2008	6.8	1.1	The 1st round of Quantitative Easing (QE1)
November 2010	9.8	1.1	The 2nd round of Quantitative Easing (QE2)
September 2011	9.0	3.9	Operation Twist, OT
September 2012	7.8	2	The 3rd round of Quantitative Easing (QE3)
December 2012	7.9	1.7	The 4th round of Quantitative Easing (QE4)

Note: The unemployment rates are those surveyed unemployment rates in seasonally adjusted terms, and the inflation rates are year-on-year CPI growth rates.

by expanding the total assets of the Fed's balance sheet (extending credit and purchasing assets). The implementation of the U.S. quantitative easing policy is shown in Table 2.

2.2. *The implementation of unconventional monetary policies in Europe*

Compared with the United States, the Eurozone was not active in adopting unconventional monetary policies (Bullard, 2015). After the European Central Bank (ECB) cut its benchmark interest rate to 1% in May 2009, it was neither willing to maintain the interest rate at zero level for a long time nor to adopt the unconventional monetary policies adopted by the United Kingdom, the United States and other countries. It was not until 2015 that the ECB began to implement quantitative easing policies.

After the outbreak of the Subprime Crisis and the European Sovereign Debt Crisis, the unconventional monetary policies implemented by the ECB can be divided into two stages.

The first stage was from the outbreak of the Subprime Crisis to June 2014. At this stage, the monetary policy of the ECB still focused on enhancing the effectiveness of its conventional monetary policy transmission mechanism. At this stage, the changes in the ECB's balance sheet only passively met the liquidity demands of commercial banks, which was quite different from the typical unconventional monetary policies taking the balance sheet as a policy instrument in the United States and Japan. From mid-2012 to mid-2014, the interest rate cut policy adopted by the ECB did not lead to the reduction of corporate borrowing costs. For example, since June 2012, the ECB has reduced the Main Refinancing Operation (MRO) from 1% to 0.05% in June 2014, with a decrease of about 95 basis points. However, in most Eurozone countries, the loan interest rate for corporate fell only slightly, with the median lending rates for small and medium loans in the median countries just falling by less than 30 basis points (Constâncio, 2015).

The second stage was after June 2014, when the ECB began to implement a more aggressive expansionary monetary policy. After January 2015, the ECB expanded its asset purchase program and formally proposed the Public Sector Purchase Programme (PSPP), which is the so-called quantitative easing monetary policy.

Constâncio (2015) summarized the transmission channels of the unconventional monetary policy in the ECB into four aspects: The first is the information display channel. The implementation of the unconventional monetary policy indicated the firm determination of the ECB to stimulate the economy. The second is the inflation expectation mechanism. The third is the credit channel, that is, to stimulate the recovery of the real economy by reducing the effective loan cost of the private sector and improving the credit availability. The fourth is the asset purchase channel, which superficially led to the expansion of the central bank's balance sheet through the purchase of long-term assets, essentially reduced the liquidity risk and duration risk of the private sector asset portfolio, and reduced the risk premium of holding assets. The leverage of the private sector was reduced, through rebalancing private sector portfolio and raising asset prices, making it easier for the private sector to obtain loans from the banking sector. Table 3 lists the ECB's monetary policy operated from 2009 to 2016.

2.3. *The implementation of unconventional monetary policies in Japan*

After the Subprime Crisis, compared with Europe and America, the expansionary monetary policy in Japan was relatively moderate and temporary (Vollmer and Bebenroth, 2012). There are mainly two reasons for it: one is that Japan is not the country where the Subprime Crisis occurred directly; the other is that Japan's monetary authorities have learned from

Table 3. Monetary Policies of the ECB

Time	Unconventional Monetary Policies
2009–2010	The 1st round of Covered Bond Purchase Programs
2010–2012	Securities Markets Program (SMP)
2011–2012	The 2nd round of Covered Bond Purchase Programs; Two Liquidity-providing Long-term Refinancing Operations in Euro with a 3-year Maturity
2011	Expanding the scope of eligible collateral
2012–2014	Open-ended Outright Monetary Transactions
2014	Targeted Longer-term Refinancing Operations (TLTROs); Outright Purchases of Private Sector Assets
2015–2016	Expanded Asset Purchase Program, including PSPP

the financial crisis in the 1990s. Relative to the monetary policy, the fiscal policy in Japan was more powerful than that of Europe. However, as Japan's economic recession continued to intensify, since April 2013, Japan has begun to implement the Quantitative and Qualitative Monetary Easing with the additional Forward Guidance, in order to achieve the goal of stabilizing the annual growth rate of CPI at 2%.

The core content of the Quantitative and Qualitative Monetary Easing includes two points. First of all, the central bank promised to stabilize the CPI growth rate at 2% as soon as possible within 2 years. Secondly, on the one hand, quantitative easing was achieved by expanding the scale of the balance sheet; on the other hand, the policy effect was improved by expanding the types of asset purchases, in order to achieve the goal of stabilizing the annual growth rate of CPI at 2%. Specifically, the quantitative easing policy is mainly reflected in the fact that the Bank of Japan will increase the monetary base by 60–70 trillion yen annually by purchasing government bonds. Quality improvement is mainly reflected in increasing the purchase ratio of assets with a higher risk profile and long-term assets. For example, the Bank of Japan has begun to purchase exchange-traded funds (ETFs) and Japan real-estate investment trusts (J-REITs), and reduced the risk premium implied in the yields of these assets by raising prices.

The most important factor in the transmission channel of the Quantitative and Qualitative Monetary Easing in the Bank of Japan is to reduce the expected real interest rate. In fact, although the Bank of Japan emphasizes the adjustment for the types of asset purchases, its

Quantitative and Qualitative Monetary Easing can be regarded as the quantitative easing policy with the additional Forward Guidance. That is, the easing monetary policy will continue until the CPI growth rate stabilizes at 2%. Setting an explicit goal of inflation and implementing an active expansionary monetary policy are conducive to forming a stable expectation of inflation in the private sector.

3. Analyses of the Reasons for the Differences of Unconventional Monetary Policies in Europe, the U.S. and Japan

After the Subprime Crisis, there are great differences in the implementation of the so-called unconventional monetary policies among the United States, the United Kingdom, Japan and the Eurozone. Generally, these differences are caused by factors from three aspects: the first is the difference in the states of the economy (including financial markets); the second is the difference in financial market structures; the third is the difference in political frameworks of decision-making bodies themselves. We will focus on comparing the differences in unconventional monetary policies among the United States, the Eurozone and Japan, due to the high similarity in the implementation of unconventional monetary policies between the United States and the United Kingdom.

From the perspective of differences in the states of economy, the United States is the country where the Subprime Crisis occurred, while the Eurozone and Japan are the countries affected by the Subprime Crisis. But that does not mean the U.S. real economy was in the worst state after the Crisis. Whether it was in 2009, at the early stage of crisis, or in 2011–2012, during the deep fermentation of crisis, the growth rate of the U.S. economy was higher than that of Japan and the Eurozone. What is more, after 2014, the growth rate of the U.S. economy was still consistently higher than that of Japan and the Eurozone. In addition to the impact of the Subprime Crisis, the Eurozone also suffered from the sovereign debt crisis after 2008. The economy in Japan has been in a downturn for a long time since entering the 21st century.

From the perspective of the difference in the financial market structures, the financial markets of the United States and the United Kingdom are mainly direct finance, while the financial markets of the Eurozone and Japan are mainly indirect finance represented by the banking system. The difference in the financial market structures leads to the difference in the transmission of monetary policies, which in turn leads to the difference in the formulation of monetary policies. For example, the Bank of England (2009) pointed out that as commercial banks are not dominant in financial markets, the Bank of England should not be limited to the assets of commercial banks when purchasing assets.

From the perspective of the difference in the political frameworks of the decision-making bodies themselves, the United States and Japan are sovereign countries with unified fiscal and monetary policies. The Eurozone is a non-sovereign transnational organization. Although its monetary policy has been unified, there is no unified government and fiscal policy. Meanwhile, within the political framework of the Eurozone, there are many restrictions on the implementation of monetary policy. For example, the central bank is prohibited from providing monetary financing, public institutions and governments have no priority when borrowing from financial institutions, and another example is the "no-bailout" clause, etc.

3.1. *Differences in unconventional monetary policies between the United States and Japan*

Bernanke (2009) specifically analyzed the difference between the unconventional monetary policy adopted by the Federal Reserve and the quantitative easing policy adopted by the Bank of Japan from 2001 to 2006. Bernanke summarized the Fed's unconventional monetary policy as "Credit Easing". Compared with the quantitative easing policy adopted by Japan in 2001–2006, what they have in common is that both policies led to the expansion of the balance sheet of the central bank. However, there are also huge differences between the unconventional monetary policy of the United States and that of Japan.

3.1.1. *Differences in policy objectives*

Under the Japanese pure quantitative easing policy, the monetary policy is dedicated to expanding commercial bank reserves, while the reserves are the liabilities of the central bank. The composition of loans and securities on the asset side of the central bank changes passively. In contrast, the credit easing policy adopted by the Federal Reserve focuses on influencing credit conditions for residents and businesses through the portfolio management of loans and securities in the asset side of the Federal Reserve. The reason for such policy differences is that after the Subprime

Crisis, the United States is facing more severe credit market distortions than Japan did in 2001–2006. Compared with the situation in Japan at that time, there is larger gap of spreads in American credit market, and the loss of credit market function is more serious. The Fed has to devote more energy to restoring the normal function of the private credit market.

3.1.2. *Differences in policy transmission mechanisms*

In an economic crisis, because the balance sheets of financial institutions, households and businesses may suffer significant damage, the effects of different types of expansion policies of the central bank are quite different. Through the central bank's portfolio management of lending programs and securities, the Fed's credit easing policy not only contributes to maintaining the security of financial institutions and the stability of the financial market but also replaces the role of some commercial banks in fact, and promotes the recovery of private credit market function as soon as possible. Because Japan's financial system mainly relies on commercial banks, Japan's unconventional monetary policy achieves the transfusion for economy mainly through pumping liquidity into commercial banks. However, after the Crisis, the investment inclination of enterprises decreases and the investment risk of real economy increases, due to the increase of economic uncertainties. Therefore, the willingness of banks for credit supply and the willingness of enterprises for loan demand are all not strong. A large amount of liquidity pumped by the central bank stays in the account of the central bank in the form of excess reserves and has not entered the real economy.

3.1.3. *Attitudes on adopting unconventional monetary policies or not*

After the Subprime Crisis, although Japan's interest rate has been maintained at a low level, the time for Japan to restart quantitative easing policy lagged far behind, compared with the United Kingdom, the United States and other countries. Even in the case of insufficient liquidity in Japan's interbank market from 2007 to 2008, the Bank of Japan did not expand its balance sheet on a large scale. From 2007 to 2008, the overnight unsecured call rate in Japan's interbank market rose to about 0.5%, and had maintained for nearly 2 years. During that period, the Bank of Japan mainly increased short-term loans to commercial banks, which had a very limited effect on easing credit terms for households and businesses, and did not include low-interest asset-backed securities as eligible collateral either. It can be said that from the outbreak of the Subprime Crisis in 2008–2013 before the quantitative easing policy was formally implemented, the Bank of Japan had very limited intensity in its expansionary monetary policy.

Then why was the Bank of Japan so reluctant to adopt American quantitative easing, after the Subprime Crisis? For the Bank of Japan, the expansionary monetary policy in the 1990s caused asset bubbles. Meanwhile, the return from the easing policy in the 1990s to the normal policy has also been proved to be a very long and difficult process, making the Bank of Japan excessively cautious when adopting the quantitative easing monetary policy. For the Bank of Japan, it is still an unresolved problem on how to withdraw from the quantitative easing monetary policy when the unconventional monetary policy is introduced.

3.2. *Differences in unconventional monetary policies between the United States and Europe*

In response to the Subprime Crisis or for the implementation of unconventional monetary policies, the ECB was indecisive, mainly due to the following reasons.

First of all, the Eurozone has congenital defects in its institutional arrangements. The Eurozone is a non-sovereign transnational organization. Although its monetary policy has been unified, there is no unified government and fiscal policy. Regarding the purchase behavior of sovereign debt of member States by the ECB Bank, there are no relevant provisions in the Maastricht Treaty. The current situation of using the same currency in multiple sovereign states makes the governments of member states lack incentives to adopt fiscal and structural policy reforms to maintain financial market stability (Cour-Thimann and Winkler, 2013). Under these circumstances, the ECB took a wait-and-see attitude towards the low interest rate policy, attempting to eliminate the impact of the Subprime Crisis only through the low interest rate policy. However, the European sovereign debt crisis broke out in 2009 and reached its peak in 2011 and 2012. The unemployment rate in the Eurozone also peaked at 12.1% in the second quarter of 2013, and was still as high as 10.8%[1] by September 2015.

[1] The unemployment rate data is the surveyed unemployment rate.

Secondly, the ECB implements a single-objective monetary policy. Although stabilizing inflation is the primary objective of a monetary policy, it is not the sole objective. What the Federal Reserve actually implements is a dual mandate monetary policy framework for stabilizing both employments and prices; while the ECB implements a single-objective monetary policy rule, that is, to stabilize the inflation rate at 2% by setting an explicit goal of inflation (Bullard, 2015). For example, under the circumstances that the year-on-year CPI growth rate reached or exceeded 3% and the unemployment rate maintained at 10%, the ECB raised its benchmark interest rate twice in 2011. It was not until December 2014, when the CPI growth rate fell to zero years on year, that the ECB began to consider the implementation of unconventional monetary policy. After January 2015, the ECB began to implement an open-ended quantitative easing monetary policy similar to QE3 in the United States, and planned to continue the policy at least until September 2016.

4. Conclusion

This chapter summarizes the characteristics of the implementation of unconventional monetary policies and their differences in effects in major economies such as the United States, the United Kingdom, Europe and Japan, and on this basis, analyzes the causes of these differences.

From the perspective of the implementation of unconventional monetary policies in various countries, the United States and the United Kingdom are the most active in the implementation of unconventional monetary policies. The United States and the United Kingdom implemented their unconventional monetary policies in 2008 and 2009, respectively, and the main reason is that the United Kingdom and the United States are the countries directly hit by the Subprime Crisis. The Bank of Japan just began to implement its quantitative easing monetary policy after 2013, for fear of the negative impact of the expansionary monetary policy and the difficulty to withdraw from it. At that time, it had been 5 years since the implementation of quantitative easing policies in the United Kingdom and the United States. However, the Eurozone is even more lagging behind in the implementation of unconventional monetary policies. The Eurozone formally implemented the PSPP after January 2015, due to institutional barriers in the implementation of unconventional monetary policy.

From the perspective of the effect of unconventional monetary policy, there is an asymmetry for the unconventional monetary policy in two aspects of stabilizing inflation and its expectation and stimulating economic growth. From the perspective of the existing empirical findings, the quantitative easing policy is effective in stabilizing prices and inflation, but its effect in stimulating economic recovery is limited. Deflation is extremely harmful to economic stability. From this perspective, it is necessary to implement the unconventional monetary policy, but considering the need to stabilize (economic) growth and reduce unemployment, it is not enough to just adopt unconventional monetary policy.

Chapter 4

Development Trends of World Service Industry & Trade and Opening up of China's Service Industry*

After the Second World War, world service industry and service trade developed rapidly, along with the generation and development of the third scientific and technological revolution, the emergence of a large number of transnational corporations and the globalization of the financial and information technology revolution. It can be said that, currently world economy and trade show the tendency of inclined development toward service industry and service trade. It is an inevitable result of social productivity development that the service industry has become an important pillar industry in all countries. The service industry accounts for an increasing proportion of economies in all countries. According to statistics, at present, the output value of the service industry accounts for more than 70% of GNP or GDP in developed countries on average, more than 55% in middle-income countries, and 35%–55% in low-income developing countries. According to the report of the International Labor Organization, the proportion of service sector employment in the total employment population reached 72% in the rich countries of the northern hemisphere, as well as more than 45% in the developing countries of the southern hemisphere in 2009.

With the further development of the division of labor in the service industry, the service exchanges among countries are expanding increasingly.

*This chapter was written by Han Yujun and Wang Li.

In 1970, the export volume of world service trade was less than 71 billion dollars. In 2014, the export volume of world service trade reached 4.94 trillion dollars, with an increase of about 68.6 times. At present, the service trade accounts for about 1/4 and 1/5 of total world commodity trade and total world trade, respectively. The important role of service industry and service trade attracted the attention of the negotiators of trade agreement. The Uruguay Round Negotiations also included it in important new topics, and the General Agreement on Trade in Services (GATS) was signed. Its aims and objectives are to expand the international service trade on the basis of transparency and progressive liberalization.

The characteristics and trends of the development of world service industry and service trade have been changed or are undergoing some changes. What do these characteristics and trends mean for the economic development of various countries, in particular, what are the impacts on China? What are the problems in the competitiveness of China's service industry and service trade, as well as in the opening of its service market? How should China's service sector response to these trends? Based on the qualitative analysis to the aforementioned problems, this chapter makes an empirical analysis on the competitiveness of service industry and service trade, as well as on the openness of service market.

1. Characteristics and Trends of World Service Industry and Trade Development

The service industry often develops at a faster speed, along with the continuous development of science and technology and the constant adjustment and optimization of economic structure. At present, the service industry in most developed countries has already accounted for 70%–80% of the whole national economy, whether in terms of output value or employment, and makes world economy and trade development present a kind of new characteristics and trends.

1.1. *Characteristics of world service industry and trade development*

1.1.1. *Rapid development and increased proportion*

As world service industry generally develops faster than manufacturing and agriculture, the service industry accounts for an increasing proportion of economies in all countries. For example, the share of service industry (tertiary industry) in GDP accounted for 82.0% in the U.S.A. (in 2013), 78.4% in Japan (in 2013), 73.6% in Germany (in 2014), 84.5% in France (in 2014), 84.6% in the U.K. (in 2014), 79.3% in Italy (in 2014), 80.5% in Spain (in 2014), 81.5% in the Netherlands (in 2014), 64.9% in the Czech Republic (in 2014), 67.9% in Russia (in 2013), and 69.6% in Mexico (in 2013), 74.0% in Brazil (in 2011), 78.3% in South Africa (in 2013), 45.5% in Thailand (in 2013), 51.3% in India (in 2013), 63.4% in South Korea (in 2014), 74.9% in Singapore (in 2013), 92.7% in Hong Kong (in 2013) and 48.2% in China (in 2014, excluding construction), respectively (see Table 1).

The growth rate of world service trade was also faster than that of goods trade in the same period in most years. Especially in the 1980s and several years after the GATS of the World Trade Organization (WTO) was signed in 1994, the average growth rate of world service trade exports was higher than that of goods trade. In 1970, the export volume of world service trade was less than 71 billion dollars. In 1992, it exceeded 1 trillion dollars for the first time, reaching 1.01 trillion dollars. In 2000, it reached 1.44 trillion dollars, with an increase of about 19 times over 1970. In 2014, world service trade made great progress, with exports reaching 4.94 trillion dollars, about 68.6 times that of 1970. However, since the beginning of the 21st century, the growth rate of service trade has been slightly lower than that of goods trade in some years. For example, in 2005, the growth rate of world goods trade was 13%, slightly higher than the 11% that of service trade. After the outbreak of the global financial crisis in 2008, the growth rate of world trade slowed down. From 2009 to 2011, the average annual growth rate of global goods trade was 5.1%, however, from 2012 to 2014, the average annual growth rate was only 2.4%. In 2015, the growth rate of global trade was lower than 3% for the fourth consecutive year. In 2014, the growth rate of global service trade was 4.2%, and the growth rate of global goods trade was only 2.8%. On the whole, the proportion of service trade in the whole world trade has increased to a certain extent, being 1/7 in the early 1980s and gradually increasing to about 1/5 after entering the 1990s. At present, the proportion still remains at the level of over 1/5.[1]

[1] International Statistical Yearbook (1990, 2010, 2015).

Table 1. The Composition of GDP of Major Countries and Regions in the World (%)

Countries and Regions	Primary Industry			Secondary Industry			Tertiary Industry		
	1995	**2008**	**2014**	**1995**	**2008**	**2014**	**1995**	**2008**	**2014**
U.S.A.	1.6	1.2	1.4[a]	26.8	19.5	16.6[a]	71.7	79.3	82.0[a]
U.K.	1.6	1.0	0.7	28.2	23.3	14.7	70.2	77.7	84.6
Germany	1.2	0.9	0.7	30.1	29.0	25.7	68.7	70.1	73.6
Japan	1.9	1.3	1.2[a]	38.2	29.4	20.4[a]	59.9	69.3	78.4[a]
France	3.0	2.0	1.7	24.4	20.5	13.8	72.6	77.5	84.5
Italy	3.0	2.0	2.2	28.3	27.1	18.5	68.7	70.9	79.3
Spain	4.3	2.8	2.5	28.5	29.1	17.0	67.2	68.1	80.5
Netherlands	3.3	1.7	1.8	25.9	25.4	16.7	70.8	72.9	81.5
Czech Republic	5.0	2.3	2.7	44.2	37.6	32.4	50.8	60.1	64.9
Russia	7.9	5.0	4.0[a]	39.2	37.2	29.0[a]	52.9	57.8	67.9[a]
Australia	3.4	2.6	2.5[a]	25.2	29.1	18.6[a]	71.5	68.4	78.9[a]
Mexico	5.5	3.8	3.3[a]	27.9	37.1	27.1[a]	60.6	59.1	69.6[a]
Brazil	9.0	6.7	5.1[b]	36.7	28.0	20.9[b]	54.0	65.3	74.0[b]
South Africa	3.9	2.8	2.4[a]	34.8	31.3	23.8[a]	61.3	65.9	78.3[a]
Thailand	11.2	11.7	12.0[a]	39.1	44.1	42.5[a]	49.7	44.2	45.5[a]
India	28.4	17.6	18.0[a]	27.9	29.0	30.7[a]	38.9	53.5	51.3[a]
South Korea	6.2	2.6	2.3	43.2	37.1	33.3	47.0	60.3	63.4
Singapore	0.2	0.1	0.0[a]	34.0	27.8	25.1[a]	65.9	72.2	74.9[a]
Hong Kong, China	0.1	0.1	0.1[a]	16.1	9.8	7.2[a]	68.0	90.1	92.7[a]
China	19.9	11.3	9.2	47.2	48.5	42.6	28.7	40.1	48.2
The World	5.4	3.0		34.5	28.0		59.4	69.0	

Note: [a]Represents the data of 2013; [b]Represents the data of 2011.
Source: OECD statistics (http://stats.oecd.org/), International Statistical Yearbook (2001, 2010, 2011, 2014) and China Statistical Yearbook (2015).

1.1.2. *The scope continuously expanded and the structure further improved*

After the Second World War, with the completion of the third industrial revolution, the rapid development of telecommunications, finance, transportation, tourism, information industry, intellectual property protection, etc., service trade has been accelerated to expand into these fields. If the currently recognized international service trade items are classified according to their correlation with commodity trades and direct investments, then there can be three categories of service trade items.

The first category is the traditional international service trade items directly related to the goods trade, such as international transportation, international repairs and maintenance, international financial services (mainly trade settlement services), etc.

The second category is the international service trade items that are closely related to the international direct investments and characterized by element transfer, such as securities investment income in the form of stocks and bonds, profit income from operation and management, labor export such as construction and engineering contracting, and international credit in financial services, etc.

The third category is service trade items in emerging industries, which are relatively independent of the goods trade and the direct investments, such as services provided by international tourism, information network services, audio-visual products and intellectual property services, etc.

In terms of structure, the structure of world service industry and service trade has also been further improved, due to technological progress and the development of economic globalization. Not only the labor-intensive and resource-intensive service industries such as transportation and tourism have been constantly expanding their trades due to the adoption of advanced technology but also many emerging service industries separated from the manufacturing industry and operated independently, have also been developing very fast. Those service industries which are capital intensive, technology intensive and knowledge intensive with high-tech as the carrier have been developing at the fastest speed, such as finance, insurance, information, consulting, data processing and so on.

1.1.3. *The unbalanced development around the world*

The development of service industry and service trade is very unbalanced worldwide, whether from the type of country or from the structural division of service industry and service trade. This imbalance is determined by the imbalance of world economic development.

From the perspective of country type, the developed countries are the main body in the international service trade, while the service trade of the developing countries is still at a disadvantage, which is far from that of developed countries and extremely unbalanced. According to the statistics of WTO, in 2014, the service exports of developed countries accounted for 75% of the global service exports, while the service imports accounted for 72.5% of the global service imports. In 2014, the top 10 countries for international service exports, including the United States, the United Kingdom, Germany, France, China, the Netherlands, Japan, India, Singapore and Spain (which are all developed countries except China and India), accounted for 52.8% of world service exports. In 2014, the top 10 countries for international service imports, including the United States, China, Germany, France, the United Kingdom, Japan, the Netherlands, India, Ireland and Singapore (which are all developed countries except China and India), accounted for 49.8% of the global service imports (see Table 2).

The reasons why the developed countries are well ahead in their service trades are as follows: (1) Nowadays, the service industry and service trade are driven by high-tech, and the developed countries are in a leading position in technology. (2) There are differences in the production structure, and the output value of the service industry or the tertiary industry in the developed countries accounts for a much higher proportion of the national economy than that of the developing countries. At present, the output value of the service industry accounts for generally 60%–80% of the GDP in the developed countries, and 40%–60% in the developing countries. (3) There are differences in the economic development level and consumption structure. In the developed countries, the per capita income level is much higher than that of the developing countries, and the proportion of services in consumption structure is much higher than that of the developing countries. (4) International service trade is constantly developing in the process of international investments as well as development of multinational companies, and the international investments and the development of multinational companies are all dominated by the developed countries.

Since the beginning of the 21st century, the status of the developing countries and regions in world service trade has risen gradually, the growth of service exports has accelerated significantly, and the proportion of the developed countries and regions as a whole has declined. From 2000 to 2010, the average annual growth rate of service exports from the developing countries and regions was 8%, which was more than double that of the developed countries. Among them, the development of service trade in Asia was particularly rapid, with significant growth in the maritime transport industry, tourism and labor export, etc.

Table 2. Top 10 Countries of World Service Trade in 2014 (In 100 Million Dollars)

	Export				Import			
2014 Ranking	**2004 Ranking**	**Country (Region)**	**Exports**	**Proportion of Totals (%)**	**2004 Ranking**	**Country (Region)**	**Imports**	**Proportion of Totals (%)**
1	(1)	United States	7,094	14.4	(1)	United States	4,783	9.8
2	(2)	United Kingdom	3,415	6.9	(8)	China	3,836	7.9
3	(3)	Germany	2,715	5.5	(2)	Germany	3,278	6.7
4	(4)	France	2,684	5.4	(5)	France	2,484	5.1
5	(9)	China	2,335	4.7	(3)	United Kingdom	2,037	4.2
6	(8)	Netherlands	1,888	3.8	(4)	Japan	1,919	4.0
7	(5)	Japan	1,625	3.3	(7)	Netherlands	1,566	3.2
8	(16)	India	1,562	3.2	(15)	India	1,479	3.0
9	(12)	Singapore	1,404	2.8	(9)	Ireland	1,419	2.9
10	(6)	Spain	1,344	2.7	(14)	Singapore	1,415	2.9
		Total of the above countries	26,066	52.8		Total of the above countries	24,216	49.8
		World total	49,404	100		World total	48,603	100

Source: The United Nations Conference on Trade and Development (UNCTAD) database (http://unctadstat.unctad.org/).

In terms of the service trade structure, there are obvious differences between the developed countries and regions and the developing countries and regions. What the developed countries and regions export mostly are capital intensive, technology intensive, knowledge intensive services such as financial, insurance, information, consulting, data processing, etc. However, what the developing countries and regions export are labor intensive and natural resource intensive services such as tourism and labor services, etc. This kind of structural feature reflects the differences in economic development levels and stages.

1.1.4. *Diversified development of international service trade market*

With the development of world economy, in recent years, the demand and scope of international service trade have expanded increasingly, and the geographical distribution has become increasingly widespread. Before the 1970s, the Western countries were the main market for labor imports. In the late 1970s, several major oil-producing countries in the Middle East and North Africa, which needed a large number of foreign workers each year, increasingly became the major markets for the import of labor services. Since the 1980s, the economies of some countries in Asia, Africa and Latin America have grown rapidly, and the demand for overseas services has increased. In the 1990s, especially since the 21st century, Asia has become a hot spot of world economic growth; especially, the general opening policy has brought about a large amount of overseas service imports.

The service export market also shows a diversified trend. There have been fierce competitions among the developed countries, between the developed countries and the developing countries, and within the developing countries, in order to expand their service market share. Although the developed countries have an advantage in general, this situation is gradually being broken.

1.1.5. *The coexistence of international service trade liberalization and trade barriers*

The GATS, signed in 1994, provided institutional arrangements and guarantees for the liberalization of service trade for the first time. The WTO has been striving to promote the process of liberalization of service trade in the past 20 years after its establishment, in order to comply with the economic globalization. Today, the liberalization of service trade covers all traditional service sectors and emerging service industries, from commerce, tourism, transportation, engineering contracting and labor service export, to information, finance, insurance, law, consulting, accounting, communication, etc., all kinds of professional services have become the object of negotiation and expansion of market access among various countries.

At the same time, with the rapid development of service trade, the competition in this field has intensified and protectionism is prevalent. Many countries have adopted non-tariff barrier measures such as entry restrictions, technical standards, and foreign exchange controls, in order to protect their own service industries. Some sensitive fields, such as finance, insurance, communications and air transportation, are often related to the sovereignty and national security of the importing countries of service trade, and many countries have even imposed more restrictions on their imports.

1.2. *Development trends of world service industry and service trade*

1.2.1. *The development of service industry and service trade has become an important symbol to measure the modernization of a country*

Generally speaking, the more developed the economy of a country, the higher the proportion of its service industry. Since the service industry reflects the development level of productivity, and marks the expansion of consumer demand and the change of consumption structure, its proportion has become an important basis for measuring the level of economic development and the rationality of industrial structure in various countries. Among the 10 standards for a modern country proposed by Professor Morkles of Stanford University in the United States, one of which is that the tertiary industry, namely the service industry, accounts for more than 45% of GNP. Therefore, the development of service industry represents the level of economic development for a country.

1.2.2. *The service industry and service trade have become a guarantee for the sustained growth of the national economy*

The modern economy is based on the high development of the primary, the secondary and the tertiary industries as well as the deepening of social division of labor. After the growth rate of the primary and the secondary industries, as material production sectors, reaches a certain level, the growth will gradually slow down due to the restriction of various factors. At this time, the industry and agriculture will inevitably put forward more and higher requirements on the social service industry, not only requiring the matching and coordinated development of the tertiary industry but also requiring the service industry to develop in advance, guide market consumption and create new demand.

The development of service industry has also complied with the needs of the improvement of residents' consumption level and the transformation of consumption structure. The improvement of residents' living standards will inevitably lead to the transformation of consumption structure to advancement and diversification. The proportion of consumption for food and clothing is gradually decreasing, meanwhile, there are greater increases in expenditures on education, health care, transportation, tourism, culture and entertainment, etc. Because the service industry can provide people with services that are more convenient, more comfortable and conducive to comprehensive development, it is bound to become an important industry to raise the consumption level and prosper the market.

1.2.3. *The service industry absorbs the most labor force, which is the main way to solve employment problems*

The service industry plays an important role in maintaining the stable development of the economy and society. The characteristics of the service industry itself determine that it can widely absorb multiple-level employments such as physical labor, medium technical service and high-tech development, research and application, etc., and has a strong ability to accommodate employment. In the process of transforming the industrial structure to a high-tech intensive one, factories generally implement automation, and enterprises carry out labor-saving and efficient rationalized production and operation, which makes the demand for employment in the manufacturing industry increase little, moreover, many enterprises are also constantly reducing their staff. At this time, the service industry has become a container for absorbing labor force in the adjustment of the industrial structure. The service industry not only absorbs the surplus labor in the material production sectors but also reduces the cost of material production, which plays a role in improving the efficiency of industrialization.

1.2.4. *The development of service-oriented economy shows certain periodicity and regularity*

From the perspective of the development history of the service industry, the development of the service industry can be divided into the following four stages:

(i) The stage of mainly consumer-oriented life service. The service industry was in a secondary position in the national economy and only played a supplementary role. The three industries in the national economy were characterized by "the first, the second, and the third".
(ii) The stage of development in commerce, transportation and communication. During this stage, the role of the service industry was enhanced, but it still accounted for a low proportion in the national economy, and industry began to occupy an important position. The three industries in the national economy were characterized by "the second, the first and the third".
(iii) The stage of rapid growth in finance, insurance and professional services. During this stage, the secondary industry still played a dominant role in the national economy, but professional services such as finance became important for adjusting social resources. The three industries in the national economy were characterized by "the second, the third and the first".
(iv) The stage of comprehensive development of the service industry. At this time, the tertiary industry plays a leading role in the national economy, and science and technology and information industry become the main driving force of economic growth. The three industries in the national economy are characterized by "the third, the second and the first". At present, most of the developed countries have reached this stage, and China has also entered this stage.

1.2.5. *Technological progress has become a leading factor in growth of the service industry*

The vigorous development of contemporary service industry is the result of the extensive penetration of modern science and technology. The application of new technology in service sectors not only greatly improves the operation efficiency and promotes the increase of social productivity but also contributes to the development of differentiated service products. Moreover, many important scientific and technological inventions are often first applied in the service sectors, such as steam engine, computer and Internet, etc. Today, all countries regard the promotion of technological progress and the development of service industry as an important means to prosper the economy and increase employment. In fact, services such as law, information, management, finance and technology have become the main driving forces of economic development.

1.2.6. *The Information Technology industry has become the most promising industry in service industries*

The vigorous development of information industry is the most important content of service industry expansion. Information has become an indispensable and valuable resource for social production and life, and the information industry has become the key to improving economic competitiveness. The year 1991 is known as the watershed between the industrial age and the information age in the United States. In that year, the investment in computers and communications by American companies exceeded their investment in industrial manufacturing for the first time. In early 1993, the United States announced the plan to build the "Information Highway". This kind of electronic information network, which can connect businesses and households across the country and even all over the world and provide various services, has had a great impact on world economic life and also provided an unprecedented opportunity for the development of information industry. Since the 1990s, the United States has been in the leading position in information technology. It took the lead in putting forward the plan of developing the "Information Highway" and put it into action, which revived the economy that was once in recession. Since 1994, the international competitiveness of the United States has been stronger than that of Japan, which previously ranked the first. Just as what Kenneth Arrow (an economist at Stanford

University and Nobel economics laureate) said, the role of information is changing the nature of the economy.

1.2.7. *The service industry has become a new focus of international market competition*

As a part of the market demand, services have been no longer only valued by the service industry but have begun to be concerned by industrial production enterprises. The service economy has three outstanding characteristics as follows:

(i) The product-based economy should be transformed to the service-based economy.
(ii) Enterprise competition strategies should not only focus on the competition of tangible products but also the competition of intangible services.
(iii) The service economy requires the construction of a new vocational training system, so that employees can receive various professional education and training, have modern scientific and technological knowledge, skills and literacy, and are capable to face new challenges.

It is not difficult to see that the service economy is a knowledge-based economy. The competition in services is essentially the competition for technology and education, and the competition for talents. Only under the condition that cultural education and scientific technology has been greatly improved, can the competitiveness of services be rapidly improved.

1.2.8. *The service trade is growing rapidly, and the service industry is developing toward globalization and liberalization*

Driven by the revolution of information technology, the service industry is breaking through the restrictions of borders and regions, and developing rapidly towards globalization. World service trade volume will develop at a faster speed than the commodity trade volume. Another important manifestation of the globalization of service industry is that, in overseas investments of developed countries, the proportion of investment in the service industry has increased continuously, and multinational service companies have emerged. In the developed countries such as the United States, the investment in the service industry has already exceeded investments in heavy industries such as automobiles, and the proportion of investment in service industry has already taken the first place in outward foreign investments.

With the constantly improving importance of service trade in global trade, for various countries, especially for the developed countries, the desire to remove service trade barriers and accelerate the process of international service trade liberalization is becoming more and more urgent. This is also the reason why the GATS was signed, which is an important symbol of the development of international service trade liberalization.

2. Impacts of Rapid Development in World Service Industry and Service Trade on China

The rapid development of world service industry and service trade, especially the liberalization, is a major issue generally concerned by both developed and developing countries in the field of contemporary world economy. The so-called liberalization of service trade is to enable various countries to remove the barriers restricting the service trade and realize the free international exchange of services to the maximum extent. In the international trade, compared with the trades of goods and commodities, China is at a great disadvantage in terms of the service trade. Although China has some advantageous service industries, in most modern service industries and service trade, China is facing severe challenges. Individual service industries in China may even be seriously damaged, and endanger the national security, which must be paid attention to.

The reason why China is at a great disadvantage in world service trade is not only because China is still at a disadvantage and has a large deficit in the volume of service trade, but more importantly, because the development of world service industry and service trade since 1980s is not conducive to China. The development of contemporary service industry is characterized by the closer integration of the service industry and the material production, on the basis of advanced science and technology. Producer services, especially information services, play a more and more important role in international service trade. However, it is difficult for China to keep up with this development trend. First of all, the social division of labor is underdeveloped in China's domestic economy, and the service industry is still dominated by consumer services, with low internationalization. Secondly, on the whole, the cultural, educational and technical qualities of China's labor force are still lagging behind, and the technical level of the whole economy is relatively low. Today, as the service industry is increasingly relying on technical knowledge for international competition, it is difficult for China's comparative advantage derived from cheap labor resources to obtain competitiveness in the service market. All of these have made it difficult for China to further expand the volume of service trade and improve its structure.

The development of world service trade liberalization has influences on China from both economic and non-economic aspects. In terms of its influence from the economic aspect, there are both advantages and disadvantages, which are mainly reflected in the following aspects.

Firstly, the influence on economic efficiency.

The service trade liberalization can promote China's economic efficiency through the following ways:

(i) Due to the effect and influence of the Anti-driving Mechanism, with the entry of foreign service providers, China's service enterprises must keep up with the international advanced level, absorb advanced service technology and experience abroad, strive to reduce costs, improve quality and competitiveness, improve the economic efficiency of enterprises, and provide the market with more high-quality and low-cost services.
(ii) China can import producer services that are urgently needed for the economic development but are unable to meet the demand in its own country, which is conducive to solving the contradiction between the development of production and the backwardness of the service industry.
(iii) It is conducive to the development of China's own advantageous service industries and the import of services that are relatively not advantageous, thus promoting the effective allocation of economic resources and creating more opportunities for China's advantageous service sector exports.

Secondly, the influence on balance of payments.

The service trade liberalization has double influences on the balance of payments. On the one hand, as China reduces restrictions on service imports, imports may increase significantly in the short term, resulting in the deterioration of the balance of payments. On the other hand, China can take advantage of the free international environment, to expand its own service exports. As a result of being able to adopt high-quality and low-cost import services, China is likely to reduce the cost of its material products, improve the quality, and enhance its international competitiveness in the exports of goods and commodities, thus increasing its revenue. At the same time, appropriately opening up the financial services market will also be conducive to the inflows of foreign capitals and improvement of the balance of payments.

Thirdly, the influence on technological progress.

The service trade liberalization can promote the technological progress mainly in two aspects:

(i) The service trade itself can become a channel for technology transfer. Since technological progress tends to occur first in the field of services, advanced technology and other information can be obtained through technology introduction, consultation, training and other forms of technical services. At the same time, foreign direct investment in the service industry is often accompanied by certain technology transfers.
(ii) The pressure of international competition will force China's service industry to speed up the technological progress in order to improve its competitiveness, and thus drive the technological progress in other sectors. Of course, the service trade liberalization may also have a negative influence on technological progress. For example, if there is over-reliance on foreign high-tech services, it may inhibit the domestic research and development in this area. But generally speaking, the service trade liberalization has a positive influence on technological progress.

Fourthly, the influence on employments.

China's service industry is characterized by low labor productivity, high labor intensity and poor labor quality, which makes it difficult to transfer to other sectors. Therefore, the service trade liberalization may deteriorate the employment situations of the domestic service industry and its related material production sectors. Moreover, it may cause damage to the high-tech service sectors in China that have not yet grown up, such as computer software, telecommunications, law, financial insurance, information consultant and other service industries, thus affecting the development of these service industries and domestic employment. However, with the expansion of service imports and exports, it may also increase part of the employments, especially by expanding the export of labor services, which can alleviate the pressure of the domestic employment to a certain extent.

Fifthly, the influence on economic security.

(i) The influence on the economic independence or economic sovereignty of a country. The service trade liberalization may weaken the economic independence of China. The reason is that, first of all, the commitment to open up the service market will make China lose part of the autonomy in its economic decision-making to a certain extent. In particular, for certain important services, such as communications, finance and transportation, etc., they may be controlled and dominated by multinational corporations of developed countries, thus damaging China's sovereignty. Secondly, the competition of foreign services may inhibit the development of weak emerging service industries in China, especially the high-tech producer service industries and the related high-tech industries, and make it difficult for them to improve their own industrial structure, thus relying on the developed countries in high-tech services.

(ii) The influence on the stability of economic development. The stability of economic development is related to its independence. Unreasonable industrial structure and high external dependence will affect the long-term stable development of the economy. In addition, the service trade liberalization also increases economic instability through the following two aspects. The first is that, the service trade liberalization encourages a country to develop its own service industries with comparative advantages according to the principle of comparative advantage, which may enhance China's dependence on a certain service sector, and is not conducive for China to improving its resilience to the international market. The second is that, the opening up of financial service markets such as the banking will link China's domestic financial system with world financial market. Once there is a strong turmoil in the international financial market, it will inevitably have an impact on China's national economy. For example, the Southeast Asian financial crisis in 1997 and the global financial crisis in 2008 quickly caused the turmoil in the financial markets across Asia and even in the whole world, leading to an economic downturn.

3. An International Comparative Analysis on Competitiveness of China's Service Trade and Openness of China's Service Industry

3.1. *A competitiveness analysis on service trades*

Since the Reform and Opening up, China's service industry has developed rapidly, playing an increasingly important role in China's economic development. The overall service trade in China has been continuously expanding. According to the statistics of the WTO, the imports and exports of China's service trade in 2014 reached 606.95 billion dollars, an increase of 12.6% over that of 2013. The exports and imports of China's service trade ranked fifth and second, respectively, in the world. Among the various sectors of China's service trade, traditional service sectors such as tourism services and transportation services account for relatively large proportions and have always been dominant, and modern service sectors such as financial services, computer and information services, account for relatively low proportions. The international competitiveness of China's service trade is still weak, and modern service industries are at a disadvantage in the international competition. The RCA index and TC index are used to analyze the competitiveness of service trade in this section.

3.1.1. *Revealed comparative advantage index (RCA Index)*

The revealed comparative advantage index (RCA Index) can effectively measure the competitiveness of a country's products or industries in the international market. The export competitiveness of some industries of a country can be determined through the RCA index, and thus a country's comparative advantage in the international trade can be revealed.

The calculation formula of the RCA index is as follows.

$$\mathrm{RCA}_{ij} = \frac{X_{ij}/X_{it}}{X_{wj}/X_{wt}} \tag{4.1}$$

Where, RCA_{ij} stands for the revealed comparative advantage index of the *jth* industry in Country *i*. X_{ij} stands for the export value of the *jth* industry in Country *i*, X_{it} stands for the export value of all industries in Country *i* in Year *t*, X_{wj} stands for the export value of the *jth* industry in the world, and X_{wt} stands for the export value of all industries in the world in Year *t*. When the RCA index is greater than 2.5, it indicates that the industry has strong competitiveness; when the RCA index is between 1.25 and 2.5, it indicates that the industry has a medium level of competitiveness; when the RCA index is less than 1.25, it indicates that the industry has relatively weak competitiveness.

According to the statistics of the UNCTAD, nine major service trade countries in the world are selected in this section, namely, the United States, the United Kingdom, Germany, Japan, South Korea, Italy, Australia, Canada and India, for calculating the overall RCA index of service trades of these nine countries from 2001 to 2014, and comparing with the RCA index of service trade of China, so as to analyze the gap in service trade competitiveness between China and these countries. As can be seen from Table 3, the RCA index of China was relatively low from 2001 to 2014, and there has been a downward trend in recent years. The RCA indexes of the United Kingdom and the United States are both higher than 1.25, indicating that the competitiveness of the service trade of these two countries is relatively strong. Although the RCA index of Japan is less than 1, its RCA index has increased continuously in recent years, indicating that the competitiveness of Japan's service trade is on the rise. The RCA indexes of South Korea, Italy and Canada are less than 1, but higher than the RCA index of China. India, which is also a developing country like China, has a higher RCA index and stronger competitiveness in service trade.

In this section, the RCA indexes of China's traditional and emerging service trade sectors are examined, from the perspective of the industry, in order to further explore the reasons for the low RCA index of China's service trade and effectively analyze the international competitiveness of various sectors in China's service trade. The specific calculation method is the ratio of the proportion of export value of an industry in China's service trade export to the proportion of export value of the industry in world service trade export. The calculation results are shown in Table 4.

Among the various industries in China's service trade, the traditional trades, including transportation services, construction services and tourism services, have obvious competitive advantages, among which, the

Table 3. Comparison of RCA Indexes between China and Major Service Trade Powers

	China	Germany	Japan	U.S.A.	U.K.	ROK	India	Italy	Australia	Canada
2001	0.560 808	0.681 603	0.725 174	1.387 885	1.537 911	0.838 742	1.405 602	0.959 827	1.115 223	0.629 207
2002	0.533 715	0.704 215	0.700 145	1.425 742	1.578 175	0.769 894	1.353 383	0.941 539	1.136 349	0.652 559
2003	0.475 415	0.698 81	0.727 86	1.421 906	1.676 785	0.734 972	1.390 044	0.956 388	1.242 249	0.662 284
2004	0.486 765	0.688 182	0.756 789	1.454 693	1.783 726	0.721 641	1.625 992	0.957 592	1.215 865	0.652 736
2005	0.446 587	0.717 406	0.816 533	1.470 851	1.760 372	0.735 756	1.705 539	0.972 657	1.129 619	0.655 576
2006	0.443 251	0.724 076	0.818 485	1.478 216	1.765 197	0.739 159	1.843 208	0.978 685	1.071 125	0.670 194
2007	0.452 224	0.700 887	0.795 061	1.474 444	1.964 6	0.783 827	1.793 759	0.908 058	1.099 651	0.652 44
2008	0.471 277	0.741 294	0.840 338	1.472 905	1.931 781	0.874 354	1.775 688	0.890 008	0.978 466	0.653 579
2009	0.436 164	0.761 915	0.854 986	1.449 208	1.886 657	0.763 225	1.588 897	0.843 138	0.929 448	0.751 761
2010	0.453 167	0.761 659	0.791 075	1.470 299	1.919 212	0.774 391	1.635 879	0.874 278	0.871 702	0.766 334
2011	0.435 984	0.759 681	0.801 587	1.502 171	1.960 381	0.755 459	1.595 066	0.874 651	0.821 368	0.761 728
2012	0.430 705	0.770 654	0.805 447	1.491 447	1.928 692	0.848 848	1.668 734	0.876 917	0.867 203	0.742 732
2013	0.418 899	0.779 497	0.875 929	1.483 528	1.895 614	0.816 115	1.610 99	0.869 735	0.853 54	0.719 129
2014	0.369 263	0.708 775	0.911 388	1.686 510	1.923 589	0.717 747	1.842 414	0.849 266	0.865 422	0.698 560

Source: Calculation based on data from the United Nations Conference on Trade and Development (UNCTAD) database.

Table 4. RCA Indexes of Various Industries in China's Service Trade from 2001 to 2014

Industry	2001	2002	2003	2004	2005	2006	2007	2008	2009	2010	2011	2012	2013	2014
Transportation services	0.625 22	0.663 028	0.800 097	0.852 6	0.937 177	1.045 054	1.167 709	1.148 249	0.934 203	1.017 943	1.001 719	1.023 574	0.952 03	0.860 14
Tourism services	1.741 98	1.720 342	1.296 281	1.404 512	1.441 209	1.409 437	1.213 966	1.128 818	1.242 948	1.156 858	1.128 455	1.058 815	1.000 006	0.986 23
Construction services	1.200 96	1.451 756	1.320 592	1.122 237	1.599 921	1.261 746	1.774 573	2.451 662	2.377 071	3.503 238	3.424 325	2.674 445	2.316 59	3.067 01
Communication services	0.341 10	0.604 417	0.575 042	0.363 155	0.282 515	0.327 124	0.404 114	0.427 695	0.352 123	0.301 709	0.402 396	0.377 039	0.316 368	—
Insurance services	0.348 05	0.193 569	0.253 352	0.238 828	0.384 641	0.282 065	0.336 372	0.440 882	0.458 075	0.428 987	0.710 339	0.746 981	0.902 467	0.750 27
Financial services	0.048 43	0.020 991	0.051 276	0.021 721	0.027 819	0.020 409	0.022 143	0.028 057	0.037 227	0.113 368	0.066 439	0.142 886	0.216 792	0.233 36
Computer & information services	0.396 84	0.444 107	0.596 303	0.621 635	0.612 998	0.745 006	0.794 82	0.852 684	0.941 409	1.040 164	1.210 076	1.292 362	1.232 845	—
Technology patent royalties & royalty services	0.055 63	0.055 379	0.037 477	0.059 25	0.034 089	0.037 201	0.047 948	0.066 399	0.049 917	0.078 106	0.063 471	0.083 147	0.066 401	0.048 67

Source: Calculation based on data from the United Nations Conference on Trade and Development (UNCTAD) database.

RCA index of the construction service was more than 2.5 from 2010 to 2012, indicating that it is very competitive internationally. The RCA index of computer and information services is on the rise and has exceeded 1 since 2010, indicating that China's computer and information services have increasing competitiveness. It is relatively small for the RCA indexes of technology patent royalties and royalty services, as well as of communication services and financial services, and their competitiveness is relatively weak. In recent years, the RCA index of financial services has increased significantly, indicating that the international competitiveness of China's financial services is constantly improving.

3.1.2. *Trade competitiveness index (TC Index)*

The trade advantage index, also known as the trade competitiveness index (TC index for short), refers to the proportion of the balance between the import and export trades of an industry or a commodity in the total volume of imports and exports, in a country. The formula is as follows.

$$\mathrm{TC} = \frac{X - M}{X + M} \tag{4.2}$$

where, X stands for the export volume of an industry or a commodity, and M stands for the import volume of the industry or the commodity. The TC index is a relative value, excluding impacts from macro aspects such as inflation and economic fluctuations, etc. No matter what the absolute volume of import and export is, the value of the TC index is between −1 and 1, and there is comparability among different countries. If the TC index of a country is less than 0, it indicates that the country is a net importer of products or services, with small competitive advantages. If the TC index of a country is greater than 0, it indicates that the country is a net exporter of products or services, with large competitive advantages. The closer the TC index is to 1, the stronger the competitiveness is; the closer the TC index is to −1, the weaker the competitiveness is. When the TC index is close to 0, it indicates that its competitive advantage is equivalent to the international level.

As can be seen from Table 5, from 2001 to 2014, the TC indexes of China were all less than 0, with a large fluctuation range; the TC indexes of the United States and the United Kingdom were greater than 0, indicating that the United States and the United Kingdom have large competitive

Table 5. TC Indexes of China and Major Service Trade Powers

	China	Germany	Japan	U.S.A.	U.K.	South Korea	India	Italy	Australia	Canada
2001	–0.081 72	–0.234 06	–0.248 8	0.121 317	0.089 904	–0.046 85	–0.073 78	0.000 287	0.020 915	–0.060 97
2002	–0.078 63	–0.174 34	–0.235 77	0.112 285	0.096 298	–0.095 36	–0.038 53	–0.023 44	0.031 744	–0.053 63
2003	–0.083 74	–0.170 62	–0.167 61	0.095 843	0.109 502	–0.076 47	–0.020 01	–0.018 22	0.039 542	–0.084 93
2004	–0.056 73	–0.148 11	–0.149 34	0.098 283	0.137 429	–0.062 69	0.035 715	0.008 824	0.009 618	–0.077 85
2005	–0.060 38	–0.129 77	–0.098	0.112 293	0.120 668	–0.090 93	0.052 506	–0.003 71	0.008 806	–0.081 59
2006	–0.045 77	–0.092 83	–0.072 03	0.113 876	0.147 999	–0.104 96	0.085 917	–0.007 97	0.013 302	–0.093 21
2007	–0.031 35	–0.081 5	–0.075 94	0.144 02	0.179 08	–0.075 76	0.102 22	-0.041 7	0.007 309	–0.117 81
2008	–0.038 6	–0.068 17	–0.065 01	0.140 096	0.170 092	–0.030 66	0.096 084	–0.051 79	–0.033 11	–0.130 02
2009	–0.101 9	–0.043 88	–0.073 83	0.141 567	0.205 232	–0.043 18	0.071 753	–0.058 57	–0.026 73	–0.112 01
2010	–0.087 64	–0.041 18	–0.053 94	0.156 329	0.219 356	–0.047 09	0.010 761	–0.058 66	–0.048 38	–0.137 89
2011	–0.148 73	–0.042 27	–0.070 5	0.178 209	0.241 291	–0.029 79	0.053 218	–0.035 37	–0.085 76	–0.136 82
2012	–0.189 94	–0.044 7	–0.096 8	0.188 674	0.233 315	0.026 376	0.062 94	–0.004 5	–0.093 26	–0.144 61
2013	–0.232 36	–0.043 66	–0.051 85	0.198 716	0.243 712	0.027 257	0.092 745	0.007 614	–0.086 09	–0.143 2
2014	–0.264 619 254	–0.085 436 059	–0.081 168 571	0.196 245 099	0.249 938 226	–0.036 793 79	0.106 116 96	0.003 550 386	–0.080 268 411	–0.107 602 575

Source: Calculation based on data from the United Nations Conference on Trade and Development (UNCTAD) database.

advantages in service trade; the TC index of South Korea has increased in recent years, and its TC indexes in 2012 and 2013 were both greater than 0, indicating that the competitive advantage of service trade of South Korea is on the rise. Although the TC index of Japan was less than 0, its absolute value has continuously decreased, indicating that the competitive advantage of the service trade in Japan is constantly increasing. The TC index of India has been greater than 0 since 2004, with an overall upward trend, and its service trade has obvious competitive advantages. Although the TC index of Germany was less than 0, its absolute value has decreased continuously, and the competitiveness of its service trade is gradually rising. The TC indexes of Australia since 2008 and those of Canada from 2001 to 2014 were all less than 0. Since 2013, the TC index of Italy has been greater than 0, indicating that the service trade competitiveness in Italy is in a rising period.

As can be seen from Table 6, the TC indexes of construction services were all greater than 0 except that in 2001, and had an overall upward trend, with a relatively large competitive advantage; before 2009, the TC indexes of tourism services were all positive values, since 2009, the TC index of tourism services has been negative values, indicating that the competitive advantage of China's tourism services is weakening; the TC index of computer and information services has been increasing gradually year by year. Since 2003, the TC indexes have been all greater than 0, which indicates that the competitive advantages of computer and information service in China are constantly increasing; the TC indexes of communication services were basically above 0, and reached a peak in 2011, indicating that the international competitiveness of China's communication services is increasing; the TC index of transportation services is less than 0, indicating that the competitive advantage of transportation services is relatively weak. After 2001, the TC indexes of insurance services and financial services are both less than 0, but the competitiveness of financial services is stronger than that of insurance services. Among various industries in China's service trade, the TC indexes of technology patent royalties and royalty services are the smallest ones, which are the closest ones to −1, indicating that China's technology patent royalties and royalty services have the weakest competitiveness.

3.1.3. *Conclusion*

Firstly, on the whole, China has a relatively small competitive advantage in its service trade. Developed countries in Europe and the United States

Table 6. TC Indexes of Various Industries in China's Service Trade from 2001 to 2014

Industry	2001	2002	2003	2004	2005	2006	2007	2008	2009	2010	2011	2012	2013	2014
Transportation services	−0.419 17	−0.408 22	−0.395 05	−0.340 78	−0.296 88	−0.241 11	−0.160 21	−0.134 22	−0.327 97	−0.298 01	−0.386 8	−0.376 28	−0.429 62	−0.430 48
Tourism services	0.122 488	0.139 368	0.068 072	0.131 972	0.147 623	0.165 217	0.111 118	0.060 857	−0.048 3	−0.090 04	−0.199 27	−0.341 86	−0.427 18	−0.486 63
Construction services	−0.010 14	0.127 85	0.043 031	0.045 847	0.231 124	0.146 37	0.297 732	0.406 05	0.234 511	0.481 58	0.595 894	0.543 802	0.461 841	0.515 48
Communication services	−0.092 13	0.078 085	0.197 999	0.077 064	−0.108 55	−0.017 45	0.041 166	0.019 346	−0.004 69	0.035 186	0.183 686	0.042 486	0.017 608	−0.119 22
Insurance services	−0.845 47	−0.879 04	−0.861 78	−0.882 91	−0.858 2	−0.881 75	−0.843 76	−0.804 22	−0.751 7	−0.802 43	−0.734 77	−0.721 75	−0.690 95	−0.662 97
Financial services	0.125	−0.275 7	−0.209 54	−0.190 27	−0.046 75	−0.719 5	−0.414 57	−0.284 98	−0.286 41	−0.020 67	0.064 233	−0.010 43	−0.075 56	−0.089 11
Computer & information services	0.143 921	−0.279 32	0.031 043	0.133 015	0.063 651	0.259 522	0.326 07	0.327 797	0.336 519	0.514 736	0.520 268	0.579 905	0.444 035	0.367 09
Technology patent royalties & royalty services	−0.892 58	−0.918 18	−0.941 46	−0.900 12	−0.942 54	−0.940 19	−0.919 71	−0.895 22	−0.925 28	−0.880 25	−0.903 78	−0.888 88	−0.917 94	−0.945 76

Source: Calculation based on data from the United Nations Conference on Trade and Development (UNCTAD) database.

have relatively strong competitive advantages in their service trades, and India, which is also a developing country like China, has a relatively large competitive advantage in its service trade. There is a big gap between China's service trade and international competitiveness.

Secondly, from the perspective of trade structure, the competitive advantages of China's service trade are concentrated in the traditional service trade sectors, such as transportation services, construction services and tourism services. The service trade structure is at a relatively low level, and the competitive advantages are relatively small in capital-intensive and technology-intensive service trade sectors, such as the technology patent royalties and royalty services. The service trade structure is relatively simple and vulnerable to the international situation.

Thirdly, from the perspective of changes in competitive advantages, the competitive advantages of modern service trades, such as computer and information services, have been continuously enhanced, and the competitive advantages of traditional service trade sectors such as transportation services and tourism services have begun to weaken. The computer and information service trade has greater potential for development. The changes of competitive advantages are conducive to the adjustment of China's service trade structure and the enhancement of competitiveness in the service trade.

3.2. *An empirical research on the openness of China's service industry*

In order to demonstrate the openness of China's service industry more clearly, in this section, a more intuitive evaluation will made by establishing comprehensive indicators and selecting countries with higher development level and higher openness of service industry in the world, to compare with China.

In this section, the weighted sum method is adopted, to obtain the comprehensive indicator for evaluating the internationalization level of the service industry, by assigning weights to various statistical indicators that can reflect the internationalization level of the service industry, and then adding them together.

3.2.1. *Parameters selection*

In this section, three indicators are selected, which are commonly used to evaluate the openness of a country's service industry, namely, the service trade indicators, the service FDI indicator and the service offshoring (SO) indicator.

(i) The service trade indicators. In this section, the service trade imports (SIM) and the service trade exports (STE) are selected, which represent the overall status of a country's service trade.

(ii) The Service FDI indicator (SFDI). The economic globalization and the development of multinational corporations have promoted the rapid growth of FDI, which has promoted the global flow of capital, talents and technology. The inflow of service FDI is an important symbol of the openness of a country's service industry, so the service FDI inflow is selected as the service FDI indicator.

(iii) The SO indicator. In recent years, with the rapid development of global service outsourcing, the SO, as an important part of service trade, can effectively reflect the openness of a country's service trade. Therefore, the SO indicator is selected in this section. Considering that the statistical work of service outsourcing is relatively backward and the statistical data of various countries are difficult to be obtained, other services in the service trade include communication services, construction services, insurance services, financial services, computer and information services, patent fee and technology transfer fee services, consultancy services and accounting service, etc., while the outsourcing services are mainly communication services, computer and information services, financial and insurance services, consultancy services, accounting services, legal services, etc.; the outsourcing services are a major part of other services in the service trade. Therefore, the export volume of other service trade in the export volume of service trade is selected as a proxy variable for the volume of undertaking SO, so as to facilitate an international comparison.

We selected eight OECD member countries (the United States, the United Kingdom, France, Germany, Italy, Japan, South Korea and Australia), as well as India and China, which have a good momentum of service outsourcing development, for an international comparative study of 10 countries in total.

In order to avoid the subjectivity and arbitrariness of artificial selection, in this section, the principal component analysis (PCA) method is adopted to analyze the openness of service industries in various countries.

Given the availability of data, in this section, the relevant data of various countries in 2012 are selected for the PCA, to determine the weights of various indicators, and horizontally analyze the level of openness for service industries in different countries; then these weights are used to calculate the values of the comprehensive indicators of various countries in other years, so as to facilitate the longitudinal analysis of the changes in the openness of service industries of various countries in different years.

The basic principle of the PCA method is that, through the orthogonal transformation, the original random vector whose component is correlated, is transformed into a new random vector whose component is uncorrelated. This is expressed algebraically as transforming the covariance matrix of the original random vector into a diagonal matrix, and geometrically as transforming the original coordinate system into a new orthogonal coordinate system, making it point to the orthogonal direction where the sample points are most widely dispersed, and then the dimensionality reduction is performed on the multi-dimensional variables, so that they can be converted into a low-dimensional variable system with a higher precision, then through constructing appropriate value functions, the low-dimensional system is further transformed into a one-dimensional system.

With the PCA method, each variable is standardized, in order to avoid ignoring the information provided by small dimensional variables when there are too many dimension differences of variables. However, after the data of each year are standardized respectively, they cannot reflect the changes of the same variable in different years. (The PCA is the analysis of cross-section data, without considering time changes. However, in this book, we want to compare the changes of different years, if the data of each year are respectively standardized to make the variance become 1, it will be difficult to reflect the increase or the decrease of variables in different years.) In order to achieve the purpose of longitudinally comparing the openness of the service industry in various countries in different years, in this section, the variance and the mean value used in the standardization of all variables in 2012 will be adopted uniformly to replace the variance and the mean value in those years for data of other years, to do standardized calculation. The PCA was completed with STATA10.0 statistical software.

3.2.2. *Empirical findings*

The data of the four indicators selected for various countries are shown in Table 7.

Table 7. Data of the Indicators Selected for Various Countries

Country	SIM (In US $100 Million)	STE (In US $100 Million)	SFDI (In US $100 Million)	SO (In US $100 Million)
China	191,430.4	281,203.8	57,196.26	102,490.3
Germany	270,441.5	295,749.4	876,047.5	174,446.9
Japan	145,589.7	176,796.7	117,527.4	90,847.95
U.S.A.	651,492	444,674	1,536 856	407,933.4
U.K.	291,863	181,435.2	859,126.2	220,383.3
South Korea	111,558.5	105,824.8	61,480.45	56,434.9
India	146,143.7	128,836.5	8,686.552	106,783.6
Italy	105,138.7	106,089.5	233,366.4	49,923
Australia	53,245.39	64,197.68	216,740.9	16,090.87
France	236,499.4	204,625.6	925,138.5	117,459.5

Source: China's service industry FDI data come from the China Statistical Yearbook over the years, the OECD member countries' data come from the OECD database, and the Indian FDI data come from the Bloomberg database. China's statistics are generally on the same caliber as the OECD statistics (referring to the overall data comparison of the UNCTAD). Since the division of service industries in India is slightly different from that of other countries, with smaller caliber, there is a certain degree of underestimation for it. However, the scale of service FDI inflow in India is relatively small, compared with that of other sample countries, so it has little impact on the analysis results.

Kaiser Meyer Olkin (KMO) is an important indicator to measure whether the correlation between variables is strong or weak, which is obtained by comparing the correlation coefficient and partial correlation coefficient of two variables. The KMO is between 0 and 1, and the greater the KMO value is, the stronger the commonality of the variable is. If the partial correlation coefficient is relatively large compared with the correlation coefficient, then the KMO is relatively small, and the PCA cannot have a good data reduction effect. According to Kaiser (1974), the general judgment criteria are as follows: 0.00–0.49, is unacceptable; 0.50–0.59, is very poor; 0.6–0.69, is barely acceptable; 0.70–0.79, is acceptable; 0.80–0.89, is better; 0.90–1.00, is acceptable.

The SMC is the square of the multiple correlation coefficients between one variable and all other variables, that is, the coefficient of determination of the multiple regression equation. The larger the SMC is, the stronger the linear relationship of the variables is, the stronger the commonality is, and the more appropriate the PCA is.

The results of the KMO test and the SMC test for PCA are as follows: The KMO value is 0.77>0.70, which indicates the selected variable can be used for PCA. The SMC value of each variable is large, and close to 1, which also indicates that each variable is suitable for PCA. The diagonal value of anti-image correlation matrix is 1, and most other values are very small, which also indicates that the PCA results are credible.

In view of the low contribution rate of cumulative variance of other components in the PCA, only Component 1 (denoted as the PCA) is selected as the principal component in this section, and the formula of contribution degree of each indicator is obtained as follows:

$$\begin{aligned} PCA = {} & 0.484\,3SIM + 0.520\,9STE + 0.480\,1SFDI \\ & + 0.513\,4SO \end{aligned} \tag{4.3}$$

According to Equation (4.3), it can be seen that there is not much difference among various indicators, which are basically equal. Because the coefficients obtained above are the results[2] of the standardization of each variable, the formula for standardization of each variable is substituted into Equation (4.3), and the quantitative relation between the PCA and the original data is obtained as follows:

$$\begin{aligned} PCA = {} & (4.235SIM + 3.072STE + 9.197SFDI + 4.542SO) \\ & \times 10^{-6} - 2.579 \end{aligned} \tag{4.4}$$

It can be seen from Equation (4.4) that, the quantitative relation between the PCA and the original data indicates that the service industry has the largest FDI inflow (with the coefficient of 9.197), undertaking SO is the second (with the coefficient of 4.542), and the service trade import is the third (with the coefficient of 4.235), the service trade export is the smallest (with the coefficient of 3.072). In a practical sense, the amount of FDI inflows in the service industry is an important indicator to measure the openness of a country's service industry. The FDI in the service industry brings capital, technology and talents to the development of the country's own service industry, and promotes the flow of international capital, knowledge and technology. The FDI is conducive to improving the openness of a country's own service sector. Offshore service outsourcing is conducive to improving the internationalization of a country's

[2]The standardization of a variable is to first subtract the mean value of the variable, and then divide it by the standard deviation of this variable.

service industry, which is of great significance to promote the technical level of the industry and accelerate the upgrading of domestic industrial structure. The import of service trade reflects a country's ability to utilize the resources in the global service industry market, which is conducive to promoting the flow of economic factors, promoting the development of national economy, importing high-tech service products, promoting domestic technological progress, and improving the level of modern service industry. The export of service trade reflects the advantages of a country's service products, which is conducive to actively participating in global division of labor, improving the status of domestic service industry in the global value chain, as well as promoting the convergence of domestic services production and global services production.

In Table 8, the PCA scores of various countries show that the United States had the highest PCA score of 2.402 (rounded to the third decimal place on the basis of the data in Table 8), which indicates that the openness of the Service industry in the United States is far ahead of other countries, and also reflects the international competitive advantages of the service industry in the United States. Germany and the United Kingdom ranked the second and the third, respectively, with a PCA score of 0.579 for Germany and a PCA score of 0.461 for the United Kingdom; China ranked the fifth, with a PCA score of –0.148, and France ranked the

Table 8. PCA Scores and Rankings for Various Countries

Country	PCA score	Ranking
China	–0.148 277 61	5
Germany	0.579 058 635	2
Japan	–0.453 204 166	6
U.S.A.	2.402 013 95	1
U.K.	0.460 725 466	3
South Korea	–0.775 251 003	9
India	–0.573 595 318	7
Italy	–0.717 495 857	8
Australia	–0.983 236 954	10
France	0.209 262 858	4

fourth in PCA scores, with a PCA score of 0.209. The PCA scores of Japan and India were –0.453 and –0.574, respectively. As Italy and South Korea have relatively small scale of offshore service outsourcing, their PCA scores were low, ranking the 8th and the 9th, respectively. Australia had the lowest score because both imports and exports of its service industry are very small.

Equation (4.4) is used to calculate the score of service industry openness in various countries from 2005 to 2012, and the results are shown in Table 9.

Given the availability of data, in this section, the data of 10 countries from 2005 to 2012 are selected and the trend chart is drawn for the international comparison. As can be seen from Figure 1, the PCA scores of the United States over the years have been very high, much higher than those of other countries; the PCA scores of Germany have been on the rise; before 2007, the PCA scores of Germany were lower than those of the U.K.; after 2007, the PCA scores of Germany surpassed those of the U.K. The PCA scores of China increased continuously, but its PCA scores were all below 0 from 2005 to 2012. The PCA scores of China were the closest to those of Japan. Since 2010, the PCA scores of China have exceeded those of Japan. The service FDI inflow in Japan was relatively low, so its total score has not been high. The SO in India is relatively strong, but its service FDI inflow is relatively low, which affects the total PCA score of India. The service trade of South Korea has developed well, but its service FDI inflow has not been high, so the PCA scores of South Korea ranked the ninth, and both the imports and the exports of service industry in Australia are relatively low, so its PCA scores have always been the lowest, ranking the 10th.

From the perspective of the overall trend of PCA scores of various countries, the United States had the most obvious upward trend, with a large range. China and France had overall upward trends. Germany, the United Kingdom and India showed the upward momentum in the fluctuation. Australia was basically stable, without an obvious upward trend, and Italy was is in downward state. After the financial crisis in 2008, the PCA scores of the United States, the United Kingdom and China all declined. The United States has been on the rise since 2009, the U.K. has been on the rise since 2010, and the decline for China was small.

In summary, China's service industry has a good momentum of development, and the openness of the service industry has been constantly

Table 9. PCA Scores for Various Countries from 2005 to 2012

Country	2005	2006	2007	2008	2009	2010	2011	2012
Australia	−1.166 72	−1.148 35	−1.104 4	−1.091 85	−1.092 06	−1.040 01	−1.001 36	−0.983 14
China	−0.970 01	−0.884 11	−0.725 26	−0.583 75	−0.615 98	−0.443 09	−0.292 19	−0.148 51
Germany	−0.123 67	0.046 718	0.305 632	0.462 871	0.373 095	0.399 164	0.569 595	0.578 655
Japan	−0.705 8	−0.667 86	−0.590 43	−0.463 9	−0.553 27	−0.503 01	−0.453 69	−0.453 16
South Korea	−1.078 6	−1.030 35	−0.951 55	−0.892 37	−0.946 64	−0.875 02	−0.829 01	−0.775 04
U.K.	−0.103 87	0.130 863	0.440 701	0.331 251	0.222 238	0.262 201	0.425 813	0.460 942
U.S.A.	0.941 966	1.243 336	1.562 064	1.772 889	1.690 046	1.940 445	2.248 793	2.401 912
India	−1.070 87	−0.983 63	−0.894 42	−0.782 29	−0.860 49	−0.708 66	−0.620 42	−0.574 94
Italy	−0.859 77	−0.787 51	−0.656 14	−0.660 82	−0.750 14	−0.742 39	−0.701 56	−0.717 4
France	−0.441 81	−0.325 53	−0.123 01	−0.013 77	0.010 602	0.053 126	0.221 717	0.209

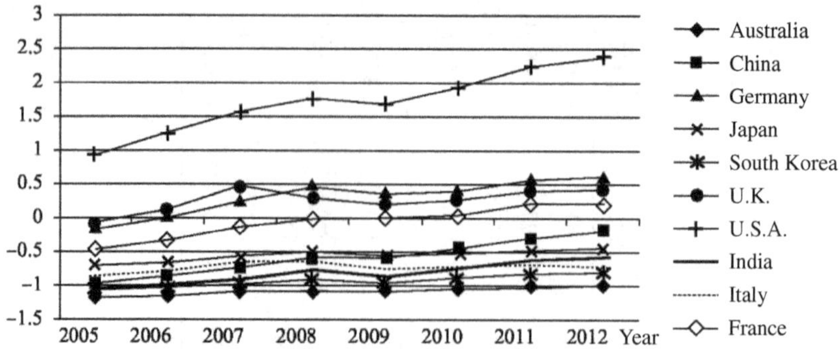

Figure 1. Changes of PCA Scores for Various Countries from 2005 to 2012

improving. Compared with other countries with better development and higher openness of their service industries, China is still in the middle reaches. There have been huge impacts of the global financial crisis in 2008 on service industries in various countries. Compared with other countries, China was less affected, and China's service industry has developed steadily.

The import and export of service trade, the services FDI and the SO are all positive factors to promote the development of a country's service industry, and its development level represents the openness of service industry in a country (region).

(i) In this section, 10 countries with a high level of development and openness of the service industry in the world are selected, namely, Australia, China, Germany, Japan, South Korea, the United Kingdom, the United States, India, Italy and France, the PCA method is used to construct the comprehensive evaluation indicators, and analysis and comparison are carried out. The conclusion shows that the service FDI inflow has the greatest impact (with the coefficient of 9.197), followed by undertaking the SO (with the coefficient of 4.542), the import of service trade is the third (with the coefficient of 4.235), and the last is the export of service trade (with the coefficient of 3.072). Thus, it can be seen that, it is of great significance to absorb foreign direct investments and undertake the SO, for the improvement of the openness of service industry in a country (region).

(ii) In terms of the rankings of various countries, China was ranked the fifth, and the United States, Germany and the United Kingdom ranked the first, the second and the third, respectively; Japan, India and Italy ranked the sixth, the seventh and the eighth, respectively; and South Korea and Australia ranked the ninth and the tenth, respectively, indicating that China's service industry openness is currently in the middle reaches of the world, and the openness of China's service industry has risen steadily.

(iii) From the perspective of future development, although China's service industry suffered from the impact of the financial crisis in 2008 and its openness has declined, since 2009, China's service industry has maintained a good momentum of development, and its openness has been constantly improving. The financial crisis in 2008 caused a certain impact on the openness of service industries in all countries in the world. The PCA score of the United States, which has the highest openness of its service industry, has declined, but has begun to rise since 2009. The PCA score of the United Kingdom, which has a higher openness of its service industry, has begun to rise since 2010. At present, China should seize the opportunity of service industry development, vigorously develop the service trade, improve the quality of services FDI, focus on promoting the development of high value-added and high-tech emerging service industries, improve the quality of domestic service industry development, and promote the openness of China's service industry.

4. China's Countermeasures and Principles for Opening up Its Service Industry Market

The service industry and the service trade play an important role in the economic development of the developed countries, and are also of great significance to China's economic development. Therefore, regardless of the impact of liberalization of the world service trade, China must face up to the reality of gradually opening up its service market. In this context, the basic guiding ideas for China to formulate the countermeasures for service trade liberalization is to break the limitations of the original comparative advantages, narrow the technical gap, improve its own service industry and service trade structure, so as to promote the development of domestic service industry by taking the advantage of the service trade liberalization as much as possible, and at the same time, to minimize the negative impact of liberalization. From the perspective of the international competition, the following points are the most noteworthy.

Firstly, the foothold of China's service industry should be on promoting the development of the whole national economy, rather than simply for the sake of earning foreign exchange through exports, and increasing revenue.

In accordance with the principle of comparative advantage, the development of a few traditional services such as engineering construction, labor service export and tourisms can quickly obtain economic benefits, by taking the advantages of natural conditions and cheap labors. However, in the long run (especially for large countries), it is difficult for such a service export strategy to gain a foothold in the international market for a long time. As we all know, the international competition in the contemporary service industry is connected with the international competition in the material production sector, and international service trade powers are also powerful countries in the material production. The core of the modern service trade is the producer services with information technology services as the main body. If traditional non-information services can rely more on those factors, such as labor force or geographical environment, to obtain their comparative advantages, the improvement of the international competitiveness in information service is associated with the development level of the whole social productivity. Therefore, China cannot separate the service industry from the material production, and should pay special attention to the development of the producer services, organically combine the development of the service industry with the development of the material production, enable them to promote and support each other, and let the service industry play a more active role in the economic development. On the one hand, the development of the producer services can help improve the competitiveness of export commodities. On the other hand, the enhancement of the self-competitiveness for producer services can improve the structure of service exports and reduce the dependence on foreign services. When implementing this strategy, we must avoid rushing for quick success and instant benefits by all means. For certain knowledge-intensive and technology-intensive services that play an important role in promoting the development of production, they should be supported even if they do not conform to the principle of comparative advantage and it is difficult for them to enter the international market for a while, because only in this way can we guarantee the sustainability of the service industry in the international competition.

Secondly, China should have a clear understanding of its own advantages in cheap labor forces.

With the development of social productivity and science and technology, for human beings, it has entered an era with information, culture and knowledge as the major means of production — the era of knowledge economy. In such an era, to compare the advantages of labor forces, it depends on not only their prices but also their qualities. Although the cost of labor forces is low in China, their technical quality is poor, and most of them are engaged in labor-intensive, namely, low-value-added service activities. In the developed countries, although the labor forces are with high cost, they are engaged in knowledge-intensive and technology-intensive services with high added value, and create high value. Therefore, China must make great efforts to improve the qualities of its labor forces; otherwise, they can only be engaged in labor-intensive services in the competition of service trade liberalization. Of course, this does not mean that China cannot develop labor-intensive services. In fact, developing labor-intensive services first is the only way generally for the developing countries to enter the international service market. However, it must be made clear that the development of labor-intensive services is not an end in itself, but it is a means, to accumulate funds and create conditions for improving the technical level of services in the future.

Thirdly, China should give full play to the role of its service trade as a channel of the technology transfer in the process of opening up its service market.

During the opening up of the service market, what have suffered the greatest impact in China's economic security and its national sovereignty are those high-tech service fields such as communications, finance, computers and cultural services, etc. However, China needs to introduce such services most as well, and it is also most likely to get the benefits of technology transfers from such services. If a country is closed to international intercourse for fear of being impacted, then it will always fall behind. The only choice is to introduce technology under the condition of opening up, and cultivate its own high-tech services. The author believes that, it is more advantageous for China to introduce high-tech services by adopting the mode to absorb foreign direct investments, in the early stage of developing China's high-tech services, because the form of direct investment is more conducive to the technology transfer. Among those technology transfers from the United States to the developing countries, 80% of which is carried out through the direct investments of multinational corporations. However, for the introduction of high-tech services by means of trade, it can only obtain results rather than introduce production processes. On the contrary, it is easy to cause the dependence on imports, which is not conducive to the development of China's high-tech services from scratch. However, it is worth noting that the introduction of direct investments in the high-tech services will also involve a series of issues related to the national economic sovereignty and security, which requires China to take appropriate policies to seek advantages and avoid disadvantages.

The foothold of protecting the domestic service market should be to improve the technical level of domestic service industry and cultivate its own high-tech services; and the foothold of opening the domestic service market should be the introduction of technology, and it must be recognized that technology transfers are the greatest interests that China may gain from the liberalization of service trade.

Fourthly, China should strive for the initiative in international negotiations.

The GATS requires all members to implement the unconditional most-favored-nation (MFN) treatment. However, considering the particularity of service industries and service trades, the form of specific commitments can be adopted in the opening up of service markets, and all members are allowed to make exceptional arrangements for the MFN treatment. Therefore, in the multilateral negotiations on trade in services, China should adhere to the principles of specific commitments and of efforts to create conditions for implementing the exceptional arrangement of unconditional MFN treatment, strive to obtain a favorable position in international negotiations, and safeguard its own interests.

In the international negotiations on the liberalization of trade in services, currently, China is too passive, denying many proposals from the developed countries and taking few specific measures of its own. On the basis of adhering to the principle of differential treatment, China should make its own analysis of existing barriers to trade in services and put forward its positive counter-proposals. For example, from the Cancun Conference in September 2003 to the Bali Conference in 2013 of the WTO, the majority of the developing countries adhered to their own positions and principles in the fields of agricultural products and service trades, which made the developed countries have to give up their original requirements. The author believes that, China should have two main objectives in international negotiations: one is to safeguard the right to appropriately protect its own service industry and service market; the other is to improve the openness of its own service market and strive for favorable conditions for its own service industry to proceed to the world.

Chapter 5

The Influences on World Economy by Multinational Companies after the Financial Crisis*

1. Expansion Strategy and Operation Mode of Multinational Companies

1.1. *Production strategy*

The emergence of multinational companies has broken through the limitations of their parent countries' borders, which enables companies to find production sites with comparative advantages in various production procedures around the world. Multinational companies have extended the value chain of their production and sales worldwide on the basis of advantages of their domestic production scale and local market. They can have new production portfolio advantages and develop a broader international sales market through the division of labor and the collaboration in the economy, so as to take advantage in the global value chain. During the formation of the actual global production system, multinational companies gradually build their own unique multinational production strategies.

*This chapter was written by Luo Laijun and Mao Zeqing.

1.1.1. *Strategy for global distribution of production*

Enterprises are profit-seeking. The way how multinational enterprises pursue profits in production is to search for locations where they can produce with the most comparative advantages, the most abundant production resources and the lowest production costs worldwide. For instance, electronic products are designed in Silicon Valley of the United States, financed on Wall Street in New York, specifically produced in the vertical production systems in Japan, China and Southeast Asia, sold in mature markets in the developed countries in the United States and European countries, processed profits in tax havens and finally disposed of in production waste. At the same time, there is an increasing trend of industrial agglomeration for the overseas production of the multinational companies due to the intensified international competition and the drive for further reducing cost. The multinational enterprises can stimulate the production vitality and stronger creativity in their enterprises by sharing the specialized labor markets, the related service industries and low-cost wisdom collision among talents. In addition, the collaboration among multinational enterprises can also effectively cut the costs of information and communication, which is conducive for the enterprises to develop new technologies and find new sources of economic growth. Although a monopoly may be formed by the collaboration among multinational enterprises that produce similar products, resulting in output control and price manipulation, in general, the interaction among the multinational companies is of benign dominance, which plays an irreplaceable role in the process of global economic recovery.

1.1.2. *Strategy for localization of marketing and sales*

Economic globalization has brought much larger international markets for multinational companies and has laid the foundation for enabling productions on a larger scale. However, the products sold by multinational enterprises in different countries and regions should also be continuously adjusted to meet the demand of localization due to different levels of economic development, differences in cultural traditions, customs and legal restraints in different countries. For example, a new type of Old Beijing Chicken Wrap was created in China by KFC, with cucumber and sweet soybean paste added to the traditional Mexican Chicken Wrap to cater for the needs of Chinese consumers. In addition, in the early days, there was no Gaifan (i.e., rice topped with dishes) in KFC in China. The current Gaifan was gradually offered after being tested and recognized in Hong Kong. Due to the existence of Economies of Scope, which means that the cost of producing two products at the same time is lower than the sum of the costs of producing each product separately, multinational enterprises have effectively expanded their markets and improved the welfare to local consumers without increasing the cost significantly.

1.1.3. *Flexible production*

With the increasingly fierce global competition and the constantly changing market demand, more lean-oriented requirements have been put forward for the production of multinational companies. Therefore, based on the flexible manufacturing, the flexible production system has been further established by the multinational companies. The flexible production refers to the multi-type and small-batch production method that is realized by primarily depending on highly flexible manufacturing equipment which is mainly with CNC machine tools. In 1965, Molins, a British company, first put forward the concept of flexible production. Flexible production is an advanced production method of market-oriented and on-demand production, which was produced in order to adapt to the changing market demand and fierce market competition. Its advantages are that it can enhance the flexibility and adaptability of manufacturing enterprises, shorten the production cycle, improve the utilization of equipment and the labor productivity of employees, and improve the quality of products. Specifically, it has the characteristics as follows.

(i) It can adapt to diversified production and realize economies of scope.
(ii) Multinational companies are responsible for the essential part of production, and the rest parts are completed by the offshore sourcing or the outsourcing. For example, Nike headquarters in the United States is mainly responsible for the design and publicity of products, while the specific products are produced by factories in China or Southeast Asia.
(iii) With order management systems, orders can be transferred to the factory which is closest to the customer in the area, which can not only shorten effectively the delivery time of products and reduce the

inventory cost of the factory but also reduce the waiting time of customers and improve the customer experience.

(iv) Mature production system can make timely adjustments to new products faster and take the lead in rapidly changing markets.

1.2. *R&D*

It is the production technology and the business model that are the core competitiveness of multinational enterprises. Therefore, only those enterprises that pay attention to the continuous technological development and model innovation can keep their vitality forever and win in the big globalized market. Since the 1990s, many multinational enterprises have set up their research and development institutions all over the world. For example, Microsoft Research China is a scientific research institution established by Microsoft with a huge investment in Beijing on November 5, 1998, which was then upgraded to Microsoft Research Asia on November 1, 2001. Microsoft China Research Institute is Microsoft's second overseas basic research institution and the only basic research institution in Asia. Founded in August 2000, Samsung Electronics China Communications Research Institute is an R&D institution with independent legal personality invested and established by Samsung Electronics in China. Specifically, the research and development strategies overseas of multinational companies have features as follows.

1.2.1. *R&D localization and information collection*

For the traditional R&D model in a multinational company, the technology development is mainly carried out in headquarters in the parent country. And the feasibility tests of the technology are carried out in the host country. Then the technology is tried to be applied to specific products and the standardization and maturity are realized in the production process. However, as the global market develops, overseas consumers have turned gradually from the passive takers for new things into the demanders actively putting forward new requirements for products. Therefore, one of the main purposes which the multinational companies set up research institutions all over the world is to capture information worldwide; the technical information is collected, sorted out and processed, and sent back to the headquarters of the multinational companies, for reference of and used by technical departments. Meanwhile, those regional research institutions undertake the research projects designed for different regions by their headquarters, conduct the feasibility experiments locally and send back the results to their headquarters. For example, in order to cater for the needs of Chinese consumers, for some car brands such as Mercedes-Benz, BMW and Audi, their cars sold in China have been lengthened correspondingly; as a result, there is a "Li" with a Chinese characteristic on the rear of each car.

In addition, with the limitation of teams and locations of R&D departments in the headquarters of multinational companies in their parent countries, the technology and designs in the headquarters cannot be fully personalized and differentiated. However, modern intra-industry trade is established on the basis of product differentiation to a large extent. Therefore, the globalization strategies of multinational companies have not been implemented thoroughly, and the resources of enterprises have not been fully utilized. Strategically, there is room for Pareto improvement. In fact, the establishment of R&D institutions in different regions of the world is the inevitable result of the vertical integration implemented worldwide by multinational companies. Its role is to make adjustments to the upstream and downstream technical intermediate products for differentiation within the production systems of multinational companies according to the characteristics of the host markets or local regions, so as to enhance their local competitive advantages.

1.2.2. *Local cooperation and talent recruitment*

Out of the demand for talents, multinational enterprises often cooperate with local top universities in academic exchanges, research and development as well as career development, and constantly take in local talents through internship and direct recruitment. For example, on August 30, 2008, HSBC donated RMB 150 million to support Peking University in building a world-class business school. Shenzhen Business School of Peking University was officially renamed as Peking University HSBC Business School, and the opening ceremony was held on October 22 in the same year. In January 2003, Microsoft Asia Research Institute and National Taiwan University officially signed a cooperation program to establish the first "Dot NET Research Center" in Taiwan, and announced the signing of the academic exchange and cooperation programs with National Chiao Tung University and National Tsing Hua University. In August 2006, the "Carnegie Mellon University-Shanghai Jiaotong University-Microsoft Asia Research Institute Joint Talent Development Project" was launched, which takes Microsoft Asia Research Institute as the link and the important base, connecting the international and domestic top computer schools, in order to form the "Industry-University-Research" transnational cooperation.

Discovering and developing talents is an important part of the globalization strategy in multinational enterprises. That the research institutions of multinational enterprises in various regions search for talents in the local areas can continuously reserve talents for the headquarters of multinational companies, so as to lay a solid foundation for their long-term international competitiveness. Meanwhile, technology development departments in multinational enterprises tend to be human capital intensive with high salaries and multiple promotion channels, which have a strong appeal for local talents.

1.3. *Competition methods*

1.3.1. *Strategic alliances*

The strategic alliances refer to a kind of loose cooperation mode. With this mode, two or more companies that have common strategic interests and equivalent business capacity form partnerships that are of complementary or mutually beneficial advantages, risk-sharing, and horizontal two-way or multi-directional flows of production factors through various agreements and contracts in order to achieve the strategic goals of owning markets and sharing resources. At present, each of Fortune Global 500 has about 60 major strategic alliances on average. With the development of more than 30 years, the strategic alliances have shown some advantages: firstly, they can help multinational enterprises to complement each other's advantages and have comprehensive advantages; secondly, they can help multinational enterprises to improve their local recognition and rapidly increase their local market shares; thirdly, they are conducive to achieving diversified structures for production and investment of multinational companies; fourthly, they can reduce business risks of multinational companies in local markets.

1.3.2. *Cross-border mergers and acquisitions* (*M&A*)

Since the late 1980s, both the number of global M&A cases and the amount of M&A have increased steadily, in which the volatility has increased significantly in global M&A transactions since 2001. The number of global M&A was 1,174, and the M&A turnover was 97.31 billion dollars in 1987; the number of global M&A increased to 8,098, with a turnover of 730.44 billion dollars in 2001; the number of global M&A reached a record 10,145, with a turnover of 1.64 trillion dollars in 2007. At present, the cross-border M&A mainly has the following trends. (i) The number of cross-border M&A is rising up rapidly, with a huge amount for M&A. Volkswagen acquired 49.9% shares of Porsche at 3.9 billion euros in 2009; Google acquired YouTube with shares worth 1.65 billion dollars in 2006; HP acquired Compaq for 18 billion dollars in 2002. (ii) There is a wide range of fields involved in cross-border M&A. There are not only global M&A cases in industry, but also a series of mergers and restructurings in the fields of finance, media, entertainment, etc. (iii) The main objective of multinational M&A is to set up world-class super enterprises. Multinational companies can effectively reduce their transaction costs with external transactions "internalized", avoid the risk of supply fluctuation in external markets through internal "imperative" modes of production, and increase their corporate profits by transfer pricing. (iv) Cross-industry M&A. The M&A cases before the 1980s were mainly mergers and restructurings among enterprises in the same industry. However, there were a large number of cross-industry M&A cases after the 1990s, among which the acquisition of CBS by Westinghouse Electric is an example.

As an approach for multinational companies to implement their global strategies, cross-border M&A plays an irreplaceable role, mainly including: (i) To expand the scale of enterprises themselves. Multinational companies can quickly expand their business scales and increase their market shares through cross-border M&A in a short time. (ii) When acquiring a large enterprise in a host country, a multinational company can not only get around the local market barriers in the host country and directly get access to the local market but also obtain the extensive sales network of the original company as well as the local market information and legal knowledge, helping the multinational company to save considerable time and money. (iii) To enhance the competitive advantages of multinational enterprises. Multinational enterprises can reduce local competitors in host countries, expand their production scale and increase their market share through acquiring enterprises in the host countries. This will improve the abilities of multinational companies to resist business risks, thus enhancing their competitive advantages.

2. The *Status Quo* of Multinational Companies Worldwide and Their Influences on the Overall World Economy

2.1. *The* status quo *of multinational companies worldwide*

According to the World Investment Report 2006 of UNCTAD, there were about 77,000 multinational companies and at least 770,000 foreign branches worldwide. Among them, there were about 55,490 multinational companies established in the developed countries, accounting for more than 70% of the total number of global multinational companies, and the internal business networks of multinational companies covered almost every country and region in the world. In 2011, there were only five companies that came from the developing countries and regions, among world's Top 100 non-financial multinational companies ranked by overseas assets, including Hutchison Whampoa in China, Sinopec Group, CBMM, PETRONAS, and CEMEX in Mexico. These five companies covered a wide range of industries, including not only traditional industries such as oil and transportation but also industries in the "new economy", such as electricals and electronics. This indicates that the developing countries have the potentials to become global competitors in various industries. However, there is still a large gap compared with the developed countries. From 2000 to 2011, the overall scale of world's Top 100 non-financial companies had greatly increased. In 2011, the averages of their overseas assets, sales and the number of employees increased by 10.6%, 8% and 2%, respectively, compared with those in 2000. However, the scale of each company was quite different. By contrast, their overseas assets tended to be close, but the difference in the number of employees was widening. In 2011, for world's Top 100 non-financial multinational companies, the average number of overseas employees was 90,585, (of which) Wal-Mart Stores Inc. had the largest number of 800000 overseas employees, while British Gas had the smallest number of 4,495 only; the average overseas sales were 56.963 billion dollars, of which American

Exxon Mobil had the highest ones of 316.686 billion dollars, and LBTYA, an American cable operator had the lowest ones of 9.366 billion dollars only; the average overseas assets were 77.76 billion dollars of which General Electric Company had the highest overseas assets of 502.612 billion dollars and the U.K. BAE Systems had the lowest ones of 29.783 billion dollars. Among world's Top 50 financial multinational companies ranked by the geographical distribution index (GSI) in 2011, except Bank of China Ltd., the remaining 49 companies were all from the developed countries.

In 2011, there were big differences in the scale of world's Top 50 financial multinational companies. The average total assets of these companies were 1075.588 billion dollars of which Deutsche Bank in Germany had the highest total assets of 2809.328 billion dollars and Swiss Reinsurance had the lowest ones of 225.899 billion dollars only. The average overseas branches of these companies were 264.58, of which Deutsche Bank had the largest number of overseas branches, up to 1027, while Bank of China had the smallest number, with only 12 ones. The developed economies referred to in the World Investment Report Database of UNCTAD include 38 countries and regions, of which there are 2 in Asia, namely Japan and Israel; 2 in North America, namely the United States and Canada; 31 in Europe, namely France, Britain, Germany, Italy, Sweden, Finland, Denmark, Norway, Netherlands, Belgium, Switzerland, Austria, Greece, Iceland, Ireland, Luxembourg, Portugal, Spain, Bulgaria, Cyprus, Czech Republic, Estonia, Hungary, Latvia, Lithuania, Malta, Poland, Romania, Slovakia, Slovenia and Gibraltar; 2 in Oceania, namely Australia and New Zealand; and the last one is Bermuda. According to this classification, UNCTAD counted the foreign direct investments of various developed economies and the status of some multinational companies. The multinational companies in the developed economies were not only abundant in numbers but also large in scales. The Top 100 non-financial multinational companies and the Top 50 financial multinational companies in the world were mainly from the developed countries in Europe and North America. World's Top 100 non-financial multinational companies from the developed economies were distributed in 19 countries and regions. Among them, the numbers and the total overseas assets of Top 100 companies in the United States, France, Britain, Germany and Japan ranked Top 5, and they enjoy 68 world-class top multinational companies in total, with the total overseas assets accounting for 71.9% of those in all Top 100 companies. Among these countries, the United States was the most outstanding one, and had 22 Top 100 non-financial companies, with the total overseas assets accounting for 1/4 of those in all Top 100 non-financial companies. From the perspective of the industries invested, the Top 100 non-financial companies from the developed economies mainly engaged in business activities in the industries such as automobiles, petroleum, pharmaceuticals, food, beverages and tobacco, and electrical and electronic equipment (EEE). World's Top 50 financial multinational companies from the developed economies were distributed in 14 countries and regions; among them, the number and the total assets of the Top 50 financial companies in the United States ranked the first, and the United Kingdom ranked the second, with its 6 Top 50 financial companies, but the total assets could not match those of France and Japan. The scale of single Top 50 financial companies in France was relatively large. Although there were only 4 Top 50 companies, they had the largest number of foreign branches, and their total assets are second only to those of the United States.

2.2. *The influences of multinational companies on the world economy*

2.2.1. *The integration of world economy has been further promoted by multinational companies*

Multinational companies emerged with economic globalization. Their development has promoted the internationalization of production and that of capitals to a great extent. The globalization strategies and internationalization of multinational companies have further promoted the collaboration in production, exchange, circulation, consumption, and R&D of technical products among various countries in the world. Currently, the total output value of multinational companies has accounted for more than 1/3 of that in the capitalist world. They have been in control of 50% of international trade, 80% of technology development and 30% of international technology transfer. The sales of their branches (subsidiaries) (excluding their internal sales) are equivalent to 70% of the total exports in the world. Quite a few turnovers and assets in multinational companies are from abroad and the proportions are still increasing constantly. With the development of the internationalization of production, capital flows have been accelerated among various countries. The economic relations have been made closer and a global economy of interpenetration and interdependence has been gradually formed. At the same time, with their monopoly advantage, internalization advantage and location advantage of investment choice, multinational companies have organically connected production, distribution, consumption, finance, insurance and so on, making the economies increasingly interconnected among various countries.

2.2.2. *International trade has been expanded and promoted by multinational companies*

Deepening the international division of labor has resulted in the development of multinational companies. Meanwhile, they also further promote the international division of labor. A significant portion of the traditional division of labor among enterprises has been transformed into the internal division of labor of companies, which makes the internal trades in production factors surging, including intermediate products, technology, services, information and so on between the parent companies and overseas subsidiaries of multinational companies. At present, the internal trades of multinational companies contribute to nearly 80% of the total world trade. In addition, as multinational companies continually introduce new technologies and products as well as make internal transfers, the international trade flows will increase constantly and new technologies and new commodity trades will be discovered continuously.

2.2.3. *The global technological progress and productivity improvement have been promoted by multinational companies*

Multinational companies must keep investing in R&D and developing new products and new technology if they want to stay ahead in the drastic international competition and continue to expand their market share. Large multinational companies are in control of most of the modern advanced and cutting-edge technologies. According to statistics, world's Top 500 multinational companies control 90% of production techniques in the capitalist world. In addition, while multinational companies develop and apply new technologies independently, they also selectively transfer and sell their technologies according to the product life cycle. As the biggest owners and disseminators of science and technology in the world, multinational companies push forward the progress of international science and technology, thus promoting the development of productivity in the world.

2.2.4. *The resource allocation worldwide has been optimized by multinational companies*

The globalization strategies of multinational companies not only facilitate the search for production factors with international comparative advantages worldwide but also promote the factors to flow globally and optimize their allocation. This is mainly because with the advantages of internalized information and instruction, multinational companies can effectively reduce the information asymmetry in the international market and cut the cost for the global flow of factors, which makes production factors such as goods, services, capital, information and management smoothly flow and properly allocate around the world.

The transnational flows of factors reflect most significantly in the international flow of talents. By the end of 2011, there were about 69 million employees hired in the foreign branches of multinational companies. With training from multinational companies, these employees began to have a vision of globalization and have gradually become international talents, although they were mainly from the host countries. With central dispatching by the headquarters of multinational companies, global flows of these international talents have not only promoted the internal exchanges of information, technology, management and culture in multinational companies but also enabled employees to get closer to each other and made the culture and tradition of the countries represented by employees more widely spread.

2.3. *The influences of multinational companies on their parent countries*

2.3.1. *Capital stock and employment wages*

When a multinational company invests abroad, if it raises funds in its parent country, then the capital stock of its parent country will be reduced, resulting in the decrease in the capital stock per capita and the decline of average wages in its parent country; if it raises funds in the capital markets outside its parent country, then there will be fewer impacts on the capital stock of its parent country. When a multinational company makes overseas investments, it will use cheap overseas labor force to replace a part of the homogeneous high-cost labor force in its own country (this part of the labor force may face structural unemployment in the short term). Whether the labor market in the parent country can fit the new labor demand brought by the overseas investment of the multinational company determines whether the employment in the parent country will increase or decrease; whether the labor market in the parent country can successfully embed into the higher value-added link of the value chain, quickly improve labor productivity and create greater value determine whether the wages of workers in the parent country will rise or fall.

2.3.2. *Technical and industrial structures*

With their overseas expansion, multinational companies realize economies of scale and provide the basis of production and practice for the progress and effective usage of technology. Meanwhile, they lay the foundation of talents and intelligence for innovation and technological progress of enterprises through absorbing and training overseas high-end talents.

For the overseas investment of multinational companies in the developed countries, the traditional labor-intensive and resource-intensive industries are often transferred to the developing countries, while the capital-intensive and technology-intensive industries are developed in their own countries. The decrease in the share of traditional industries can release additional factors of production to develop emerging industries and take advantage in the global value chain. However, at the same time, excessive transfer of the real industries to foreign countries will easily lead to the "industry hollowing-out" in the parent country, which makes the proportion of non-material production service industries and material production manufacturing industries imbalanced. In peacetime, the parent country can effectively bring its comparative advantage into full play and improve world welfare by importing foreign material products and exporting domestic service products with advantages. However, in wartime or during economic blockades, it is prone to imbalances between supply and demand, so there are potential economic risks.

2.3.3. *National income*

In the case that the political situation of the host country is stable and there is sufficient infrastructure and strong undertaking capability of human capital there, the transfer of capital from the parent country can obtain higher incomes than that in the parent country (pursuing a higher return of investment is the core motivation for overseas investment by a multinational company), thus increasing the income of its own country. In addition, multinational companies can get around the trade barriers set by the host country, expand actual exports and output, and increase the level of national income potentially.

2.4. *The influences of multinational companies on their host countries*

2.4.1. *Capital transfer*

The overseas investments of multinational companies can increase the capital stock in host countries and improve the capital per capita and average wages in the host countries. This is a very important opportunity for the host countries with the capital shortage in their development period. In addition, what flows in is not just capitals in the abstract meaning. The specific equipment, technologies and patents purchased by multinational companies from their parent countries, factories invested and established in the host countries and employees trained have more or less technology spillover to the host countries based on the different levels of confidentiality and regulation of multinational companies, so there is the positive externality (this requires the host countries to attract investments from multinational companies with subsidies in disguise such as preferential policies).

2.4.2. *Employment and talent development*

That multinational companies set up subsidiaries and factories in the host countries can have a great demand for labor force in the host countries and increase employments effectively in the host countries. Furthermore, the investment and production of the multinational companies in the host countries can also bring about upstream and downstream industries and related service industries, thus improving the employments in the host countries significantly. The business activities of multinational companies in the host countries tend to be not short-term, which means that multinational companies can adopt localization strategies and make long-term investments. Among them, the more significant one is the development of local talents. In addition to productive talents, multinational companies will also hire a large number of local management talents in the host country to take part in the management of enterprises and provide trainings to them, so that they can get access to, understand and master the advanced management modes of global companies. And these management talents also have adequate mobility. They will gradually penetrate into various industries and sectors in the host countries by job-hopping or self-employment.

2.4.3. *Tax revenues*

Multinational companies have production and management activities in the host countries, pay their taxes according to law, and contribute new tax revenues to the host countries. At the same time, the vigorous development of upstream and downstream industries and related service industries brought about by multinational companies will also increase government revenues. New employment and higher-end employment opportunities due to multinational enterprises can increase the labor income of native workers and non-native workers working in the countries through two channels of total wages and wage levels, thus increasing government revenues.

2.4.4. *Potential risks and disadvantages*

First of all, multinational companies have remarkable advantages in many aspects such as capital scale, intangible assets, technology and operational experience, compared with the enterprises in the infant industries of the host countries. This is an insuperable barrier for the development of national enterprises in the host countries. Multinational enterprises can gradually control a certain industry in the host countries by means of shareholding, M&A, and form a monopoly. This will lead to the dependence on foreign enterprises by host countries in terms of economy and people's livelihood and become a serious threat to the economic security and national security of the host countries.

Secondly, the developed countries tend to implement higher standards for environmental protection in their own countries than those in the developing countries. Therefore, multinational companies in the developed countries have transferred a large number of resource-intensive and industries with serious environmental pollution to the developing countries, such as chemical industry, petroleum and steel, etc. This will cause serious pollution to the air, water resources and food of the host countries. At the same time, the plundering exploitation of resources in the host countries will also speed up the loss of their resources.

Thirdly, once an economic crisis occurs in the host countries and factor prices fluctuate continuously, multinational companies will choose to transfer their production to regions with more economic and political stability, since multinational companies can allocate capitals and carry out production around the world. As a result, the original income and effective demand often decline in the host countries, and further increase the existing economic risks.

Finally, what multinational companies pursue is to maximize their own interests, so there is often inconsistence between the business objectives and strategies of enterprises and the economic development objectives of the host countries, which causes contradictions and even conflicts between the two parties. To the host countries, after all, multinational companies are overseas enterprises with the background and support of the governments in other countries, and multinational companies represent more interests of other countries. Therefore, the business activities of multinational companies in the host countries could challenge the sovereignty of the host countries in a sense.

3. Opportunities and Challenges Brought to China by Multinational Companies

As the country with the largest population in the world, China has always been the main destination of international investment and overseas production for multinational companies. With further opening up of China since 1992, multinational companies have begun to surge into China comprehensively, based on the extension of their global strategies and the expansion of their global management network coverage. At present, as the second largest economy in the world, China has a huge consumption-population base in its domestic market, and foreign products are also in great demand; at the same time, with advancing science and technology, improving business environment and improving the quality of education in China, it is also likely to become the birthplace of new global new growth engines increasingly. Therefore, China will still be an important part of the international strategy for multinational companies in the predictable future. Multinational companies will have a far-reaching influence on China in various aspects including its macro-economy, industrial structure and micro-enterprise as they surge into China.

3.1. *China's economic development has been promoted by multinational companies*

With the Reform and Opening-up in China over the past 30 years, China has achieved its economic boom. To a large extent, this is due to the combination of foreign capital inflow and abundant labor force in China, which have released huge productivity. And multinational companies are the main body of overseas direct investments. Multinational companies have become an important impetus for the economic development in China through cross-border M&A, greenfield investment, output management, technology transfer and so on. According to the statistics of China's Ministry of Commerce, from January to December 2014, 23778 foreign-invested enterprises were established in China with a year-on-year increase of 4.4%, and the actual utilization of foreign capital was 119.56 billion dollars (which was equivalent to 736.37 billion yuan) with a year-on-year increase of 1.7%; from January to May 2015, 9,582 foreign-invested enterprises were established in China with a year-on-year increase of 9.6%, and the actual utilization of foreign capital was 53.83 billion dollars (which was equivalent to 330.95 billion yuan), with a year-on-year increase of 10.5%. In addition, the industrial output value, tax revenue, imports and exports created by foreign-invested enterprises which are mainly represented by multinational companies accounted for about 30%, 20% and 55% of the nation's total value respectively (of which the exports of high-tech products were about 80%), and the number of direct employments was about 54 million. China has also introduced the factors which have positive spillover effects, such as technology and management while introducing investment from multinational companies. This is of profound significance for the transition of economic structure in China and its ascent in the global value chain.

3.2. *China's economic system transformation has been promoted by multinational companies*

In "The CPC Central Committee's Decision on Major Issues Concerning Comprehensively Deepening Reforms" approved at the Third Plenary

Session of the 18th CPC Central Committee, it is pointed out that "economic system reform is the focus of comprehensively deepening reform, and the core issue is to handle the relationship between the government and the market properly, make the market play a decisive role in the allocation of resources and better play the role of the government."

At present, China has not yet established an internationally recognized market economy system, which makes China frequently face many disadvantageous conditions in the anti-dumping of international trade. Therefore, to promote the establishment of the economic system in the domestic market comprehensively can not only promote commodity circulation and economic prosperity in the domestic market but also better link the Chinese market with the international market, turning disadvantageous conditions into equal ones or even advantageous ones.

The multinational companies invested in China are mainly from the developed countries in Europe and America with a mature market economy system and have rich experiences of business operations under the market economy. At the same time, as active business entities in the market economy, multinational enterprises can improve the diversity of market entities and enrich the content of market supply. Therefore, the advanced concepts and international rules brought by multinational companies will promote the reform of the economic system and the establishment of market operation mechanism in China.

3.3. *Multinational companies and environmental pollution*

With the continuous development of Chinese economy, the Chinese government and the public in China have gradually shifted their concerns to environmental protection issues. On March 1, 2015, *Smog Investigation by Chai Jing: Under the Dome*, a documentary of an in-depth investigation on air pollution caused a strong reaction in the society with the video played over 200 million times within 48 hours.

One of the motivations for multinational companies to invest in China is that their production and business activities are restricted with strict environmental protection standards in their parent countries. Therefore, parts of the production with serious environmental pollution have been transferred to China, which had a negative impact on the natural environment and living environment in China.

According to a report in *Southern Weekly* on October 26, 2006, 33 well-known multinational companies in China were discovered to have violated regulations in the national environmental protection laws. In Shanghai, Japanese Shanghai Kao Co. Ltd. was listed in the second batch of illegal enterprises investigated and punished by environmental protection authorities in 2005, due to arbitrary discharge of over-standard wastewater. In Fujian, a company invested by German Nuoer Lifting Equipment Co. Ltd. was in the list of enterprises listed for supervision in Fujian Province due to unauthorized production without building pollution control facilities and thus causing severe pollution. In Zhejiang, the subsidiary of British Purolite Group (the world's largest multinational group specializing in ion exchange resins) in China was listed as one of the provincial main polluting enterprises in 2005. In Hunan, a solely-invested subsidiary of Yamaha Motor Co. Ltd. in Japan has become one of the 20 large polluters listed for supervision due to major environmental safety hazards in the electroplating production line.

Whether multinational companies transfer polluting industries is their own economic choice or out of the political consideration of the governments behind them, the objective result is severe pollution caused to China's environment. Therefore, we should balance the comprehensive benefits of economic development and environmental protection in China while encouraging the introduction of foreign investment. Only in this way can the common environmental rights and interests of the people be safeguarded and the sustainable development can be achieved.

Chapter 6

Regional Economic Cooperation Toward Deep Integration*

More and more economies have turned from multilateral economic cooperation at the global level to bilateral or plurilateral economic cooperation at the regional level in order to meet the need of further development in intra-product international division of labor and adapt to the stagnation of the multilateral trading systems. In the new tide of regional economic cooperation, the focus of policy coordination has turned from at-the-border barriers to behind-the-border barriers with the purpose of coordinating the differences and conflicts in domestic rules among various countries. The competition for the right to make new international rules among participating countries is fully reflected by the regional economic cooperation characterized by deep integration. Especially for the regional economic cooperation which great powers participate in and dominate, it is particularly noticeable for the competition for international rule-making power out of consideration for economic interests.

1. A New Wave of Regional Economic Cooperation Has Emerged

Since the 21st century, with the development of intra-product international division of labor and the formation of the global value chain, the interdependence of product trade, international investments and services

---

* This chapter was written by Yu Chunhai and Zhu Dan.

have become the core of international economic and trade exchanges. It is necessary not only to improve the market access of various countries but also to form a new international rule that can support the interdependence of product trade, international investment and services based on coordinating domestic policies, rules and regulations of various countries in order to maintain and facilitate such complicated international economic and trade exchanges (Baldwin, 2011).

Subject to a variety of factors, the efforts to build global rules within the multilateral framework have not made progress and the stagnation of the Doha Round negotiations has caused international economic and trade activities since the 21st century to face a "rule gap". In this context, more and more World Trade Organization (WTO) members choose to "vote with their feet", turning from multilateral actions at the global level to bilateral or plurilateral actions at the regional level and striving to build new international rules in the regional scope. A new tide of regional economic cooperation has swept across major economies in the world. Since 2000, the number of new Regional Trade Agreements (RTAs) has increased rapidly. Among the 275 RTAs that are still valid, 193 ones took effect after 2000, according to the statistics of the WTO Regional Trade Agreement Information System.

What's more, the United States and East Asian economies, with distinct preference for multilateralism in history have also shown great enthusiasm for participating in RTAs since the 21st century. There were 46 RTAs participated by East Asia from 2000 to 2010, while only 5 ones participated in the past 50 years.[1] Of the 15 free trade agreements signed by the United States so far, there are 12 ones which has been negotiated and implemented since the 21st century. The Transatlantic Trade and Investment Partnership Agreement (TTIP) still under negotiation also emerged only later the Subprime Crisis.[2] As an emerging global economic center, China participated in regional economic cooperation only

[1]The Data is from the WTO (2011).

[2]At present, the free trade agreements already signed by United States include: U.S.–Panama (2012), U.S.–Colombia TPA (2012), U.S.–Korea (2012), U.S.–Oman (2009), U.S.–Peru (2009), U.S.–Central American countries and the Dominican Republic (CAFTADR) (2006, 2007, 2009), U.S.–Bahrain (2006), U.S.–Morocco (2006), U.S.–Australia (2005), U.S.–Chile (2004), U.S.–Singapore (2004), U.S.–Jordan (2001), North American Free Trade Agreement (1994), U.S.–Israel (1985), TTIP (2015). The information was from the website of Office of United States Trade Representative.

after it joined the WTO in 2001. Up to now, there are 14 free trade agreements already signed by China and 8 free trade agreements are still under negotiation.[3]

What is particularly noticeable is that the giant RTAs participated and dominated by great powers have become the direction for developing the regional economic cooperation increasingly. The TPP negotiations were initiated in 2009 with 12 countries including the United States, Australia, Brunei, Chile, Malaysia, New Zealand, Peru, Vietnam, Singapore, Japan, Canada and Mexico, which covered 40% of global GDP and 30% of total global trade. In 2013, the United States and the European Union initiated TTIP negotiations which covered 50% of global GDP and 30% of total global trade.[4] The Regional Comprehensive Economic Partnership (RCEP) negotiations were initiated in 2013, with 16 countries including China, Japan, South Korea, Australia, New Zealand and India, which covered 32% of world GDP and 30% of total world trade. What is more, the Free Trade Agreement of the Asia-Pacific (FTAAP) in conception is to establish a free trade area (FTA) which will cover all Asia-Pacific economies based on the integration of TPP, RCEP and other bilateral and small free trade agreements.

2. Characteristics of "Deep Integration" in the New Round of Regional Economic Cooperation

There have been two waves of regional economic cooperation in history. The first wave was mainly about the economic integration of the European region, which emerged in the 1950s–1960s; the second one was mainly about the deepening of the European economic integration and the emergence of the North American Free Trade Agreement in the 1980s–1990s. It has been the third wave since the 21st century (WTO, 2011; Baldwin, 2011, 2012). The third wave of regional economic cooperation is obviously more extensive and deeper than the previous two waves. The improvement of the extensiveness is mainly reflected in two aspects: firstly, East Asia and the United States which traditionally

[3]The information is from the website of the Ministry of Commerce of the People's Republic of China.

[4]The information is from the website of United States International Trade Commission (USITC).

preferred multilateral coordination are actively participating in regional economic cooperation; secondly, the economies participating in regional economic cooperation are no longer subjected to geographical proximity, and cross-regional RTAs increase significantly. The improvement in depth is mainly reflected in the content of policy coordination for regional economic cooperation, including two changes: one is to further improve market access and reduce at-the-Border Barriers that restrict the development of international trade and investment; the other is to transfer the focus of policy coordination from at-the-Border Barriers to behind-the-border barriers and coordinate the differences and conflicts of domestic rules among various countries. These changes make regional economic cooperation with the characteristics of "deep integration" (Baldwin, 2012).

From the main content of policy coordination, the focus of the new round of regional economic cooperation surpasses the WTO agreement in two aspects. On the one hand, stronger commitments and rules are given in RTAs regarding those 14 specific areas already involved in the WTO agreement such as industrial product tariffs, agricultural products and customs procedures, etc. Such clauses in RTAs are called "WTO+ clauses." On the other hand, those issues that are not covered by the WTO agreement are introduced into RTAs, including competition policy, investment policy, environmental protection, labor standards, government procurement, personnel mobility, domestic legislation and intellectual property excluded from the TRIPS agreement. Such clauses in RTAs are called "WTO-X clauses".[5] The number of WTO+ and WTO-X clauses included in the new RTAs signed since 2001 has increased significantly, compared with those before 2000. According to the WTO data, the number of WTO + clauses has increased from 234 to 646 and the number of

[5]Since the Doha Round negotiations in 2001, about 1/3 of RTAs have contained clauses on competition policy, intellectual property and capital flow. Among them, 47% included competition policy clauses, 39% included capital flow clauses, 37% included intellectual property clauses not involved in TRIPs, and 31% included investment clauses. The WTO-X clause is also known as the "second generation" of trade policy. Its main purpose is to reach a commonly recognized minimum standard through the coordination and regulation of the domestic policies of the participating countries, and achieve fair competition and eliminate economic distortions, based on the rules. Therefore, the direction of policy change is gradually from low standard to high standard, with the nature of upward competition (or positive integration). See Horn *et al.* (2010), Sheng Bin and Guo Ting (2014), WTO (2011).

WTO-X clauses has increased from 221 to 534.[6] Deep integration is especially obvious in RTAs signed between the developed and the developing economies.[7] Since the 1990s, the status and influence of the developing economies have constantly risen in the complicated global trade as they joined the intra-product international division of labor system. Intellectual property protection, law and infrastructure are relatively weak in emerging economies due to the low level of internal governance. In such cases, it is a particularly serious issue for lack of new international rules. Therefore, it becomes more urgent for the developed and the developing countries to construct new international rules through RTAs. Since 2000, among those vertical RTAs signed by developed and developing economies, the number of WTO + clauses has increased from 109 to 422 and the number of WTO-X clauses has increased from 123 to 378.[8]

The issues addressed by WTO-X clauses are typical domestic rules, whose original motive is to regulate domestic production, investment and sales. Then, why have domestic rules become the emphasis on regional economic cooperation since the 21st century? From international trade and international investment in general logic, the first thing is to break through at-the-Border Barriers in order to get access to overseas markets and get benefit from them, which is related to whether the foreign market can be entered. Only after entering the foreign market will we have the problem of the internal rules in the foreign market. Therefore, at-the-Border Barriers will be the first within the scope of international economic policy coordination. During the multilateral and regional economic cooperation in the 20th century, how to reduce at-the-Border Barriers is the focus on policy coordination, while behind-the-border barriers are relatively less involved in coordination. Domestic rules have gradually become the focus on international policy coordination in the 21st century due to the changes in several aspects. First of all, the previous multilateral, regional and bilateral economic cooperation had significantly reduced at-the-Border Barriers, and then behind-the-border rules have naturally become the focus on further coordination. Secondly, changes in the form of international division of labor and those in the content of international

[6] It was compiled based on the data of the WTO Regional Trade Agreements Information System (RTA-IS).

[7] WTO, World Trade Report 2011: The WTO and Preferential Trade Agreements, 2011.

[8] It was compiled according to the data of the WTO Regional Trade Agreement Information System.

economic and trade exchanges have further highlighted the importance of reducing behind-the-border barriers.

If product trade is more restricted by at-the-Border trade barriers, then service trade and investment activities will be more subject to behind-the-border rules. Suppose that an enterprise provides patent licensing and technical consulting services, there are optional ways to provide services to foreign customers as follows. (i) To save patents and technical solutions in electronic media, and provide them to foreign customers remotely through the network. (ii) To send employees abroad to meet with customers and provide patent and technical services face to face. (iii) To invest abroad and establish branches and realize the local supply of services. For this service enterprise in this assumption, domestic rules, such as intellectual property protection, short-term personnel mobility and visa policy, investment policy and competition policy, are more important issues than at-the-Border barriers such as tariff and customs procedures. Domestic rules will naturally become the focus on international policy coordination as the importance of service trade and international investment increases, especially when they become the necessary conditions to maintain the international division of labor and global value chain.

According to the theory of international economics, enterprises need to pay extra costs for market entry, in order to get access to the foreign market, including cross-border transportation costs, trade costs caused by border barriers and internal transaction costs. Costs for cross-border transportation have been significantly reduced with the advances in transportation and communication technology. Border barriers have been greatly reduced with the development of multilateral trading system. The cost of cross-border transportation and the trade cost caused by border barriers can be avoided with international direct investment. Therefore, how to cut down transaction costs after entering the market of a country has become the most important and most urgent problem. After entering the foreign market, enterprises need to adapt to the new rules system and make various adjustments and changes due to the differences in domestic rules of various countries, which will bring additional transaction costs. Therefore, to coordinate the domestic rules in various countries and reduce the differences and conflicts of rules should be the righteousness of international policy coordination.

It can be regarded that "deep integration" is a necessary requirement under the new situation of the international division of labor. But why could "deep integration" take the lead in making headway in regional economic cooperation? The reason is very simple. Whether it is to further cut down border barriers or to coordinate domestic rules, it is to construct new international rules for international economic and trade exchanges under the new division of labor. This is an issue of supply in an international system. Within the multilateral framework, the differences in benefits and power of different countries make the building process of rules full of speculation, free rides and interest conflicts, with low efficiency of system supply. In regional economic cooperation, negotiations can be focused on a few countries with similar interests, so as to solve the problem on the supply of institutions more effectively.

3. Competition for International Rules Behind "Deep Integration"

It is usually the most effective and sustainable means to compete for the dominance of international rules to obtain maximum economic benefits in international economic and trade exchanges. In the short run, international rules have an influence on whether the existing competitive advantage of a country can be brought into full play; in the long run, international rules will have an impact on whether the competitive advantage of a country can be sustained and whether it can develop its competitive advantages. All these are the essential guarantee for a country to obtain benefits from international economic and trade exchanges. The role of rules is not only to regulate the market conduct but also to change the comparative advantages of various countries based on their endowments and have profound effects on the final distribution of benefits. Therefore, the international competition that various countries participate in is not only the market competition of microcosmic entities but also the competition of governments in making international rules. The competition of participating countries for the right to make new international rules is fully reflected in the new wave of regional economic cooperation. The competition of rule-making power is especially obvious in the regional economic cooperation dominated by great powers in particular.

In fact, since the 1990s, the characteristic of "deep integration" and the competition for the right to make international rules have already shown in the RTAs signed by major European and American countries and the developing economies (Li Xiangyang, 2003). In those RTAs signed, a common practice is that the major European and American countries bring the developing economies closer to themselves in terms of political and economic systems, regulations and policies by transferring market shares and giving up traditional trade interests. The purpose of this is to build up their bargaining power for the dominance of international rules through the construction of regional economic cooperation organizations led by themselves. The characteristic of deep integration and the competition for international rules behind it in the new round of regional economic cooperation have been essentially different from those in the 1990s. For great powers, their motives for economic interest become more and more important, especially those for non-traditional economic interests other than trade interests as great powers initiate and sign RTAs. With the intra-product international division of labor, the economic interests concerned by the great powers have already surpassed the traditional trade interests. To maximize the added value of domestic factors globally is the most important consideration of economic interests for great powers to promote deep integration through RTAs. With the consideration of realistic economic interests, the great powers are no longer satisfied with building up their bargaining power for the dominance of international rules by using regional initiatives, but substantively initiate the process of making new international rules beyond the existing multilateral trading system.

The competition for dominance of international rules is particularly obvious in the giant RTAs initiated and dominated by great powers, especially in TPP and TTIP initiated and dominated by the United States (Meltzer, 2015; Sapiro, 2015). Of the 27 issues involved in TPP, only 5 are directly related to trading and the others are mainly issues of domestic rules. Therefore, many people think that TPP is a "rules agreement" rather than a free trade agreement (Meltzer, 2015). Definition of TPP importance given by Mr. Obama is also very straightforward: "If we don't make the rules for global trade, China will make them for us, and China will make them in a way that benefits its own businesses and its own labors." In TTIP which were initiated by Europe and America, besides the goal of reducing traditional trade barriers and improving regulatory coordination, the other goal is to cope with global challenges together such as labor standards, environmental standards, state-owned companies and competition policies, and strengthen the dominance of the new rules for global trade (Office of United States Trade Representative, 2013).

The competition for international rules is not an illusive goal. It takes consideration of realistic and long-term potential economic interests. The service industry in the United States has realistic international competitive advantages. Large-scale service exports have become technologically possible, with the advancement of transportation, information and network technology. However, the policy or regulatory barriers of service trade are still very high in terms of market opening, personnel mobility and intellectual property protection. Overseas investment and local sales are effective means to avoid border barriers. This is the so-called overseas institutional transaction, which is of more importance than service export. In order to make use of this channel, branches in other countries and regions should be established at first, and then relevant services will be provided for the local market. This is more affected by behind-the-border barriers in the host country, including investment policy, competition policy, commercial convenience, intellectual property protection and so on (Baldwin, 2011).

From a long-term perspective, intelligent manufacturing technology and technological innovation in energy and environment will become the basis of competitive advantages of the United States in the future.[9] We must realize that the greatest value to the United States, whether of new manufacturing technology or of new technologies in energy and environment, is not to improve the supply capacity of final products. With consideration of the endowment restriction of the United States, the effective carrier is not the products produced with new technologies, but the equipment and services for the application and diffusion of new technologies, in order to achieve the potential benefits of technological advantages. In addition, the direct transfer of technology is not the best way to achieve the benefits of comparative advantages, although it can bring about benefits. On the one hand, the transaction cost is relatively high for cross-border technology transfer; on the other hand, the direct cross-border technology transfer makes less contribution to domestic production and

[9] Mr. Obama once proposed that the United States should be made as the center of the next revolution in manufacturing by creating a network of a series of manufacturing hubs, in his State of the union address 2013. The United States has set up its first manufacturing innovation center in Youngstown, Ohio, and its main task is to train skilled workers for 3D printing. The U.S. government also announced to start the construction of three new manufacturing centers, at the same time, also proposed that the Congress help create a network of 15 manufacturing centers. This indicates that the focus of future technological changes in the United States is the new generation of manufacturing technology and technological innovation in energy and environment, which will become the basis of competitive advantages of the United States in the future.

employment. A better way is to turn new technologies into corresponding equipment and services and provide key equipment and service inputs for the diffusion and extensive application of new technologies.

Outside the U.S., with the increase of labor costs, the emerging economies urgently need to reconstruct the manufacturing value chain based on the usage of new technologies to revamp the production process; with the increasing pressure on energy and environment, it is an urgent need for them to apply new technologies to improve the energy utilization structure, change energy exploitation modes, and improve the energy efficiency and environmental protection level of existing industries. This has brought about a huge demand for the application and diffusion of new technologies. Based on this, the promotion and implementation of environmental protection and labor standards in emerging economies will be conducive to further stimulating demands and cultivating markets. If environmental protection and labor standards can be strengthened worldwide, then this will be put together with the rapidly rising labor costs and deteriorating environmental and energy problems in emerging economies, making the demand of emerging economies for new technologies, equipment and services of the United States increase rapidly.

All these need to coordinate by using foreign trade policies, lower at-the-Border trade barriers, promote the opening of foreign service market, eliminate behind-the-border barriers of external market, and connect more effectively the advantageous supply capacity of the United States with the expanding external demand. Through dominating in the process of making new international rules and even directly expanding the domestic rules of the United States into international rules, the United States can not only reduce the cost to access foreign markets so as to maximize the added value which is generated by U.S. factors globally but also create favorable institutional conditions for cultivating long-term potential advantages and achieving economic benefits of the United States.

It is necessary to select appropriate strategies and means in order to compete for the right to make international rules more effectively, and even dominate the process of building international rules. As the conventional focus of regional economic cooperation, the bilateral FTA can coordinate bilateral rules and regulate the bilateral economic and trade relations. The great powers can also maintain obvious dominance. However, it is difficult for bilateral rules to upgrade directly to global rules. It is an approach toward global rules by carrying out bilateral coordination with different countries respectively and further coordinating multiple bilateral relations and bilateral rules. However, the biggest issue with this approach is that the transaction cost is too high. The multilateral coordination within the WTO framework is another approach to make global rules, but this approach also faces high transaction costs. It is difficult to promote effectively the formulation of global rules under the constraints of the realistic international politics and economy (Baldwin, 2011). More importantly, for the United States, it cannot dominate the rule-making process within the multilateral framework at all due to the uncertainty of balance of power within the multilateral framework (Baldwin, 2009).

Giant RTAs such as TPP and TTIP are the most effective ways for the United States to compete for the dominance of international rules with the constraints of the realistic politics and economy (Baracuhy, 2015; Sapiro, 2015; Hamilton, 2014; Tellis, 2015). The trans-Pacific and trans-Atlantic economic and trade relations are the key parts of the U.S. foreign economic and trade relations. The European region is the conventional focus of U.S. foreign economic and trade relations, and the Asia-Pacific region is the emerging focus of U.S. foreign economic and trade relations. However, in these two kinds of relations, the difficulties of coordinating rules are not the same. The developed economies in the America and Europe have relatively small differences in rules and have similar goals and values. Moreover, the rule systems in Europe have been gradually unified during its integration, and the policy coordination between the United States and Europe is more like a kind of bilateral one with relatively small transaction costs. These two factors determine that it can be easier for the United States and Europe to form unified rules. There are great differences in the level of economic development and the improvement of domestic rules among different economies in the Asia-Pacific region, and there is a lack of a unified rule system. This makes it more difficult to coordinate rules between the United States and the Asia-Pacific region. It must be noted that the Asia-Pacific region, especially East Asia has a strong dependence on the developed economies in America and Europe in terms of key technical equipment and final markets, although it has formed a relatively complete regional value chain. The coordination of rules and the formation of uniform rules between the United States and Europe can not only have a demonstration effect on the Asia-Pacific region but also have a competitive effect, increasing the pressure of the Asia-Pacific region to accept unified rules. Moreover, large emerging economies such as China, India, Brazil and Russia are not involved, which makes the United States have power dominance in the process of rule coordination with developing economies in the Asia-Pacific region.

Similarly, policy coordination between the United States and the Asia-Pacific region will also have a demonstration effect and a competitive effect on the policy coordination between the United States and Europe, due to the important influence of the Asia-Pacific region as an emerging market in the global market. The demonstration and competition effect between TPP and TTIP is not only conducive to making regional rules but also improving their compatibilities. With the principle of "Critical Majority", the regional rules made by the United States, Europe and the Asia-Pacific region can be upgraded to global rules with institutional arrangements within the WTO framework, and can also naturally become global rules with the demonstration effect and competition effect, based on the roles of the Asia-Pacific region, Europe and the United States in the global economy. Thus, the United States not just promotes the building process of global rules with TPP and TTIP, but more importantly, dominates the making process of these rules.

Moreover, regional policy coordination between the United States and emerging markets can avoid the complicated balance of power within the multilateral framework. In the balance of power pattern dominated by the United States, it is easier for the domestic rules of the United States to extend directly to the emerging markets and become the rules that regulate the regional division of labor, trade and investment relations. This will not only be conducive to amplifying the competitive advantage of the United States, but also help the United States to obtain greater economic benefits from the established advantages. Therefore, it is easy to understand why the United States deliberately excludes large emerging economies such as China, Brazil, India and Russia when the United States pays close attention to the emerging economies in its policy coordination of foreign trade. As a Brookings report says, both TPP and TTIP are the reactions of the United States to the emerging economic power such as China which challenges the U.S. dominance within the multilateral framework (Meltzer, 2015).

In the process of building complicated global trade rules, regional action and multilateral action are complementary to each other, leading to a complex global rule system at multiple speeds in various ways. This provides another feasible approach for the building of new international trade rules under the background of the slow progress of the multilateral trading system. However, various parallel regional actions will lead to the diversification, decentralization, inconsistency and non-transparency of rules in the process of competing for the right to make new international trade rules. As a result, the uncertainty of rules and the frequent changes among different rules will greatly increase the cost of international economic and trade exchanges. The giant RTAs, dominated by the United States are not only characterized by deep integration, especially TPP and TTIP negotiations but also tend to be multilateralized at the same time. It not only fully reflects America's intention to compete for the right to make new international rules but also is the strategic choice for the United States to get "the first-mover advantage" in this competition. TPP and TTIP related to the existing regional actions not only have the advantage of scale, covering more than half of the global trade activities, but also take the lead in promoting the multilateral process of regional actions relative to the existing regional actions. With the combination of the advantage of scale and the first-mover advantage, the final agreement of TPP and TTIP is very likely to become the benchmark of new global trade rules.

4. Challenges and Countermeasures

With large emerging economies such as China, India and Brazil absent, the United States takes an obvious dominant status in TPP and TTIP negotiations. This means that there is an obvious "power asymmetry" in the process of building new international rules. For the emerging economies which play an important role in global economy and trade, their influences and heterogeneous interest appeals cannot be fully reflected during the game behind the rule-making. The absence of checks and balances and the convergence of interest appeals will no doubt contribute to the negotiations in progress and the final agreement reached. However, the rules mainly reflect the interest appeals of the United States and even directly extend and apply the internal rules of the United States. Such a model of making international rule is similar to the "hegemony model" of the 19th century to a certain extent. This will have a very adverse effect on the competitive advantages of the emerging economies including China and the benefits of the international division of labor. It has been calculated that the new standards on intellectual property, labor, environment, competition policies and so on in TPP will increase the production costs of the emerging economies by 20% to 50% (Meltzer, 2015).

Meanwhile, for the regional economic cooperation that China currently participates in, the issue of market access is still the focus of negotiations with few deep integration arrangements involved. Among the 14 free trade agreements that China has reached, only those bilateral free trade agreements signed with Switzerland, South Korea and Australia involve deep integration arrangements such as competition policies, environmental standards, labor standards, investment policies and so on. RCEP is the only giant RTA that China has participated in and comes into a substantive stage of negotiations. RCEP still focuses on traditional issues such as goods trade, service trade, investment as well as economic and technological cooperation. For issues on deep integration such as intellectual property, competition policies and investment policies, RCEP emphasizes "recognition of the individual differences and circumstance differences of participating countries". The FTAAP in conception is still in the stage of "joint strategic research" and has not come into the substantive stage of negotiations, much less the determination of specific negotiation issues.

There are two main reasons that arrangements of deep integration have not become the focus of China's regional economic cooperation. First of all, overcapacity, economic rebalancing and domestic reforms have put great pressure on economic growth in the short term. The economy in transition is more dependent on the growth momentum brought by overseas markets, and there is an urgent need to improve overseas market access. Secondly, it is still incomplete in the domestic rules on intellectual property, environment, labor, competition policies, and capital flow and so on. The upward competition pressure brought by deep integration will lead to excessive impact of institutional adjustment. Therefore, it has realistic rationality to avoid too many deep integration arrangements, not only for stabilizing economic growth but also for avoiding excessive pressure on institutional adjustments.

Although this approach has its rationality in the short term, it may have a great negative impact on China in the long term. If TPP and TTIP become the platforms for making international trade rules in the future, then it means that China will be once again be excluded from the process of making international rules (Baracuhy, 2015). Needless to say, international rules have a vital influence on a country's status and benefit distribution in international competitions. Therefore, China will be in very unfavorable status in the international competition and the benefit distribution from the international division of labor for a long time in the future once excluded from the process of making new international rules. Therefore, the competition for the right to making new international rules should become one of China's international strategies in the future.

The unilateral actions similar to the Shanghai Free Trade Zone are conducive to improving China's internal trade environment and further raising its status in the international division of labor and trade. However, if China cannot be integrated into regional or multilateral actions, it can hardly change the current unfavorable status in the process of competing for the right to make new international rules. Therefore, on the basis of unilateral trade liberalization, it needs to take advantage of its own economic and trade influence to initiate and substantively promote regional economic cooperation with the characteristic of deep integration. At the same time, China should pay attention to the multilateral trade negotiations within the WTO framework, and push the multilateral trade system out of the current Doha dilemma with the alliances of interests and forces within the multilateral framework; and fight against the possible "hegemonic mode" in the process of making new international trade rules, with regional and multilateral actions.

China is capable of becoming a hub country of regional economic cooperation based on its expanding economic scale and market scale as well as its status in the East Asian production network in recent years. In line with this, the FTA strategy has been upgraded as a national strategy of China and its focus is to accelerate the implementation of FTA strategy on the basis of the peripheral areas, build a high standard FTA network for the world and actively participate in international rule-making and strive for the governance right of the global economy on this platform. In this process, we should take countermeasures in the following aspects in order to influence the international rule making process more effectively. The first one is to balance short-term and long-term benefits. We can consider transferring markets and giving up some traditional trade interests in exchange for the influence on domestic rules of other developing and emerging economies. Secondly, the biggest problem for China at present is that the domestic rules are incomplete, or even missing. Therefore, it is necessary to improve domestic rules on intellectual property, environmental protection, labor standards, competition policies, capital flow and so on as soon as possible based on the progress of existing RTAs and the pilot experience of the Shanghai Free Trade Zone. Moreover, we should be looking forward to the process of making and improving domestic rules, and considering the possibilities of integration and competition with relevant rules in giant RTAs such as TPP in the future. Finally, we should vigorously promote policy coordination with other large emerging economies, especially the coordination and integration with their domestic rules, and participate together in the competitions already begun for the right of making new international rules.

Chapter 7

Analyses of Global Technological Progress Trends and Industrial Characteristics*

With the rapid development of economic globalization, technological progress in the world today presents trends and industrial characteristics different from the past. In particular, after the financial crisis, the technological progress in the world presents even more complicated and pluralistic trends due to the implementation of the "re-industrialization" strategy and Industry 4.0 strategy in the developed countries. This chapter focuses on the global technological progress and industrial transformation and upgrading, analyzes countries and industries from the perspective of technology research and development as well as technology output, with the starting point of quantitative analysis of world technological progress, so as to clarify the general change trend, characteristics and major internal influencing factors of current global technological progress.

As the fundamental source of on-going economic growth, technological progress is the major force for improving economic performance and enhancing social welfare. From the perspective of the actual process of economic development, technological progress can not only enhance the improvement of productivity but also make a remarkable change in the industrial structure and trade structure. Therefore, it has an important realistic significance to discuss the overall trends and influence of

* This chapter was written by Yang Lianxing.

technological progress. Through the quantitative analysis of DEA non-parametric estimation, this chapter finds that global technological progress has been slowing down since the 21st century. Technological progress and upgrading are mostly subject to the improvement of technical efficiency but not technical change. The further analysis of world technology R&D investment and patent innovation shows that the scale of R&D expenditure in industries presents a significant differentiation trend. The decline of R&D investment in industries has generated an obvious constraint effect on technology upgrading and innovation, while the fields of emerging technology do not show a strong promotion of technical change.

The structure of this chapter is organized as follows. In the first part, overall quantitative analysis and discussion will be carried out on world technological progress based on the Malmquist index approach. In the second part, the overall reasons for world technological progress will be discussed and analyzed by country and industry from the perspective of technology input. In the third part, the overall trend of patent innovation will be further analyzed by country and industry from the perspective of technological innovation output, as a way of further clarifying the trends and the characteristics of the patent technology progress. In the fourth part, general analysis and clarification will be carried out on the characteristics and the trends of the current world technological progress.

1. Overall Trends and Characteristics of World Technological Progress

1.1. *Quantitative analysis method of world technological progress*

The measure of world technological progress in this chapter is based on the adoption of the Malmquist index approach of DEA non-parametric estimation. Based on this approach, this chapter selects the input and output data of the major OECD countries, carries out quantitative analysis and explanations on the overall dynamic change characteristics of total factor productivity in various countries, and then provides evidence for the analysis of the overall technological progress in the world.

The Malmquist index approach is mainly based on DEA non-parametric estimation model, mainly using the ratio of the distance function to calculate the input–output efficiency. It can estimate the changing range of the technological progress by comparing the production frontiers among different time series. In fact, the production frontier will change in different stages due to the technological progress. In other words, the same output vector will have different productivity in different stages. Taking this as the starting point, Färe *et al.* (1944) put forward the following Malmquist index based on the output:

$$M\left(x_t, x_{t+1}, y_t, y_{t+1}\right) = \left[\frac{d_{t+1}(x_{t+1}, y_{t+1})}{d_t(x_t, y_t)} \cdot \frac{d_t(x_{t+1}, y_{t+1})}{d_{t+1}(x_t, y_t)}\right]^{\frac{1}{2}} \tag{7.1}$$

In which, vectors x_t and y_t represent the input vector and the output vector at time$_t$ respectively, and d_t is a distance function used to define technological inefficiency. In the production frontiers based on the output, the corresponding distance functions for production technology at time$_t$, the input vector x_t and the output vector y_t can be defined as:

$$d_t(x_t, y_t) = \inf\{\theta : (x_t, y_t/\theta) \in S_t\} = (\sup\{\theta : (x_t, \theta y_t) \in S_t\})^{-1} \tag{7.2}$$

The distance function $d_t(x_t, y_t)$ which is defined by the production frontier based on the output actually measures the difference between the real output and the most efficient output with the same input. From this definition, it reflects the corresponding actual production efficiency to the input vector x_t and the output vector y_t at time t.

Two parts can be derived from the further decomposition of the technological progress in Equation (7.1): Part EF represents the change of production efficiency and Part TC represents the change of technical efficiency.

$$M\left(x_t, x_{t+1}, y_t, y_{t+1}\right) = \frac{d_{t+1}(x_{t+1}, y_{t+1})}{d_t(x_t, y_t)}\left[\frac{d_t(x_t, y_t)}{d_{t+1}(x_t, y_t)} \cdot \frac{d_t(x_{t+1}, y_{t+1})}{d_{t+1}(x_{t+1}, y_{t+1})}\right]^{\frac{1}{2}} \tag{7.3}$$

If the assumption of constant returns to scale in Equations (7.1) and (7.3) is further loosened, then with variable returns to scale, the technical efficiency change TC can be further decomposed to the pure technical efficiency change and the scale efficiency change. The formula is as below:

$$M_{v,c}\left(x_t, x_{t+1}, y_t, y_{t+1}\right) = \left[\frac{d_t^v(x_t, y_t)}{d_t^c(x_t, y_t)} \bigg/ \frac{d_{t+1}^v(x_{t+1}, y_{t+1})}{d_{t+1}^c(x_{t+1}, y_{t+1})}\right] \cdot \left[\frac{d_t^c(x_t, y_t)}{d_{t+1}^c(x_t, y_t)} \cdot \frac{d_t^c(x_{t+1}, y_{t+1})}{d_{t+1}^c(x_{t+1}, y_{t+1})}\right] \cdot \left[\frac{d_{t+1}^v(x_{t+1}, y_{t+1})}{d_t^v(x_t, y_t)}\right] \quad (7.4)$$

In the above equation, superscript “v” represents a variable of return to scale and superscript “c” represents an invariant of return to scale. In the “TC” equation, the first item represents the pure technical efficiency change under variable return to scale, and the second one represents the scale efficiency change. Similarly, it is in accordance with Equation (7.3) that the EF equation represents the production efficiency change.

The Malmquist index approach can work out efficiency analysis by using different sorts of input and output variables based on the use of the above equation, and it does not require either relevant price information or conditions of cost minimization and profit maximization. More importantly, it attributes productivity change to technology change and technical efficiency change. Moreover, it further classifies technical efficiency change into pure technical efficiency change and scale efficiency change (Liu Binglian and Li Qingbin, 2009).

Based on this, this chapter decomposes the changes of total factor productivity in various countries into technical change and technical efficiency change, and technical efficiency change includes pure technical efficiency change and scale efficiency change. One of the main purposes of index analysis is to find the contributions of pure technical efficiency and scale efficiency to technical efficiency change. That is to say, if there is technical inefficiency in a country, then the influence of pure technical inefficiency and scale inefficiency on technical inefficiency can be further obtained according to the Malmquist index approach, so as to enable the effective improvement of technical efficiency.

1.2. *Analyses of the general characteristics of world technological progress*

This chapter selects the input and output data of some OECD countries from 1990 to 2014 and constructs the necessary panel data to calculate the Malmquist indexes on the basis of data comparability and availability, in order to use this analysis method to estimate the overall situation of the technological progress of major countries in the world.[1] In terms of selection of specific data, this chapter uses real GDP amount denominated in US dollar in various countries as the total output data, and it uses the corresponding employed population and real capital stock as input data to work out the Malmquist indexes of various countries.

1.2.1. *Analyses of the technical change characteristics in OECD countries*

From the cross-section data of the Malmquist indexes for OECD countries in Table 1, the mean value of total factor productivity change in various countries from 1991 to 2014 was less than 1. This shows a downward trend of total factor productivity in various countries, in other words, a deteriorating trend of total factor productivity in major OECD countries. Among them, a further decomposition result of total factor productivity shows that the declining total factor productivity in major OECD countries is mainly due to the decline of the technological change (techch). It can be found that pure technical efficiency change (pech) is greater than scale efficiency change (sech) according to the decomposition result of technical efficiency change. This indicates that the decline in technical efficiency change is mainly due to the decline in scale efficiency change. In general, the decline in total factor productivity of OECD countries is mainly due to the decline in technical change (the reduction in speed of technical improvement). However, the improvement of technical efficiency plays a huge role in improving the decline in total factor productivity. A further analysis finds that the deterioration of scale efficiency in various countries is the main reason for the decline in technical efficiency change.

---

[1]The selected sample countries for analysis in this chapter on the basis of availability and comparability are Australia, Austria, Belgium, Canada, Chile, Czech, Denmark, Estonia, Finland, France, Germany, Greece, Hungary, Iceland, Island, Israel, Italy, Japan, South Korea, Luxembourg, Mexico, the Netherlands, New Zealand, Norway, Poland, Portugal, Slovenia, Spain, Sweden, Switzerland, Turkey, the United Kingdom and the United States.

Table 1. Mean Value of Malmquist Indexes in OECD Countries from 1991 to 2014

Country	Technical Efficiency Change (effch)	Technical Change (techch)	Pure Technical Efficiency Change (pech)	Scale Efficiency Change (sech)	Total Factor Productivity Change (tfpch)
Australia	1.124	0.894	1.124	1	1.005
Austria	1.088	0.879	1.088	1	0.956
Belgium	1.072	0.88	1.072	1	0.943
Canada	1.066	0.877	1.066	1	0.935
Chile	1.068	0.88	1.068	1.104	0.94
Czech	1.053	0.881	1.053	0.955	0.928
Denmark	1.052	0.876	1.052	1.014	0.922
Estonia	1.043	0.873	1.043	1.052	0.91
Finland	1.036	0.885	1.036	1.012	0.917
France	1.039	0.878	1.039	1.009	0.912
Germany	1.043	0.879	1.043	1.01	0.917
Greece	1.036	0.885	1.036	1.14	0.916
Hungary	1.031	0.875	1.031	0.772	0.902
Iceland	1.032	0.88	1.032	1.084	0.909
Island	1.023	0.886	1.023	1.01	0.905
Israel	1.027	0.884	1.027	0.94	0.908
Italy	1.028	0.876	1.028	1.078	0.9
Japan	1.027	0.876	1.027	1.003	0.899
South Korea	1.025	0.882	1.025	0.931	0.904
Luxembourg	0.875	0.891	0.877	1	0.78
Mexico	0.911	0.88	0.912	1.083	0.801
Netherlands	0.921	0.887	0.922	1.018	0.817
New Zealand	0.923	0.884	0.924	1.01	0.816
Norway	0.934	0.877	0.936	1.01	0.819
Poland	0.94	0.88	0.941	0.909	0.827
Portugal	0.94	0.877	0.941	1.107	0.824
Slovenia	0.951	0.893	0.953	0.94	0.849
Spain	0.954	0.881	0.956	1.084	0.84
Sweden	0.958	0.878	0.959	1.005	0.84

Table 1. (*Continued*)

Country	**Technical Efficiency Change (effch)**	**Technical Change (techch)**	**Pure Technical Efficiency Change (pech)**	**Scale Efficiency Change (sech)**	**Total Factor Productivity Change (tfpch)**
Switzerland	0.963	0.883	0.965	0.939	0.851
Turkey	0.959	0.884	0.961	0.977	0.848
United Kingdom	0.963	0.881	0.965	0.997	0.849
United States	0.972	0.873	0.973	1.106	0.848

Source: Database of Main Science and Technology Indicators, OECD Stat.

1.2.2. *Analyses of the annual trends and characteristics of world technological progress*

According to Fu Yong and Bai Long (2009), in terms of cross-section, the technical efficiency has a crucial effect on total factor productivity. It can be seen from the mean value of Mulmquist index of each year in this chapter that the overall total factor productivity of OECD countries was fluctuating upward, but enjoyed noticeable characteristics of stages. The total factor productivity rose at the fastest speed from 1991 to 1999, rising from 0.597 to 0.912. However, it has been lingering at around 0.9 since 2000, and the improvement was not significant (see Table 2). Furthermore, from the perspective of technical efficiency change (effch) and technical change (techch), the mean value of technical efficiency change from 1991 to 2014 was much higher than that of technical change, which was basically in accordance with the conclusion in Table 1. That is, the overall improvement of total factor productivity in various countries was mainly due to the improvement of the technical efficiency instead of the technical improvement.

From Tables 1 and 2, for the technical efficiency change, the average value of the technical efficiency change from 1991 to 2014 was almost above 1. This showed that the technical efficiency was fluctuating upward in various countries, and thus it promoted the improvement of overall total factor productivity. Among them, the technical efficiency decreased obviously from 1993 to 1997 and grew rapidly from 1998 to 2002. However, it has been lingering at around 1 since 2003 without a significant upward trend.

Table 2. Mean Value of Malmquist Indexes in OECD Countries from 1991 to 2014

Year	Technical Efficiency Change (effch)	Technical Change (techch)	Pure Technical Efficiency Change (pech)	Scale Efficiency Change (sech)	Total Factor Productivity Change (tfpch)
1991	0.993	0.511	0.993	1	0.597
1992	1.029	0.654	1.036	0.993	0.642
1993	1	0.767	1.001	1	0.767
1994	1.001	0.813	0.999	1.002	0.814
1995	0.987	0.839	0.986	1	0.828
1996	0.977	0.889	1.003	0.974	0.869
1997	0.958	0.923	0.993	0.965	0.884
1998	0.992	0.904	1	0.993	0.897
1999	1.008	0.904	1.001	1.007	0.912
2000	1.006	0.908	0.999	1.007	0.913
2001	1.029	0.886	1.015	1.014	0.911
2002	0.962	0.971	0.984	0.978	0.934
2003	1.007	0.927	1.002	1.005	0.934
2004	1.009	0.932	1.004	1.005	0.94
2005	1.005	0.935	1.002	1.003	0.94
2006	1	0.939	0.997	1.003	0.939
2007	1.007	0.942	1.004	1.003	0.948
2008	1.012	0.945	1.004	1.007	0.955
2009	1.005	0.95	0.996	1.009	0.954
2010	1.006	0.96	1.006	1	0.965
2011	1.003	0.954	1.002	1.001	0.957
2012	1.002	0.957	1.001	1.001	0.959
2013	1.002	0.961	1.001	1.001	0.962
2014	1	0.961	0.999	1.001	0.961

Source: Database of Main Science and Technology Indicators, OECD Stat.

In addition, in terms of the trend of technical change, as shown in Figure 1, before 2003, the technical efficiency index fluctuated greatly, and most of them were less than 1, and after 2003, the fluctuation of technical efficiency index is small, and most of them are greater than 1. And as shown in Figure 2, the mean values of technical change in various countries were all less than 1 from 1994 to 2014, but still enjoyed a fluctuating upward trend in general. Among them, the technical change rose

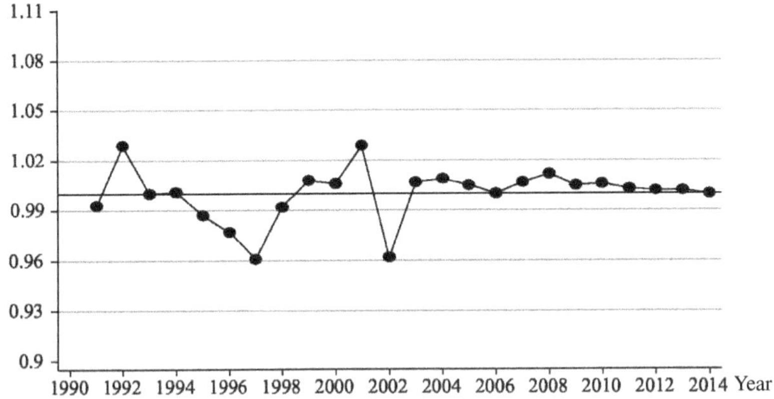

Figure 1. Indexes of Technical Efficiency Change in Sample Countries, 1991–2014

Source: Database of Main Science and Technology Indicators, OECD Stat.

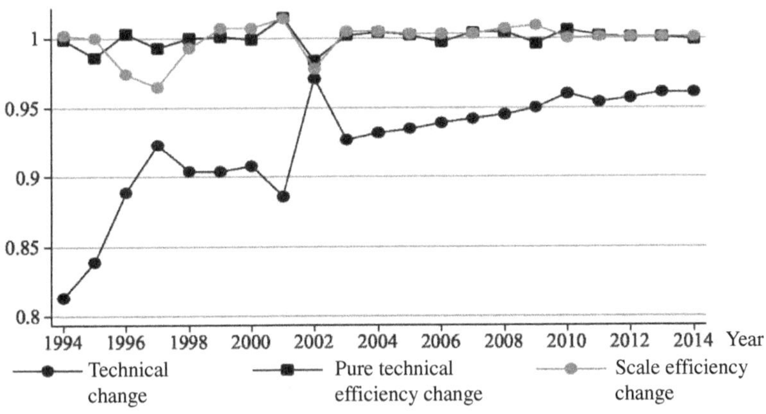

Figure 2. Indexes of Technical Change, Pure Technical Efficiency Change and Scale Efficiency Change in Sample Countries from 1991 to 2014

Source: Database of Main Science and Technology Indicators, OECD Stat.

significantly from 1994 to 1997, which was consistent with the trend of total factor productivity, then technical change lingered at around 0.95, thus greatly restricting the rise of total factor productivity. Also the trend of the pure technical efficiency change (pech) was consistent with that of the scale efficiency change (sech). However, the pure technical efficiency change (pech) exceeded the scale efficiency change to a certain extent.

On the whole, the changes of total factor productivity in OECD countries were fluctuating upward but they had noticeable characteristics of stages. Among them, the mean value of the technical efficiency change from 1991 to 2014 was obviously higher than that of the technical change. In other words, the overall improvement of total factor productivity in various countries was mainly due to the improvement of technical efficiency instead of technical improvement. The technical change rose significantly from 1991 to 1997, which was consistent with that of total factor productivity and then technical change lingered at around 0.95, thus greatly restricting the rise of total factor productivity.

2. Analyses of the Trends and the Characteristics of World Technology R&D Investment

This chapter further analyzes and clarifies the internal influencing factors on the change trend of production technology in various countries, from the perspective of R&D investment which is an important influencing factor on world technological progress, based on the analysis of the above-mentioned general change trend of production technology and productivity in various countries.

2.1. *Analyses of the overall R&D investment in world technological progress*

R&D activities are one of the major driving forces for technology research and development innovation in a country. And the proportion of general expenditure on R&D (GERD) in GDP (GERD/GDP) is one of the most important quantitative indexes relating to R&D activities. Based on this, this chapter analyzes and clarifies the trend of international technological innovation and its internal influencing factors from the perspective of R&D investment.

From the change trend of the mean value of GERD/GDP in OECD countries, GERD/GDP was fluctuating upward, but it had noticeable characteristics of stages, as shown in Figure 3 and Table 3. GERD/GDP showed U-shaped change that first declined then rose before 2000, while it changed steadily from 2000 to 2008. GERD/GDP was fluctuating upward from 2009 to 2012 and then declined obviously after 2012. Specifically, GERD/GDP declined from more than 1.5% in 1992 to less

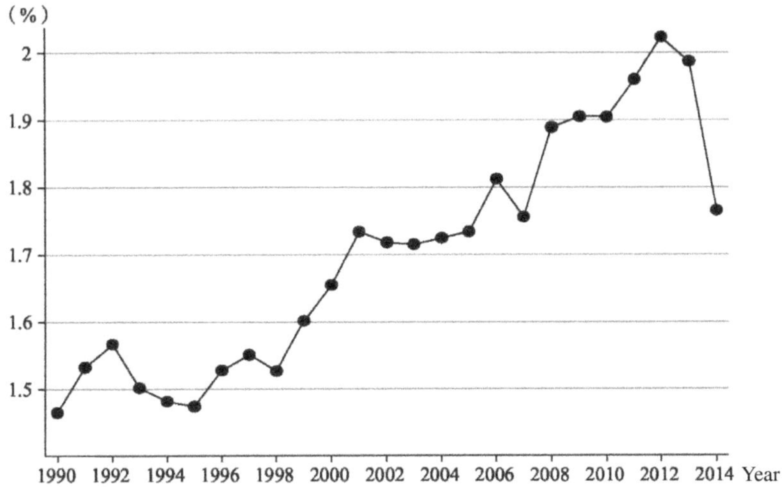

Figure 3. Mean Value of GERD/GDP in OECD Countries

Source: Database of Main Science and Technology Indicators, OECD Stat.

than 1.5% in 1995, and then rose in fluctuation to around 1.65% in 2000, which was consistent with the above-mentioned change trend of technical efficiency. GERD/GDP remained at about 1.75% from 2000 to 2008 and fluctuated around 1.9% from 2009 to 2011.

Therefore, the change trend of GERD/GDP may be one of the main factors that caused the fluctuation of the above-mentioned production technology and production efficiency. In terms of the change trend, the technical change index fluctuated greatly around 1998, 2001 and 2011, while the technical efficiency index fluctuated greatly around 1992, 1997, 2002 and 2007. The change in GERD/GDP was basically consistent with the trends of technical efficiency index and technical change index, which indicates that the R&D investment index provides a strong explanation for the trend of technical change.

Furthermore, from the distribution of the sample countries with a high proportion of GERD in GDP, for countries with a high proportion of GERD in GDP from 1990 to 2014, such as Germany, Denmark, France, South Korea, Israel, Finland and Iceland, their mean values of total factor productivity change were all higher than 0.9, and among those major stimuli to technical change, the values of pure technical efficiency change were all greater than 1. This indicates that the rise of GERD/GDP has

Table 3. Mean Value of GERD/GDP in OECD Countries (%)

Country	GERD/GDP	Country	GERD/GDP
Israel	3.549	Norway	1.604
Sweden	3.319	Luxembourg	1.531
Japan	3.056	Czech	1.232
Finland	2.959	Island	1.22
South Korea	2.636	Estonia	1.155
Switzerland	2.588	Slovenia	1.138
Germany	2.444	Italy	1.092
Denmark	2.313	New Zealand	1.07
France	2.163	Hungary	0.947
United Kingdom	2.152	Portugal	0.865
Iceland	2.117	Poland	0.67
Australia	1.976	Greece	0.561
Belgium	1.874	Turkey	0.542
Netherlands	1.818	Mexico	0.374
Canada	1.786	Chile	0.351

Source: Database of Main Science and Technology Indicators, OECD Stat.

promoted the upgrading of technical change to a certain extent, and its promotion of pure technical efficiency change was particularly evident.

Similarly, as shown in the scatter diagram of GERD/GDP and total factor productivity distribution, GERD/GDP and total factor productivity are positively correlated with each other. In other words, GERD/GDP is one of the major factors to promote the improvement of total factor productivity. Furthermore, for countries with a high proportion of GERD in GDP such as France, Germany, Denmark, South Korea, Japan and Finland, their total factor productivity was all at a high level. However, for countries with a low proportion of GERD in GDP such as Mexico, New Zealand and Poland, their total factor productivity was at a lower level (see Figure 4).

2.2. *Characteristics of R&D investment under different industrial structures*

In terms of the overall R&D investment mentioned previously, the trend of GERD/GDP was almost consistent with those of technical efficiency

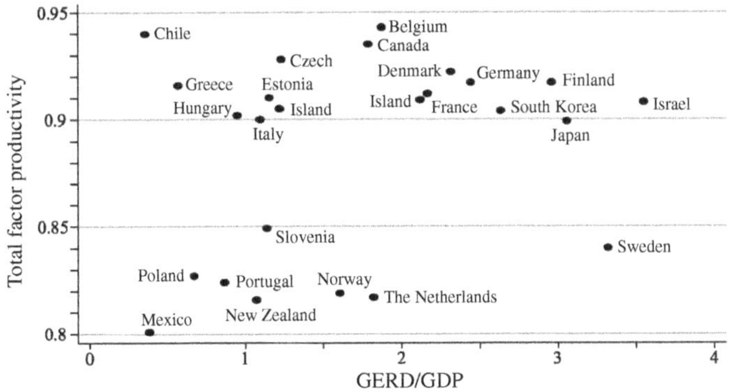

Figure 4. Scatter Diagram of GERD/GDP and Total Factor Productivity Distribution in OECD Countries

Source: Database of Main Science and Technology Indicators, OECD Stat.

change and technology change. In other words, the R&D investment index provides a strong explanation for the trend of technical change. On this basis, this chapter further analyzes the major effects of industrial structure on world technological progress, from the change trend of the scale of R&D investment under different industrial structures.

From the R&D expenditures under different industrial structures shown in Table 4 and Figure 5, the distribution of R&D expenditures in various industries saw an inverse U-shaped change that first rose then declined from 1990 to 2013. Among them, the R&D expenditures in various industries were fluctuating upward from 1990 to 2008, but it has declined obviously since 2008. This explains the stable situation of technical change and technical efficiency change in total factor productivity in 21st century to a certain extent. In other words, the decline of R&D investment in industries had an obvious constraint effect on technology upgrading and innovation.

In terms of different industrial structures, the R&D expenditure in manufacturing was the highest from 1990 to 2013, followed by that in service industry, construction industry, electric power, gas, water supply industry, mining industry and agriculture. Among them, the increase of R&D expenditure in the service industry was obviously at a higher speed than that in manufacturing, but the decrease of R&D expenditure in agriculture was most significant, declining from the peak value of 838.1 million dollars in 2007 to 46.78 million dollars in 2013.

Table 4. Distribution of R&D Expenditure in Various Industries in OECD Countries from 1990 to 2013 (In 100 Million Dollars)

Year	Agriculture	Mining	Manufacturing	Electric Power, Gas, Water Supply	Construction	Services
1990	2.495	4.059	2 136.49	13.71	16.45	172.48
1991	3.356	8.063	2 550.74	14.97	16.81	222.42
1992	2.44	4.176	2 094.11	17.03	17.81	257.56
1993	5.087	8.148	2 412.97	19.56	19.21	378.96
1994	2.326	3.761	1 975.36	16.81	15.84	451.06
1995	3.91	5.603	2 492.78	19.54	24.29	493.21
1996	2.404	4.935	2 135.26	18.88	23.94	500.8
1997	4.351	8.136	2 578.94	20.79	24.79	522.91
1998	4.19	10.79	2 342.23	20.55	19.03	567.77
1999	5.566	10.91	2 900.72	19.53	26.05	639.81
2000	2.578	9.061	3 037.68	11.64	25.26	663.56
2001	4.829	12.3	3 114.82	13.89	24.59	948.7
2002	4.172	12.07	3 041.81	13.19	30.94	1 074.17
2003	4.991	26.23	3 097.78	13.58	26.55	1 202.49
2004	4.344	16.94	3 180.27	14.49	28.12	1 228
2005	5.901	20.89	3 155.22	16.09	26.95	1 294.01
2006	6.331	29.14	3 475.58	20.37	28.09	1 372.5
2007	8.381	34.68	3 978.93	22.15	45.12	1 379.56
2008	5.839	40.68	3 804.39	19.35	41.79	1 307.5
2009	3.944	28.03	3 267.43	17.56	43.73	1 252.32
2010	2.462	37.84	3 121.65	14.8	29.45	1 008.54
2011	2.97	36.2	3 240.61	13.18	24.79	1 021.29
2012	0.848 2	0.694 1	3 136.37	11.31	20.36	164.49
2013	0.467 8	0.645 9	1 405.43	7.922	19.59	150.08
Total	94.18	373.98	67 680	390.86	619.57	18 270

Source: Database of Business enterprise R-D expenditure, OECD Stat. The industry classification standard is based on ISIC revision 3.1. Among them, the R&D expenditure data is calculated at constant prices in 2005.

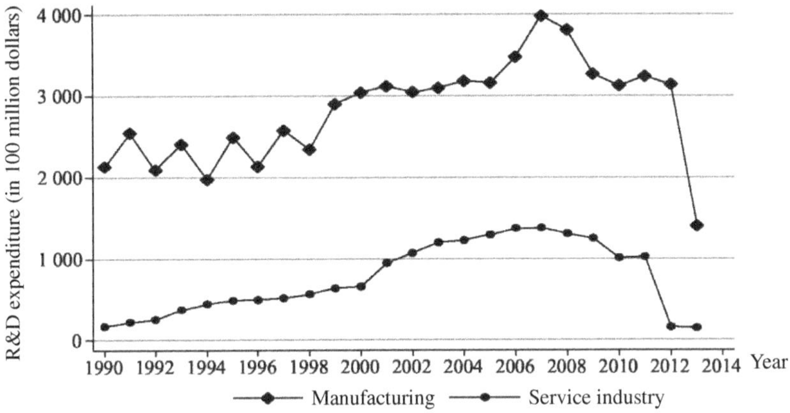

Figure 5. Trend of R&D Expenditure in Manufacturing and Service Industry in OECD Countries

Source: Database of Main Science and Technology Indicators, OECD Stat.

In terms of the scale of R&D expenditure in various industries in the sample countries, it saw a significant differentiation trend. That is, some countries had the largest R&D expenditure in manufacturing, while some countries had the largest one in the service industry. Among them, some traditional industrial powers such as the United States, Japan, Germany, South Korea, Italy, Canada, the Netherlands and Spain had much higher R&D expenditure in manufacturing than that in the service industry. However, the countries like Australia and Israel had much higher R&D expenditure in the service industry than that in manufacturing (see Table 5). On the one hand, it reflects that the slowdown of technological progress in OECD countries is mainly due to the decrease of the growth of R&D expenditure in manufacturing. On the other hand, it also shows that increasing R&D expenditure in the service industry has not enabled remarkable improvement in the general technical level.

2.3. *Characteristics of R&D expenditure in sub-sectors of manufacturing*

In terms of the change trend of R&D expenditure in different industries mentioned earlier, the R&D expenditure in manufacturing saw an obvious

Table 5. R&D Expenditure in Various Industries in OECD Countries (In 100 Million dollars)

Country	Agriculture	Mining	Manufacturing	Electric Power, Gas, Water Supply	Construction	Services
United States	0.61	39.57	31,880.00	55.67	76.07	11,570.00
Japan	11.98	34.33	18,260.00	151.44	290.49	1,699.22
Germany	11.17	9.80	5,406.14	15.33	9.00	431.81
South Korea	4.65	3.14	4,125.31	54.42	141.93	413.10
Italy	0.06	10.84	1,385.74	25.15	5.23	333.23
Canada	10.76	44.15	1 145.47	16.58	3.06	651.53
Netherlands	13.70	13.96	715.78	3.28	7.27	149.41
Spain	11.58	5.25	645.79	17.94	17.17	369.01
Sweden	2.17	1.42	518.94	4.42	0.33	127.33
Finland	0.23	1.08	443.91	3.96	4.26	97.90
Belgium	3.26	0.44	434.22	1.59	7.72	186.71
Australia	6.54	183.35	347.13	13.61	40.49	443.82
France	1.58	0.10	305.93	7.80	2.32	191.61
Israel	0	0	294.01	6.39	0	452.52
Austria	0.19	0.66	197.80	0.91	1.45	76.11
Mexico	0.23	4.41	180.68	1.83	0.68	62.46
Czech	0.89	1.27	172.18	0.40	2.91	96.23
Switzerland	0	0	163.49	0	0	32.58
Turkey	0.82	0.88	159.99	1.58	0.61	48.48
Island	0.45	0.05	115.29	0.03	0.01	26.74
Denmark	0.23	0	102.11	0.48	0.48	64.61
Hungary	4.97	0.05	98.13	0.93	0.46	32.03
Norway	2.73	13.84	91.45	0.93	2.27	102.86
New Zealand	3.00	0.16	23.11	0.04	0.18	18.70
Slovakia	0.54	0	22.53	0	0.14	31.17
Iceland	0.32	0.01	5.98	0.28	0.18	9.16
Luxembourg	0	0	5.91	0	0	7.39
Chile	0.48	0.49	2.29	0.04	0.13	7.50
Estonia	0.01	0.02	1.79	0.13	0	4.23

Source: The same as Table 4. Part of the data in sample countries are missing.

characteristic of inverse U-shaped change. Based on this, this chapter will further analyze the change trend of R&D expenditure in sub-sectors of manufacturing, so as to reveal the sub-sector characteristics of the trend of R&D expenditure in manufacturing and provide further empirical evidence in sub-sectors for the trends of world technological progress.

Firstly, as shown in Figure 6 and Table 6, the largest R&D expenditures within the manufacturing are those in its two sub-sectors, namely coke, petroleum, nuclear fuel, chemicals (hereinafter called "oil and chemicals"), metal products, mechanical equipment, tools and transportation (hereinafter called "metal products and mechanical equipment"). Their change trends were basically in accordance with the general change trend of manufacturing. Bounded by the peak value in 2008, they also showed the obvious characteristic of inverse U-shaped change. The scale of R&D expenditure and the range of change in metal products and mechanical equipment were much higher than those in oil and chemical. Among them, the changing trend in metal products and mechanical equipment saw an obvious U-shaped characteristic from 1990 to 1998, which was in accordance with the characteristics of technical change. This further proves that the change of technical efficiency, to a large extent, came from the change of R&D expenditures in these two

Figure 6. R&D Expenditure in Sub-Sectors of Manufacturing in OECD Countries

Source: Database of Main Science and Technology Indicators, OECD Stat.

Table 6. Distribution of R&D Expenditure in Sub-Sectors of Manufacturing (In 100 Million Dollars)

Year	1990	1993	1996	1999	2002	2003	2006	2009	2013
Food, Beverages, Tobacco, Textiles	23.42	46.83	29.76	50.46	62.38	69.61	84.18	85.89	24.86
Fur and Leather	7.746	10.44	7.836	16.65	16.03	14.28	22.99	23.39	15.49
Wood, Paper, Printing, Publication	10.95	14.41	12.51	19.51	18.7	21.63	24.51	41.86	6.14
Coke, Petroleum, Nuclear Fuel, Chemicals	181.09	268.38	221.04	578.63	590.31	639.3	921.82	824.32	266.75
Basic Metals	47.55	49.23	33.64	42.84	38.01	42.72	52.3	50.85	31.47
Metal products, Mechanical Equipment, Tools and Transportation	1 482.66	1 565.65	1 691.46	2 107.09	2 084.03	2 170.75	2 610.83	2 304.27	1 030.9
Furniture and Other Manufacturing	6.508	8.185	8.975	13.2	13.75	15.34	18.81	41.5	13.3

Source: The same as Table 4.

sub-sectors in manufacturing, namely metal products and mechanical equipment, oil and chemicals.

Secondly, from the change trend of R&D expenditures of other sub-sectors within manufacturing, as shown in Figure 7, the change trend of R&D expenditures of other sub-sectors was in accordance with that of the whole industry, also showing an inverse U-shape characteristic. Among them, the sectors of food, beverages, tobacco, textile and basic metals had the highest R&D expenditure among the remaining sub-sectors, while the R&D expenditure of other sub-sectors within manufacturing remained at a similar level. The changing trend of R&D expenditures in sectors of food, beverages, tobacco and textile saw an obvious U-shape characteristic from 1990 to 1998, which was in accordance with that of metal products and mechanical equipment sector. This further proves the assertion that the change of technical efficiency from 1990 to 1998 was mainly driven by the change of R&D expenditures in those two major sub-sectors in manufacturing, namely oil and chemicals, metal products and mechanical equipment.

Furthermore, from the R&D expenditures of sub-sectors in manufacturing in the sample countries shown in Table 7, as for two sub-sectors with the largest expenditures among manufacturing sub-sectors in sample

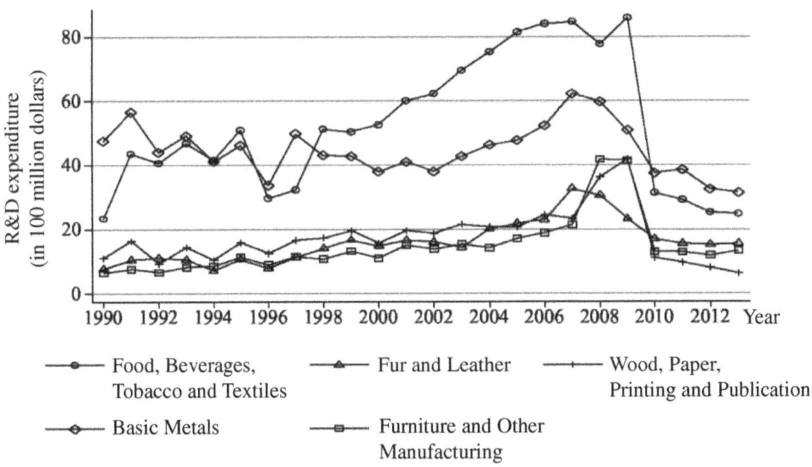

Figure 7. R&D Expenditure in Sub-Sectors of Manufacturing in OECD Countries

Source: Database of Main Science and Technology Indicators, OECD Stat.

countries, they were still metal products and mechanical equipment, oil and chemicals. For some traditional industrial powers such as the United States, Japan, Germany, South Korea, Italy, Canada and Spain, their R&D expenditure of metal products and mechanical equipment was several times more than that of oil and chemicals. On the one hand, this reflects that the slowdown of technological progress in manufacturing in OECD countries was mainly due to the decrease of the growth of R&D expenditure in these two major sub-sectors of metal products and mechanical equipment, oil and chemicals. On the other hand, it also shows that increasing R&D expenditure in sub-sectors of the manufacturing industry has not enabled remarkable improvement in the general technical level in manufacturing.

2.4. *The general characteristics of world technology R&D investment*

Overall, from the perspective of world technology R&D investment, the trend of the influence of R&D investment on world technological progress mainly enjoys several characteristics as follows.

Firstly, the proportion of world R&D expenditure (in GDP) has noticeable characteristics of stages, and the R&D investment indicators provide a strong explanation for the trend of technical change. That is, GERD/GDP saw U-shaped change that first declined then rose before 2000, while it changed steadily from 2000 to 2008; GERD/GDP was fluctuating upward from 2009 to 2012 and then declined obviously after 2012. Specifically, the trend of GERD/GDP from 1992 to 2000 was in accordance with that of the overall technical efficiency; the trend of GERD/GDP from 2000 to 2008 was almost in accordance with that of technology change. Therefore, GERD/GDP may be one of the main factors that caused the fluctuation of the aforementioned production technology and production efficiency.

Secondly, in terms of the distribution of the sample countries with different proportion of GERD in GDP, the rise of GERD/GDP promoted the upgrading of technical change to a certain extent and its promotion of the change of pure technical efficiency was especially significant. Specifically, for countries with a higher proportion of GERD in GDP from 1990 to 2014, such as Germany, Denmark, France, South Korea, Israel, Finland and Iceland, their mean values of total factor productivity change were all

Table 7. R&D Expenditure in Sub-Sectors of Manufacturing in Different Countries (In 100 Million Dollars)

Country	U.S.A.	Japan	Germany	South Korea	Italy	Canada	Netherlands	Sweden	Spain
Food, Beverages, Tobacco, Textiles	400.32	465.66	38.93	58.57	24.57	19.87	50.31	4.35	30.04
Fur and Leather	59.27	164.36	29.63	30.37	23.22	9.83	3.18	0.77	15.65
Wood, Paper, Printing, Publication	42.76	181.14	24.74	13.57	8.4	51.42	5.76	15.57	11.08
Coke, Petroleum, Nuclear Fuel, Chemicals	4 030.93	3 823.43	1 029.99	459.94	280.63	189.23	237.5	94.54	178.83
Basic Metals	140.59	606.36	46.04	78.65	17.87	30.03	8.69	9.76	13.5
Metal products, Mechanical Equipment, Tools and Transportation	18 640	12 510	3 764.73	3 432.3	1 071.61	820.91	401.43	379.4	371.07
Furniture and Other Manufacturing	49.68	195.92	20.09	15.37	10.06	9.95	2.54	1.28	9.32

Source: The same as Table 4.

higher than 0.9, and among those major stimuli to the technical change, the values of the pure technical efficiency change were all above 1.

Thirdly, from the perspective of R&D expenditure under different industrial structures, the decline of R&D investment in industries has generated an obvious constraint effect on technology upgrading and innovation. Specifically, the distribution of R&D expenditures in various industries saw an inverse U-shaped characteristic that first rose then declined from 1990 to 2013. Among them, the R&D expenditures in various industries were fluctuating upward from 1990 to 2008, but has been declining obviously since 2008. This was in accordance with the trends of technical change and technical efficiency change in total factor productivity in 21st century to a certain extent. In other words, the decline of R&D investment in industries had an obvious constraint effect on technology upgrading and innovation.

Fourthly, the scale of R&D expenditure in various industries in different countries presented a significant differentiation trend. That is, some countries had the largest R&D expenditure in manufacturing while some countries had the largest R&D expenditure in the service industry. Among them, some traditional industrial powers such as the United States, Japan, Germany, South Korea, Italy, Canada, the Netherlands and Spain had much higher R&D expenditure in manufacturing than that in the service industry. However, the countries like Australia and Israel had much higher R&D expenditure in the service industry than that in manufacturing. On the one hand, it reflects that the slowdown of technological progress in OECD countries was mainly due to the decrease of the growth of R&D expenditure in manufacturing. On the other hand, it also shows that increasing R&D expenditure in the service industry has not enabled remarkable improvement in the general technical level.

Fifthly, from the perspective of sub-sectors in manufacturing, the change of technical efficiency came from the change of R&D expenditure in sub-sectors in manufacturing, including metal products and mechanical equipment, food, beverages, tobacco and textile to a large extent. Specifically, for two sub-sectors with the largest scale of R&D expenditure, namely oil and chemicals, metal products and mechanical equipment, their R&D expenditure saw an obvious characteristic of inverse U-shaped change. Among them, for the sub-sectors of metal products and mechanical equipment, food, beverages, tobacco and textile, their R&D expenditures saw an obvious characteristic of U-shaped change from 1990 to 1998, which was in accordance with the trend of technical efficiency change. It further proves that the change of technical efficiency mainly came from the change of R&D expenditure in these two subsectors in manufacturing, namely metal products and mechanical equipment, oil and chemicals.

3. Analyses of the Trend and the Characteristics of the Technical Patent Innovation in the World

This chapter will further analyze and describe the main fields in which production technologies change in various countries from the perspective of patent innovation, an important output indicator of world technological progress, based on the analysis of the trend of R&D expenditure in the above countries.

3.1. *General state of the patent innovation in the world*

The patent innovation can greatly reflect the state of technological progress in terms of the output of technological innovation. Based on it, this chapter will describe and analyze the state of patent innovation in the world with the data from the European Patent Office (EPO) system database.

From the patent applications shown in Figure 8, the amount of EPO patent applications had noticeable characteristics of stages from 1990 to 2011. The number of patent applications was fluctuating upward from 1990 to 2000, increasing from 67,000 in 1990 to 129,600 in 2000; however, the annual EPO patent applications have fluctuated stably around 130,000 steadily since 2001, which did not increase obviously and even decreased in some periods. On the whole, the increase of patent applications after 2001 has further proved the low-speed growth of technical efficiency and technical change since the 21st century.

3.2. *Distribution of the industries for the patent innovation in the world*

From the industry distribution of patent applications from 1990 to 2011 (see Table 8), there were five fields where patent applications mainly concentrated, including network and telecommunication (ICT), electric power, physics, operations and transportation as well as human necessities. It can

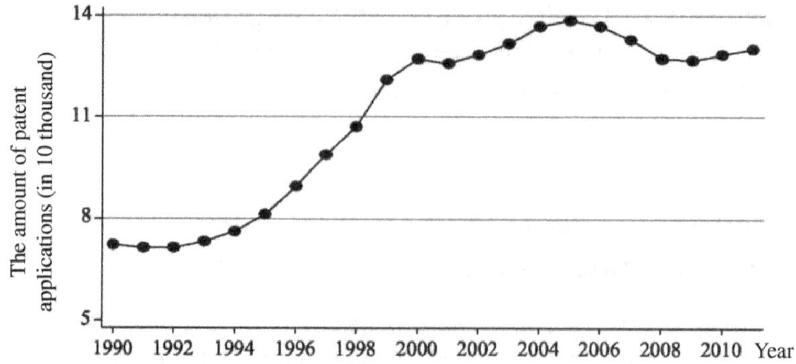

Figure 8. EPO Patent Applications from 1990 to 2011

Source: Main science and technology indicators database, OECD Stat.

be seen in these five technical fields that network and telecommunications (ICT) had a much larger proportion of patent applications than that of other technical fields, which indicates that ICT is still the core area of technology research and development. Meanwhile, there were a smaller proportion of patent applications in the fields corresponding to new technology frontiers such as biotechnology and nanotechnology, which indicates that the development in these fields is still at a less mature stage.

The patent applications had noticeable characteristics of stages from the perspective of the average annual growth rate (AAGR) of patent applications: the AAGR of patent applications from 1990 to 1999 was significantly higher than that from 2000 to 2011. On the whole, there were five technical fields with the highest average annual growth rates, that is, nanotechnology, medical technology, electric power, mechanical engineering and photothermal, as well as human necessities. However, in terms of different stages, those five technical fields with the highest average annual growth rates were nanotechnology, biotechnology, medical technology, electric power and human necessities from 1990 to 1999, and the average annual growth rates from 2000 to 2011 were mostly lower than those from 1990 to 1999 in the above five technical fields. In addition, there were a large number of patent applications only in the fields of electric power and human necessities among those technical fields with high annual growth rates, and the average annual growth rates were less than 4% in the rest of the industries with a large number of patent applications.

Overall, the patent innovation activities in various technology fields have the characteristics and trends as follows.

Table 8. Industry Distribution of EPO Patent Applications from 1990 to 2011

	Amount of Application (In 10,000)					Growth Rate (%)		
	1990–1994	1995–1998	1999–2003	2004–2007	2008–2011	1990–1999	2000–2011	1990–2011
Network and Telecommunication	9.54	11.32	17.59	18.35	20.52	9.21	2.62	2.31
Electric Power	4.91	6.24	9.22	10.08	12.52	10.29	5.49	5.12
Physics	5.41	5.69	8.46	9.59	10.83	6.52	3.79	3.37
Human Necessities	4.55	5.41	7.75	9.18	10.8	9.40	4.71	4.73
Operations and Transportation	5.92	6.09	7.62	8.49	10.15	5.18	3.09	2.85
Chemistry and Metallurgy	5.59	5.39	6.47	6.94	7.89	3.94	1.58	1.45
Mechanical Engineering and Photothermal	2.52	2.77	3.79	4.52	6.39	6.99	5.34	5.07
Biotechnology	1.83	2.4	3.68	3.28	3.42	11.37	3.49	3.42
Medical Technology	1.91	2.3	3.48	4.2	5.14	10.41	5.91	6.05
Fixed Buildings	0.96	1.03	1.23	1.42	2	6.36	4.43	3.93
Textile and Papermaking	0.67	0.62	0.71	0.76	0.83	2.50	0.98	0.75
Nanotechnology	0.18	0.21	0.45	0.57	0.51	11.83	6.20	6.20

Source: Calculated based on relevant indicators from the Main Science and Technology Indicators database, OECD Stat.

Firstly, the technological innovation activities are often immature in the fields with the rapid growth of patent applications, such as nanotechnology, medical technology, and electric power and so on, and the innovation activities account for a lower proportion in the overall scale of patent innovation. Therefore, their promotion of technological progress is not significant, especially of technological change, which leads to the slowdown in global technological progress since the 21st century.

Secondly, the patent innovation enjoys noticeable characteristics of stages. That is, the growth rates of the patent applications from 1990 to 1999 were often significantly higher than those from 2000 to 2011, and this was in accordance with the characteristic of world technological progress obtained in this chapter, that is, the characteristic of total factor productivity change. That is to say, the characteristic of technology upgrading was quite obvious before the 21st century, and the global technological progress slows down in the 21st century, in particular closely associated with the characteristic of steady fluctuation of the technical change and the technical efficiency change

Thirdly, with the slowdown in global technological progress, information technology has brought about a technological revolution, but the effect has gradually weakened, and the patent innovation has been increasing rapidly in the fields of technology frontiers such as biotechnology, nanotechnology and so on. Network and telecommunication technology are still dominant in the field of the patent technology, but their growth in technological innovation have been decreasing rapidly.

3.3. *Country distribution of the patent innovation in the world*

From the perspective of the patent innovation activities in the world, traditional industrial powers such as the United States, Germany, Japan and France played a leading role in patent applications among those five major fields where the patent applications were rather concentrated from 1990 to 2011, including network and telecommunications, electric power, physics, operation and transportation as well as human necessities. And the patent applications of the aforementioned countries were also at a high level in the emerging technology fields such as nanotechnology, medical technology and so on (see Table 9).

Table 9. EPO Patent Applications from 1990 to 2011 in OECD Sample Countries (In 10,000)

Industry	Totals	Germany	U.S.A.	Japan	France	Italy	U.K.	Switzerland	Sweden	South Korea
Network and Telecommunication	77.32	9.96	24.2	18.05	4.59	1.35	3.78	1.23	1.65	3.14
Electric Power	42.96	6.35	11.53	10.15	2.85	0.89	1.86	0.65	1.14	2.21
Physics	39.98	5.66	12.57	9.03	2.45	0.78	2.08	0.92	0.63	1.20
Human Necessities	38.26	10.31	7.66	6.57	3.07	2.17	1.65	1.19	0.87	0.34
Operations and Transportation	37.69	5.63	13.97	3.47	2.70	1.65	2.20	1.24	0.78	0.44
Chemistry and Metallurgy	32.28	5.71	10.67	5.92	1.89	0.85	1.63	0.75	0.33	0.46
Mechanical Engineering and Photothermal	19.98	5.92	3.60	3.39	1.64	1.00	0.95	0.46	0.46	0.38
Biotechnology	17.04	2.15	7.73	1.71	0.75	0.48	0.84	0.53	0.45	0.15
Medical Technology	14.62	1.57	6.50	1.56	0.79	0.27	0.84	0.28	0.22	0.18
Fixed Buildings	6.64	1.97	0.99	0.27	0.63	0.47	0.47	0.25	0.17	0.05
Textile and Papermaking	3.59	0.88	0.69	0.46	0.20	0.32	0.13	0.18	0.10	0.14
Nanotechnology	1.91	0.22	0.69	0.44	0.12	0.03	0.09	0.03	0.02	0.07

Source: Calculated on the basis of relevant indicators from the Main Science and Technology Indicators database, OECD Stat.

4. Main Conclusions of World Technological Progress

With the Malmquist index approach of DEA non-parametric estimation, it is found in this chapter that world technological progress has been slowing down since the 21st century. Based on this, from the perspective of technology R&D input and output, the reasons for the characteristics of world technological progress are further analyzed and its trends are discussed from the aspects of industry, country and technology field. On the whole, some conclusions can be drawn as follows in this chapter.

Firstly, world technological progress has been slow since 2000. The change of total factor productivity has been generally fluctuating upward, but the growth of productivity has been slow since 2000. The overall improvement of total factor productivity was mainly contributed by the increase of technical efficiency instead of the improvement of technology. The slow technological progress since 2000 had a great constraint effect on the increase of total factor productivity, which was consistent with the trend of total factor productivity.

Secondly, the proportion of the world R&D expenditure (in GDP) has noticeable characteristics of stages, and the R&D investment indicators provide a strong explanation for the trend of technical change. GERD/GDP saw U-shaped change that first declined then rose before 2000, while it changed steadily from 2000 to 2008; GERD/GDP was fluctuating upward from 2009 to 2012 and then declined obviously after 2012. Specifically, the trend of GERD/GDP from 1992 to 2000 was in accordance with that of the overall technical efficiency; the trend of GERD/GDP from 2000 to 2008 was almost in accordance with that of technology change. Therefore, GERD/GDP may be one of the main factors that caused the fluctuation of the aforementioned production technology and production efficiency.

Thirdly, the rise of GERD/GDP has promoted the upgrading of technical change to a certain extent, and its promotion of pure technical efficiency change was particularly evident. At the same time, from the perspective of sectors of the manufacturing industry, the technical efficiency change came from the change of R&D expenditure two sub-sectors, namely metal products and mechanical equipment, oil and chemicals to a large extent. Specifically, for the countries with a higher proportion of GERD in GDP from 1990 to 2014, such as Germany, Denmark, France, South Korea, Israel, Finland and Iceland, their mean values of total factor productivity change were all higher than 0.9, and among those major stimuli to technical change, the values of the pure technical efficiency change were all above 1. From 1990 to 1998, the R&D expenditure in the industries including metal products and mechanical equipment, food, beverages, tobacco and textile saw an obvious U-shaped characteristic, which was in accordance with the characteristics of technical change.

Fourthly, the scale of R&D expenditures in various industries presented a significant differentiation trend, and the decline of R&D investment in industries has generated an obvious constraint effect on technology upgrading and innovation. Specifically, R&D expenditure in various industries from 1990 to 2008 presented a significant downward trend after 2008, which was consistent with the steady trend of technical change and technical efficiency change in total factor productivity in the 21st century to a certain extent. In addition, some countries have the largest R&D expenditure in manufacturing and some have the largest R&D expenditure in the service industry. On the one hand, it reflects that the slowdown of technological progress in OECD countries is mainly due to the decrease of the growth of R&D expenditure in manufacturing. On the other hand, it shows that increasing R&D expenditure in the service industry has not enabled a significant improvement in the general technical level.

Fifthly, the field of patented technology had noticeable characteristics of stages in terms of the output of technological innovation. The slow increase of patent applications after 2001 has further proved the low-speed growth of technical efficiency and technical change since the 21st century. The number of patent applications was fluctuating upward from 1990 to 2000. However, the (annual) EPO patent applications have fluctuated stably around 130,000 steadily since 2001, which did not increase obviously and even decreased in some periods. In addition, the growth rates of patent applications from 1990 to 1999 were often higher than those from 2000 to 2011 significantly, which was in accordance with the characteristic of world technological progress obtained in this chapter, that is, the characteristic of total factor productivity change.

Sixthly, the fields of emerging technology do not show a strong promotion of technical change. The technological innovation activities are often immature in the fields with rapid growth of patent applications, such as nanotechnology, medical technology, electric power and so on, and the innovation activities account for a lower proportion in the overall scale of patent innovation. Therefore, their promotion of technological progress is not significant, especially of technological change. Information technology has brought about a technological revolution, but its effect has gradually weakened under the background of the slowdown in global technological progress, and the patent innovation has been increasing rapidly in the fields of technology frontiers such as biotechnology, nanotechnology and so on. Network and telecommunication technology are still dominant in the field of the patent technology, but their growth in technological innovation growth have been decreasing rapidly.

Chapter 8

China's OFDI Pattern within the Framework of "The Belt and Road"

The significant initiatives proposed by President Xi Jinping in 2013 to co-build the "Silk Road Economic Belt" and the "21st Century Maritime Silk Road" have been highly concerned by the international community and responded positively by related countries. China's foreign direct investment (FDI) in the Belt and Road Initiative countries (BRI countries) enjoys a rapid development correspondingly. Therefore, it is of theoretical and practical significance to study the current situation, existing problems and countermeasures of China's outward foreign direct investment (OFDI) pattern within the framework of "the Belt and Road".

1. The Scale of China's OFDI within the Framework of "The Belt and Road"

1.1. *The position of China's OFDI among global OFDI*

China's OFDI has increased rapidly since China implemented its "going globally" strategy in 2000. China's OFDI flows in 2014 was 123.12 billion dollars, ranking the third in the world for three consecutive years, accounting for 9.1% of the global total OFDI flows of 1.35 trillion dollars in that year. As of the end of 2014, 18,500 Chinese domestic investors had set up 29,700 OFDI enterprises abroad (overseas), distributed in 186 countries (regions) all over the world. In 2014, China's OFDI stock was 882.64 billion dollars, ranking the eighth in the world, accounting for

Table 1. Top 10 OFDI Countries (Regions) in the World in 2014

	Flows			Stocks		
Ranking	Country (Region)	Amount (In 100 Million Dollars)	Global proportion (%)	Country (Region)	Amount (In 100 Million Dollars)	Global proportion (%)
1	U.S.A.	3,369	25.0	U.S.A.	63,186	24.4
2	Hong Kong, China	1,427	10.6	U.K.	15,841	6.1
3	China	1,231	9.1	Germany	15,833	6.1
4	Japan	1,136	8.4	Hong Kong, China	14,599	5.6
5	Germany	1,122	8.3	France	12,791	4.9
6	Russia	564	0.4	Japan	11,931	4.6
7	Canada	526	0.4	Netherlands	9,853	3.8
8	Netherlands	408	0.3	China	8,826.4	3.4
9	Singapore	407	0.3	Singapore	5,764	2.2
10	South Korea	306	0.2	Italy	5,484	2.1

Source: World Investment Report 2015.

3.4% of the global total OFDI stock of 25.87 trillion dollars in that year (see Table 1).

1.2. *The position of China's FDI in BRI countries among its overall OFDI*

Along the routes of the "Silk Road Economic Belt" and the "21st Century Maritime Silk Road", there are 64 BRI countries and regions involved, including China, Mongolia, East Timor, Singapore, Malaysia, Indonesia, Myanmar, Thailand, Laos, Cambodia, Vietnam, Brunei, the Philippines, Iran, Iraq, Turkey, Syria, Jordan, Lebanon, Israel, Palestine, Saudi Arabia, Yemen, Oman, the United Arab Emirates, Qatar, Kuwait, Bahrain, Egypt, India, Pakistan, Bengal, Afghanistan, Sri Lanka, Maldives, Nepal, Kazakhstan, Uzbekistan, Turkmenistan, Tajikistan, Kyrgyzstan, Russia, Ukraine, Belarus, Georgia, Azerbaijan, Armenia, Moldova, Poland, Lithuania, Estonia, Latvia, Czech, Slovakia, Hungary,

Slovenia, Croatia, Bosnia and Herzegovina, Montenegro, Serbia, Albania, Romania, Bulgaria and Macedonia.

BRI countries have gradually become the important destinations of China's OFDI. In terms of flows, China's FDI flows in BRI countries rose rapidly from 200 million dollars in 2003 to 13.66 billion dollars in 2014, with an increase of 67.3 times over 12 years. And the proportion of China's overall OFDI flows in that year increased from 7.1% to 11.1%, with an average annual increase of about 51%, which was higher than the growth rate of China's investment in other regions over the same period, and the growth was particularly obvious after the financial crisis in 2008.[1] It can be seen that although BRI countries are not currently the main destinations for China's OFDI, their importance is increasing and they have become one of the important locations. In terms of stocks, as of 2014, China's FDI stock in BRI countries reached 92.46 billion dollars, accounting for 10.5% of China's overall OFDI stock, while the stock and the proportion in 2003 were only 1.34 billion dollars and 4%, respectively (see Table 2).

2. China's OFDI Structure within the Framework of "The Belt and Road"

2.1. *Regional distribution of China's FDI in BRI countries*

There are great differences in the regional distribution of China's OFDI in BRI countries (see Table 3). Among them, the largest investment was in 10 ASEAN countries. The investment flows in 5 Central Asian countries increased rapidly, presenting a dramatic increase trend especially in the year 2012 and 2013, from 454 million dollars in 2011 to 3,377 million dollars (in 2012) and 1,099 million (in 2013). However, China's investments in South Asia and Central and Eastern Europe were obviously inadequate, including those in 7 South Asian countries and especially in 16 Central and Eastern European countries. In 2014, China's FDI flows in these two regions were only 1,515 million dollars and 204 million dollars, respectively.

[1]Calculation based on the data from the annual Statistical Bulletin of China's Outward Foreign Direct Investment from China Ministry of Commerce, National Bureau of Statistics and China State Administration of Foreign Exchange.

Table 2. China's FDI stocks in BRI Countries from 2003 to 2014

	2003	2004	2005	2006	2007	2008	2009	2010	2011	2012	2013	2014
China's FDI stocks in BRI Countries (in 100 million dollars)	13.4	19.5	34.1	52.7	97.3	149.8	202.6	292.5	416.8	567.6	720.2	924.6
China's total OFDI stocks (in 100 million dollars)	332.0	448.0	572.0	906.3	1179.1	1839.7	2457.5	3172.1	4247.8	5319.4	6604.8	8826.4
Proportion of FDI stocks in BRI countries in China's total OFDI stocks (%)	4.0	4.4	6.0	5.8	8.3	8.1	8.2	9.2	9.8	10.7	10.9	10.5

Table 3. Regional Distribution of China's FDI Flows in BRI Countries (2006–2014) (in 100 Million Dollars)

Year	2006	2007	2008	2009	2010	2011	2012	2013	2014	Total
10 ASEAN countries	3.36	9.68	24.84	26.98	44.05	59.05	61.00	72.67	78.09	379.72
16 Western Asian countries	2.56	2.47	2.08	7.31	11.00	13.36	14.48	21.47	21.21	95.94
5 Central Asian countries	0.80	3.77	6.56	3.45	5.80	4.54	33.77	10.99	5.51	75.19
7 CIS countries	4.68	4.90	4.52	3.60	6.29	7.44	8.99	11.65	9.43	61.50
7 South Asian countries	−0.49	9.36	4.95	0.79	4.17	9.09	4.41	4.63	15.15	52.06
16 Central and Eastern European countries	0.19	0.32	0.38	0.39	4.19	1.30	1.51	1.02	2.04	11.34

At the end of 2014, China's FDI flows and stocks in 10 ASEAN countries were 7,809 million dollars and 47,633 million, respectively, accounting for more than half of its total investment flows and stocks in BRI regions. At the end of 2014, China established altogether more than 3,300 FDI enterprises and hired 159,500 foreign employees in ASEAN. In terms of China's FDI stocks in 10 ASEAN countries at the end of 2014, its stock in Singapore was the largest, reaching 20.64 billion dollars, while Brunei had the least stock of 70 million dollars (see Table 4).

2.2. *Country distribution of China's FDI in BRI countries*

In terms of country distribution, the top 10 destinations for China's FDI in BRI countries are Singapore, Russia, Kazakhstan, Indonesia, Laos, Myanmar, Mongolia, Pakistan, Iran and India. Since 2008, Singapore has become the country with the largest stock and flow of China's FDI in BRI countries. At the end of 2014, China's FDI flow and stock in Singapore reached 2,814 million dollars and 20,640 million dollars, respectively, far more than China's FDI scale in other countries (see Table 5). The main fields of China's investment in Singapore include wholesale and retail trade, transportation and logistics, finance and insurance, hotel and catering and so on. This is not only related to the well-developed industry, finance and entrepot trade, political stability and transparent investment

Table 4. China's FDI Stocks in 10 ASEAN Countries at the end of 2014 (In 100 Million Dollars)

Country	Singapore	Indonesia	Laos	Myanmar	Cambodia	Thailand	Vietnam	Malaysia	Philippines	Brunei	Total
Stock	206.40	67.94	44.91	39.26	32.22	30.79	28.66	17.85	7.60	0.70	476.33

Table 5. Top 10 Destinations for China's FDI Flows in BRI Countries (2006–2014) (In 100 Million Dollars)

	Flows									
Year	2006	2007	2008	2009	2010	2011	2012	2013	2014	Stocks at the End of 2014
Singapore	1.32	3.98	15.51	14.14	11.19	32.69	15.19	20.33	28.14	206.40
Russia	4.52	4.78	3.95	3.48	5.68	7.16	7.85	10.22	6.34	86.95
Kazakhstan	0.46	2.80	4.96	0.67	0.36	5.82	29.96	8.11	−0.40	75.41
Indonesia	0.57	0.99	1.74	2.26	2.01	5.92	13.61	15.63	12.72	67.94
Laos	0.48	1.54	0.87	2.03	3.14	4.59	8.09	7.81	10.27	44.91
Myanmar	0.13	0.92	2.33	3.77	8.76	2.18	7.49	4.75	3.43	39.26
Mongolia	0.82	1.96	2.39	2.77	1.94	4.51	9.04	3.89	5.03	37.62
Pakistan	−0.62	9.11	2.65	0.77	3.31	3.33	0.89	1.64	10.14	37.37
Iran	0.66	0.11	−0.35	1.25	5.11	6.16	7.02	7.45	5.93	34.84
India	0.056	0.22	1.02	−0.25	0.48	1.80	2.77	1.49	3.17	34.07

environment in Singapore but also associated with the cultural similarity between Singapore and China.

2.3. *Industry distribution of China's FDI in BRI countries*

China's FDI in BRI countries mainly focuses on the fields of energy, mineral resources, infrastructure, manufacturing, agriculture and so on with different characteristics in different regions.

China's FDI in ASEAN mainly focuses on those industries of infrastructure, leasing and business services, manufacturing, mining, wholesale and retail as well as construction, etc. In terms of industry distribution of China's FDI stocks in ASEAN countries in 2014, the production and supply industry of electricity, heat, gas and water were with 7,226 million dollars, accounting for 15.2%; leasing and business services, 6,843 million dollars, accounting for 14.4%; manufacturing, 6,133 million dollars, accounting for 12.9%, which were the most extensive industries of China's investment in those ASEAN countries involved; mining, 6,053 million dollars, accounting for 12.7%; wholesale and retail, 5,900 million dollars, accounting for 12.4%; financial industry, 5,879 million dollars, accounting for 12.3%; construction, 3,362 million dollars, accounting for 7%; agriculture, forestry, animal husbandry and fisheries, 2,444 million dollars, accounting for 5.1%; transportation and warehousing, 1,468 million dollars, accounting for 3.1%; real estate, accounting for 2.4%; scientific research and technical services, accounting for 1.4%; information transmission, software and information services, accounting for 0.3%; services for residents and other services, accounting for 0.3%; hotel and catering, accounting for 0.2%.

China's FDI flow in West Asia increased from 256 million dollars in 2006 to 2,121 million dollars in 2014, but mainly concentrated in three countries, including Iran, Saudi Arabia and the United Arab Emirates, and China's FDI in West Asia mainly concentrated in the fields of energy, infrastructure, manufacturing and so on. Among them, China's investment in Iran grew rapidly as the enterprises from Europe, Russia and South Korea withdrew their investment from Ian after the financial crisis in 2008; the average annual growth rate of the FDI stock reached up to 85% over the period from 2008 to 2014. China's FDI in Saudi Arabia was mainly in the fields of infrastructure, urban construction, energy and manufacturing. As of 2013, nearly half of the 193 overseas enterprises established by China in Saudi Arabia engaged in the architectural engineering business. The

United Arab Emirates is an important financial center and entrepot trade center in West Asia and is abundant in oil and gas resources. Enterprises invested by China in the United Arab Emirates are mostly engaged in construction projects, trade services and other businesses.

Central Asia has abundant oil and gas resources but a relatively backward light industry. Therefore, China's FDI in Central Asia mainly focuses on oil exploration and production, transportation and communications construction, chemical industry, farm and sideline products processing and other fields. As of 2013, China's FDI stock in Central Asia was close to 8.9 billion dollars. Among them, the FDI in Kazakhstan accounted for more than half of the FDI in the whole Central Asia, with large investment projects focused on oil development, automobile assembly, agricultural product processing and other fields.

From the perspective of China's FDI in Russia, China's investment in Russia has continued to grow at a high speed since 2004. In 2014, China's FDI flow and stock in Russia were 634 million dollars and 8.695 billion dollars, respectively. Russia has become one of the countries with the fastest growth in China's OFDI, and China has become the fourth largest direct investor in Russia, following Cyprus, the Netherlands and Luxembourg. China's investment in Russia has been mainly distributed in energy, mineral resource exploitation, forestry and processing manufacturing industry. Among them, the FDI in manufacturing has increased most rapidly with its proportion of investment stock increasing from 11% in 2008 to 35% in 2013. However, the growth of FDI in the field of resources has been slowing down. The slowdown was mainly related to the fact that Russia began to control foreign equity in resource exploitation in 2008 and limited China's FDI in the fields of forest and energy in Russia.

From the perspective of China's FDI in Mongolia, China has become the largest source of investment for Mongolia over many years, despite of the modest scale of direct investment. China's FDI flow and stock in Mongolia in 2014 were 503 million dollars and 3,762 million dollars, respectively. Mongolia's economy is dominated by animal husbandry and mining, coupled with rapid urbanization in recent years, China's investment in Mongolia mainly focused on mineral development, construction materials, livestock products processing and other fields.

With a large population and huge market capacity, South Asia is geographically adjacent to China. Although China's FDI in India, Sri Lanka and Bangladesh has increased rapidly, China's FDI in South Asia has lagged behind its trade growth due to the impact of the international geopolitical environment. As of 2013, China's FDI stock in South Asia was less than 10 billion dollars, in which India and Pakistan accounted for 40% and 42%, respectively. The investment was mainly concentrated in mechanical equipment manufacturing, textile, energy exploitation, infrastructure construction and other fields. Although China's FDI in India has increased rapidly from 5.6 million dollars in 2006 to 317 million dollars in 2014, the overall scale of investment was still relatively small, whether from the investment flow or stock.

Of China's FDI in BRI countries, the investment in Central and Eastern Europe accounted for the least and the investment flow was only 204 million dollars in 2014. The investment market in Central and Eastern Europe has been mainly controlled by Germany, France and Russia for a long time. However, China has seized the investment opportunities that were brought by the European debt crisis and Ukraine Crisis. China's FDI flow in Central and Eastern Europe has increased rapidly from 39 million dollars in 2009 to 419 million dollars in 2010 in the context of the encouragement given by Central and Eastern European countries to non-EU countries for investment in response to the crises. At present, nearly 500 enterprises in China have invested and established their overseas companies in Central and Eastern Europe. In recent years, China has increased its investment in transportation infrastructure (the investment in Serbia for the construction of the bridge across the Danube in Belgrade and the railway from Belgrade to Budapest) and in municipal construction in Central and Eastern Europe. Besides, China has also invested in the fields of electrical appliances, automobiles, heavy machinery and information communication in Hungary, Poland, Bulgaria, Serbia and other countries, and has built new industrial parks and business logistics parks in Belarus, Poland and other places, which has become an important platform for Chinese enterprises to invest in Central and Eastern Europe.

3. Problems and Challenges of China's OFDI within the Framework of "The Belt and Road"

3.1. *High political risks in host countries of investment*

Most BRI countries are the developing countries or regions which have not reached a high level in economic and social development. In some countries, their domestic environments are complex, religious and ethnic conflicts are severe, political situations are unstable, governmental transparency is not high, corruption is serious and administrative efficiency is low. And some countries even experience frequent anti-China and/or Chinese-exclusion incidents. All these factors force Chinese enterprises to confront so much uncertainty and sustained high political risks and increase the cost and risk of China's investment in these regions. Meanwhile, the United States, Russia and Japan have implemented strategic measures one after another to try to dominate regional affairs in the regions along the Belt and Road in recent years as the BRI countries have unique strategic locations, abundant natural resources and broad prospects for economic and social development and many other factors. China's active development of direct investment in BRI countries will inevitably enter the traditional spheres of influence of these great powers such as the United States, Russia and Japan. The complex geographical relations and game of great powers in the regions along the Belt and Road increase the complexity of China's political risk of direct investment in BRI countries. Among them, there are rampant "three forces" in Central Asia (violent terrorists, ethnic separatists and religious extremists), the turmoil in Afghanistan, the "Asia Pacific rebalancing strategy" of the United States, Russia's strategic suspicions, India's strategic non-cooperation and Japan as a strategic spoiler. All these have posed serious challenges to the security of China's FDI in BRI countries. The high political risk of the BRI countries makes China face the risk of investment obstacles or even failure, and thus directly determine the quality and efficiency of China's FDI in BRI countries.

According to statistics, among the 130 failures or cases of (investment) barriers of "going globally" from 2005 to 2014, 25% of them were caused by political reasons, of which 17% suffered losses during the operation due to the political turmoil or leadership change in the host countries. Over the same period, Chinese enterprises experienced totally 33 risk cases of investment barriers or failures in BRI countries, amounting to 56.52 billion dollars in total, involving 20 countries, with an average amount up to 1.71 billion dollars in each case involved (see Table 6).

3.2. *Unbalanced development of China's OFDI*

From the perspective of investment destinations, China's FDI in BRI countries is mainly distributed in neighboring countries and regions such as

Table 6. Number of Investment Risk Cases of China's Enterprises Globally and in BRI Countries (2005–2014)

Year	2005	2006	2007	2008	2009	2010	2011	2012	2013	2014	Total
Number of global cases	1	9	11	15	16	18	22	16	14	8	130
Number of cases in BRI countries	0	6	5	1	2	4	2	6	4	3	33
Amount involved globally (in 100 million dollars)	180	347.6	146.1	366	354.9	176.9	340.3	163.4	213.3	71.2	2359.7
Amount involved in BRI Countries (in 100 million dollars)	0	218.7	73.6	3	18.3	18.3	40.5	86.4	69.5	36.9	565.2

ASEAN and Central Asia which are adjacent to China; however, its FDI in countries with far distance is extremely insufficient, like in South Asian countries and especially Central and Eastern European countries. As of 2014, Pakistan and India in South Asia only ranked the 8th and the 10th, respectively, in the ranking of China's FDI in BRI countries, while none of the Central and Eastern European countries appeared in the top 10 list. The fast-growing investment of Chinese enterprises in ASEAN and Central Asian regions easily lead to over-competition among Chinese investment enterprises and reduce the efficiency or benefit of direct investment of enterprises, thus increasing the risk of direct investment. At the same time, the extremely insufficient direct investment in South Asian and Central and Eastern European countries is not conducive to China's further expansion of its coverage scope of the Belt and Road Initiative. From the perspective of the investment field, China's FDI in BRI countries is excessively concentrated in the fields of infrastructure, resource exploitation and preliminary processing, but less in the fields of resource comprehensive processing and high-end manufacturing. China has not given full play to its comparative advantage as a "World Factory" in modern manufacturing. Although this pattern of investment distribution helps to improve China's security guarantee of its strategic resources, it is easy to provide excuses for the so-called "China Threat Theory" and "China New Colonialism theory", arguing that China's FDI in BRI countries is mainly aimed at seeking or even plundering natural resources of the host countries.

3.3. *Ecological and environmental problems frequently occurred in host countries of investment*

Ecological and environmental problems frequently occurred in host countries of investment. In recent years, the direct investment of Chinese enterprises in BRI countries has been hampered repeatedly by ecological destruction and environmental pollution and has even been labeled as "predatory development", "China's environmental threat" or "China's ecological dumping". The reasons are as follows: On the one hand, Chinese enterprises in infrastructure, energy, mining, steel, chemical and other industries have invested in some key fields in BRI countries; most fields are environmentally sensitive industries or those that are extremely prone to environmental pollution. On the other hand, the investments made by Chinese enterprises in these fields are mostly concentrated in regions with abundant natural resources along the Belt and Road, but the ecological environment system in these regions is extremely fragile, environmental protection legal systems themselves in the relevant countries are not complete and their environmental supervision mechanism was not perfect either. In addition, Chinese enterprises have weak awareness of environmental protection and lack sufficient attention to ecological environment protection issues. Therefore, it is easy to cause ecological environment problems in the host countries, leading to serious obstacles and even failure of investment projects. One typical case was that China started a construction project called "the Myitsone Dam project" in Myanmar in 2007 with the planned investment of 3.6 billion dollars. However, the project was halted in September 2011, causing great loss to Chinese enterprises, due to the ecological and environmental problems, as well as interference caused by other non-economic factors from Myanmar domestically and even international community.

4. Policy Proposals on Adjustment and the Improvement of China's OFDI Pattern

4.1. *To take aggressive precautions to prevent and avoid the political risks in host countries of investment*

Chinese enterprises should put great emphasis on the appraisal of host countries' political risks, making this the most important part of the assessment of investment environment during the course of their FDI in

BRI countries due to the differences in specific national circumstances, political institutions, legal culture, religious belief, customs and economic development situations in various BRI countries. And aggressive precautions to prevent and avoid the risks should be taken based on the sufficient assessment of host countries' political risks. To achieve this, firstly, Chinese government should continue to promote the understanding of the Belt and Road Initiatives in the international community, especially in the BRI countries, to uphold the ideas of peace and cooperation, openness and inclusiveness, mutual learning, mutual benefit and win–win outcomes during the construction of the Belt and Road, to ensure policy coordination, infrastructure connectivity, unimpeded trade, financial integration and people-to-people bond, to enhance practical cooperation in all directions, to build a community of shared benefit, shared future and shared responsibilities with mutual political trust, economic integration and cultural inclusiveness. Secondly, Chinese governmental departments which are represented by the Ministry of Foreign Affairs and Ministry of Commerce, as well as the professional non-governmental consulting agents should make full use of their strengths on information resources and professional capabilities to establish public information service platforms, to publish information and assessment reports relating to the political risks in BRI countries and regions, and thus to provide information service of and solutions to the related political risks to Chinese enterprises during their direct investment in BRI countries. Thirdly, Chinese government should take the initiative to develop friendly relationships with the major political forces, factions or ethnic groups, to try to ensure that the political changes in host countries of investment will not become political risks to FDI from Chinese enterprises on the basis of active maintenance and development of the bilateral relationship with the BRI countries. Fourthly, given that the BRI countries have gradually become a significant platform for the global political game among great powers in the world, in particular, both the United States and Russia have regarded the related countries as their own spheres of influence. Therefore, China's FDI in the BRI countries will inevitably lead to suspicion of the United States and Russia. However, the goals of China are essentially different to those of the United States and Russia. That is, China's Belt and Road Initiatives essentially aim at economic objectives, which is for the common prosperity in economy instead of seeking any sphere of influence. Therefore, China, the United States and Russia have interest congruence in the area of economic development in the BRI countries. Three countries should make great efforts to seek common ground while putting aside differences, enhance mutual strategic trust, strengthen coordination and cooperation among themselves and realize mutual benefits and win–win results. This is exactly an important condition that China needs to meet to actively prevent and avoid the political risks in its FDI in the BRI countries. Fifthly, China should improve its overseas investment insurance schemes as soon as possible. China should set up a compensation fund against the political risks in overseas investment, and consequently improve the ability of the Chinese enterprises to resist the political risks in investing in BRI countries, in accordance with the principles of "government guidance, market operation, interest-sharing and risk-sharing".

4.2. *To avoid excessive concentration of FDI in the geographic locations in the neighboring countries and at the same time, to expand FDI in Regions of central and eastern Europe as well as South Asia*

Firstly, China should avoid excessive concentration of FDI in geographic locations in the neighboring countries when prioritizing the development of FDI in the neighboring countries. If China's FDI in the neighboring host countries is excessively concentrated, it will inevitably enter the traditional spheres of influence of the great powers such as the United States, Russia and India, causing their misinterpretation of China's strategic intention and their tense response. It will also cause concerns from the host countries over their excessive reliance on China's economy. Therefore, China should guide its enterprises to keep a moderate balance during the process of direct investment in BRI countries. Particularly in the region of Southeast Asia, Central Asia and West Asia, China should prevent its enterprises from cluster-type concentration investment in resource exploitation, leading to the check-and-balance of geo-security from the great powers as well as suspicions and concerns from the neighboring countries. China should make efforts to realize a tripartite win–win result and positive interaction with other great powers and neighboring countries. Secondly, China should expand its FDI in the Central and Eastern European region and enhance its influence and coverage of the Belt and Road Initiatives. At present, China's direct investment in the Central and Eastern European region is very small, which is quite disproportioned to the economic scale of the region and China's position in the European and global economy. In fact, with the unique geographical advantages, the Central and Eastern European region is the intermediate zone connecting Western China and Western Europe and the bridge connecting Asian and European Markets. At the same time, Central and Eastern European countries enjoy good industrial foundation, a relatively high level of economic development and the significant complementarity to the Chinese economy. Therefore, the increase of China's FDI in the Central and Eastern European region is conducive to expanding its influence scope of the Belt and Road Initiatives and optimizing China's open-up pattern. Finally, China should pay more attention to its expansion of FDI in countries with frequent economic and trade frictions with China, represented by India and Turkey. India and Turkey are two big developing countries along the Belt and Road and with huge domestic markets and great potential. At the same time, India, Turkey and China have much in common in the economic structure, the industrial structure and the level of economic development, which is easy to cause economic and trade friction between China and these two countries. India and Turkey have been the largest and the fifth largest anti-dumping sponsors against China respectively, especially since the establishment of the WTO. However, up to now, China's FDI in India and Turkey has been relatively small. Therefore, the increase of China's FDI in these two countries will not only be helpful to promote the development of the Belt and Road Initiative, but also be helpful to avoid or reduce economic and trade frictions represented by anti-dumping against China by India and Turkey.

4.3. *To handle properly the relationship between OFDI and environmental protection in the host countries*

Firstly, we should strengthen the environmental responsibility of China's OFDI enterprises. Chinese enterprises should be fully aware that only when they engage in OFDI activities coordinated with the environment can they ultimately ensure the maximum interests and long-term interests of all stakeholders involved in OFDI, ensure the profit maximization and long-term interests of Chinese enterprises engaged in OFDI, and promote the achievement of goals for environmental protection and overall economic and social development in host countries in the context that the concept of global environmental protection has been deeply rooted in the hearts of the people, countries around the world have implemented sustainable development strategy, and circular economy, low carbon economy and green economy have been developing rapidly. Meanwhile, the idea and action of Chinese enterprises to integrate foreign direct investment with environmental protection is not only a specific performance of social responsibility of Chinese enterprises but also objective requirements for enterprises to set up good international images, make enterprises bigger and stronger and even truly become multinational companies with international competitiveness. It is also a specific reflection of China's undertaking international obligations and implementing the global sustainable development strategy as a responsible developing country. Secondly, China should use domestic laws and regulations to regulate the environmental damage behavior of OFDI enterprises. The home country has the obligation to supervise its overseas investors on the premise of not damaging the sovereignty of host countries. Therefore, it not only requires Chinese enterprises to go through verification and registration procedures when making FDI in the BRI countries and comply with the laws and regulations of the host country on environmental protection and relevant international environmental protection laws but also urgently needs China to have an operable regulation or law specifically aimed at environmental protection for overseas investment, in order to regulate China's FDI activities in BRI countries and ensure the sustainable development of China's FDI in BRI countries. Thirdly, we should add environment-related clauses in bilateral investment agreements. With the Belt and Road Initiatives, as capital exporters, Chinese enterprises should not only effectively fulfill their environmental protection responsibilities but also be aware that environmental obligations may become a means for certain host countries to set environmental barriers and implement investment protectionism. We can consider adding environment-related clauses in its bilateral investment agreements in order to reduce the conflicts of interest. Thus, it can not only clarify the willingness of Chinese enterprises to fulfill the environmental obligations of the host countries in overseas investment but also promote environmental regulatory measures of host countries to be in accordance with the requirements of non-discrimination and goodwill.

Bibliography

Ali, A. S. *et al.* Dealing with High Debt in an Era of Low Growth, IMF Staff Discussion Note, 2013, No. 7.

Anderson, R. G., Gascon, C. S. and Liu, Y. Doubling Your Monetary Base and Surviving: Some International Experience[J]. *Federal Reserve Bank of St. Louis Review*, 2010, 92(6): 481–505.

Baldwin, R. 21st Century Regionalism: Filling the Gap between 21st Century Trade and 20th Century Trade Rules. WTO Staff Working Paper, 2011, ERSD201108.

Baldwin, R. Global Supply Chains: Why They Emerged, Why They Mattered, and Where They Are Going. CEPR Discussion Paper, 2012, No. 9103.

Baldwin, E. US Trade Policy since 1934: An Uneven Path toward Greater Trade Liberalization. NBER Working Paper, 2009, No. 15397.

Bank of England. Quantitative Easing Explained: Putting More Money Into Our Economy to Boost Spending. http://www.bankofengland.co.uk, 2009.

Baracuhy, B. The Evolving Geo-Economics of World Trade. March 2015.

Bernanke, B. S. The Crisis and the Policy Response. Speech at the Stamp Lecture, London School of Economics, January 13, 2009.

Bernard, M. H. and Mattoo, A. Liberalizing Trade in Services: Lessons from Regional and WTO Negotiations. EUI RSCAS Working Paper, 2013, No. 34.

Bernstein, S. Legitimacy in global environmental governance[J]. *Journal of International Lau & International Relations*, 2004 (1): 139.

Bi Jiyao, Ding Gang, Wu Runsheng, *et al. Report on China's External Economic Development (2014)*. Beijing: Publishing House of Electronics Industry, 2015.

Borchert, I., Gootiiz, B. and Matto, A. Policy Barriers to International Trade in Services: Evidence from a New Database. World Bank Working Paper, 2012, No. WPS6109.

Bullard, J. B. President's Message: A Comparison of Unconventional Monetary Policy in the US and Europe[J]. *The Regional Economist*, 2015: 3.

Calvo, G. and Reinhart, C. Fear of Floating. *Quarterly Journal of Economics*, 2002(117), 379–408.

Chen Yibo. *A Research Approach to China's Transformation from World Manufacturing Centre to Technological Innovation Centre*. Beijing: Graduate School of Chinese Academy of Social Science, 2010.

Constâncio V. Assessing the New Phase of Unconventional Monetary Policy at The ECB[C]//Panel Remarks at the Annual Congress of the European Economic Association, University of Mannheim. 2015(25): 1–15.

Cour-Thimann, P. and Winkler, B. The ECB's Non-standard Monetary Policy Measures: The Role of Institutional Factors and Financial Structure. ECB Working Paper, 2013, No. 1528.

Eichengreen, B. *et al*. The Global Productivity Slump: Common and Country-Specific Factors. NBER, Working Paper, 2015, No. 21556.

Escaith, H., Lindenberg, N. and Miroudot, S. Global Value Chains and the Crisis: Reshaping International Trade Elasticity[J]. *Global Value Chains in a Postcrisis World. A Development Perspective*, 2010: 73–123.

Färe, R., Grosskopf, S., Lindgren, B., *et al*. *Productivity Developments in Swedish Hospitals: A Malmquist Output Index Approach[M]//Data Envelopment Analysis: Theory, Methodology, and Applications*. Dordrecht: Springer, 1994: 253–272.

Findlay, C., Noedas, H. K. and Pasadilla, G. *Trade Policy in Asia, Higher Education and Media Services*. ADBI and OECD, 2014.

Frankel, J. A., Schmukler, S. L. and Serven, L. Global Transmission of Interest Rates: Monetary Independence and Currency Regime. *Journal of International Money and Finance*, 2004 (23): 701–733.

Franta, M. Identification of Monetary Policy Shocks in Japan Using Sign Restrictions within the TVP-VAR Framework. Bank of Japan Discussion Paper, 2011, No. 2011E13.

Fu Yong and Bai Long. Changes and Decomposition of Total Factor Productivity Since China's Reform and Opening Up (1978-2006) — Malmquist Index Analysis Based on Inter Provincial Panel Data [J]. *Financial Research*, 2009 (07): 38–51.

Gao Jie and Jing Xiaoyun. Global Strategies of Multinational Companies. *Productivity Research*, 2011(3): 160–161+166.

Hamilton, S. D. America's Mega-Regional Trade Diplomacy: Comparing TPP and TTIP, 2014.

Han Xiuli. *A Study on the Environmental Protection Issues in China's Overseas Investment*. Beijing: International Studies, 2013.

Han Yujun. *International Service and Trade — Theoretical Model and Positive Analysis*. Qingdao: China Ocean University Press, 1999.

Han Yujun and Liu Yijiao. International Comparison of China's Service Industry Development. *Economic Review Journal*, 2011(4): 98–100.

He Jun. *A Study on the Improvement of Internationalization of China's Service Industry*. Shanghai: Truth and Wisdom Press, Shanghai People's Publishing House, 2015.

Horn, H., Mavroidis, P. C. and Sapir A. Beyond the WTO? An anatomy of EU and US Preferential Trade Agreements[J]. *The World Economy*, 2010, 33(11): 1565–1588.

Husain, A. M. *et al*. Global Implications of Lower Oil Prices. IMF Staff Discussion Note, 2015, No. 15.

IIF. Capital Flows to Emerging Market, October 2015a.

IIF. Fed Exit and Emerging Market Crises, 2015b.

IMF. World Economic Outlook. http://www.imf.org/external/pubs/ft/weo, 2015a.

IMF. *World Economic Outlook: Adjusting to Lower Commodity Prices*. 2015b.

International Energy Agency (IEA). Medium-Term Oil Market Report 2015: Market Analysis and Forecasts to 2020, 2015.

Jiang Xiaojuan, Yang Shengming and Feng Lei. *Frontier of the Theoretical Development of China International Trade and Economic Relations III*. Beijing: Social Science Academic Press (China), 2003.

Kolstad, I. and Wiig, A. What Determines Chinese Outward FDI? *Journal of World Business*, 2012, 47(1): 26–34.

Li Daokui and Mei, Song. Tightening of US Dollar M2 Triggered World Financial Crisis: The Internal and External Causes and the Verification of the Financial Crisis. *The Journal of World Economy*, 2009 (4): 15–26.

Li Xiangyang. Neo-regionalism and Great Power Strategy. *International Economic Review*, 2003 (4): 5–9.

Lin Lan and Zeng, Gang. A Preliminary Study on Technological Diffusion and Global Dual Phenomenon in Technology. *Word Economy Studies*, 2006 (4): 23–29.

Liu Binglian and Li Qingbin. Dynamic Empirical Analysis of Urban Total Factor Productivity in China: 1990-2006 — Malmquist Index Method Based on DEA Model [J]. *Nankai Economic Research*, 2009 (03): 139–152.

Lu Jian, Liu Jianping and Cheng Shixiong. Dynamic Measurement of the Industrial Technology Gap between China and Major OECD Countries. *The Journal of World Economy*, 2014 (9): 25–52.

Meltzer, J. P. From the Trans-Pacific Partnership to a Free Trade Agreement of the Asia-Pacific? Brookings, May 5, 2015.

Ncube, M. Z. Stabilization Policy in a Developing Economy: Some Theoretical Underpinnings[J]. *BLDS Digital Library on OpenDocs*, 2014: 1–10.

OECD. Policy Challenges for the Next 50 Years. Economic Policy Paper, 2014a, No. 9.

OECD. Global Trade and Specialization Patterns Over the Next 50 Years. Economic Policy Paper, 2014b, No. 10.

OECD. Looking to 2060: Long-term Global Growth Prospects, Economic Policy Paper. 2015, No. 3.

Office of United States Trade Representative. White House Fact Sheet: Transatlantic Trade and Investment Partnership. www.ustr.gov, 2013.

Rey, H. Dilemma not Trilemma: The Global Financial Cycle and Monetary Policy Independence. The Global Dimension of Unconventional Monetary Policy, Proceedings of the Federal Reserve Bank of Kansas City, 2013.

Sapiro, M. The Geopolitical Impact of TTIP: A Transatlantic Fortress or an Open Platform? IAI Working Papers, May 2015.

Sheng Bin and Guo Ting. Comparison of Free Trade Agreement Provisions in the Asia Pacific Region and Its Enlightenment to China [J]. *Asia Pacific Economy*, 2014 (02): 94–101.

Sheng Boming. Multinational Companies and World Technology Transfer. *The Journal of World Economy*, 1996 (3): 48–51.

Tellis, J. A. The Geopolitics of the TTIP and the TPP, 2015.

The Research Group on the Topic of "the Frontier of Economic Growth". The Flow of International Capital, Economic Distortions and Macroscopic Stability — An Analysis of the Current Economic Growth Trend. *Economic Research Journal*, 2005, (4).

Vollmer, U. and Bebenroth, R. The Financial Crisis in Japan: Causes and Policy Reactions by the Bank of Japan. *The European Journal of Comparative Economics*, 2012(9), 51–77.

Wang Huiyao. *Report on Chinese Enterprises Globalization (2014)*. Beijing: Social Science Academic Press (China), 2014.

Wang Jinbin and Ma Man. Judgement on Ten Issues about Contemporary World Economy. *Journal of Anhui University*, 2015 (2): 1–10.

Wang Jinbin *et al.* Can Capital Regulation Serve a Function of Firewall? — Evidence from Cross-Country Panel Data of Emerging Economy. *Journal of Anhui University*, 2013 (3): 136–142.

Wang Zhonghong. The Current Situation and Trends of Global Technological Innovation and Its Impact on China. *Development Research*, 2013 (9): 4–8.

WTO. World Trade Report 2011: The WTO and Preferential Trade Agreements, 2011.

Xia Jiechang and Zhang Xiaobing. Strategic Thinking on Proactively Coping with the Opening-up of the Service Industry. *China Development Observation*, 2012, (3).

Xu Quanyong and Xiao Wenbin. The Preliminary Study on the Geographic Patterns of Contemporary World Technology Trade. *World Regional Studies*, 1998, (1).

Yao Zhanqi. A Study on the Current Situation, Problems and Countermeasures of China's Service Industry Opening Up: from the Perspective of FDI of China's Service Industry. *Intertrade*, 2013, (8).

Zhou Fangyin. Climate in Areas Around and China's Choice of Peripheral Strategies. *Foreign Affairs Review (Journal of China Foreign Affairs University)*, 2014, (1).

Index

I

J

K

L

M

N

O

P

CPSIA information can be obtained
at www.ICGtesting.com
Printed in the USA
LVHW080808170223
738942LV00001B/12

9 789811 247613